Studies in African American History and Culture

Edited by

Graham Hodges

Colgate University

T0347317

A Routledge Series

STUDIES IN AFRICAN AMERICAN HISTORY AND CULTURE

GRAHAM HODGES, *General Editor*

THE SELLING OF CIVIL RIGHTS

The Student Nonviolent Coordinating Committee and the Use of Public Relations

Vanessa Murphree

Routledge
New York & London

Routledge
Taylor & Francis Group
270 Madison Avenue
New York, NY 10016

Routledge
Taylor & Francis Group
2 Park Square
Milton Park, Abingdon
Oxon OX14 4RN

© 2006 by Taylor & Francis Group, LLC
Routledge is an imprint of Taylor & Francis Group, an Informa business

Transferred to Digital Printing 2009

International Standard Book Number-10: 0-415-97889-0 (Hardcover)
International Standard Book Number-13: 978-0-415-97889-7 (Hardcover)

Library of Congress Cataloging-in-Publication Data

Murphree, Vanessa.
    The selling of civil rights : the Student Nonviolent Coordinating Committee and the use of public relations / Vanessa Murphree.
        p. cm. -- (Studies in African American history and culture)
    Includes bibliographical references and index.
    ISBN 0-415-97889-0 (alk. paper)
    1. Student Nonviolent Coordinating Committee (U.S.)--Public relations. 2. African Americans--Civil rights--History--20th century. 3. Civil rights movements--United States--History--20th century. 4. United States--Race relations. I. Title. II. Series.

E185.61.M96 2006
323.1196'073--dc22   2006005652

ISBN10: 0-415-97889-0 (hbk)
ISBN10: 0-415-80580-5 (pbk)

ISBN13: 978-0-415-97889-7 (hbk)
ISBN13: 978-0-415-80580-3 (pbk)

Visit the Taylor & Francis Web site at
http://www.taylorandfrancis.com

and the Routledge Web site at
http://www.routledge-ny.com

Contents

List of Figures

Acknowledgments

Many generous people have served as academic, editorial, and personal advisors as I worked to complete this project. I am especially grateful to Jon Lindemann for his advice, friendship, insight, and editorial expertise. My dissertation committee at the University of Southern Mississippi provided a great deal of encouragement and assistance, particularly my advisor, David Davies. Other members are Bradley Bond, Arthur Kaul, Charles Mayo, and Gene Wiggins. I also offer many thanks to my friends and colleagues at Loyola University New Orleans and the University of South Alabama.

For personal inspiration and friendship, I thank the graduate student community of the School of Journalism and Mass Communication at the University of Southern Mississippi, especially Pi-yun An and Yu-Hsing Chang. My colleagues and friends associated with the American Journalism Historian's Association also offered immense support. Joseph Bernt of Ohio University encouraged the project from the start as well as provided the title. The editors and reviewers of *American Journalism* and *Journalism History* offered a great deal of insight and assistance and allowed portions of my articles to be included in this book.[1] I offer thanks to the King Center for granting permission to reproduce the eighteen figures in this book. Friends Greg Stroud and Jim Carstens also provided insight and assistance. Many thanks to them.

And finally, I am grateful to the SNCC workers who so generously shared their time and memories and added tremendous depth and wisdom to the project: Joan Browning, Robert Beyers, Connie Curry, Mary King, Jack Minnis, Jane Stembridge, and Dorothy Zellner.

Introduction

Established in 1960, the Student Nonviolent Coordinating Committee (SNCC, known to most as "Snick") emerged as part of the most important social movement in American history—the civil rights movement.[1] In the face of a daunting mission, SNCC founders purposefully put communication and publicity at the center of their initial agenda.[2] In 1962, SNCC Communications Director Julian Bond told an interviewer that the group was formed as an information agency for organizing civil rights protests at universities across the South.[3] These coordinating activities propelled and strengthened the student movement, and SNCC's communication efforts served as a foundation for the movement until the group's demise at the end of the decade.

I wrote this book in response to the lack of recognition or analysis[4] of the public relations and communications tactics that SNCC used to support student and community-led civil rights protests during the 1960s and in response to the need to examine the communications component of all social movements. The tendency among public relations historians has been to focus on corporate and government organizations, thus overlooking the successes of civil rights groups in their efforts to develop grassroots communication campaigns. Furthermore, social movement and African American historians have emphasized individual leaders and incidents rather than the communication devices that were used as organizing tools. SNCC communication projects are particularly noteworthy not only because they played an essential role in the civil rights movement, but because they serve as a case study for public relations professionals, historians, and students. Analyzing public relations from the context of the civil rights movement provides an example of how public relations has been used to change the social fabric of the country in a positive and long-standing fashion. This research, therefore, contributes to the study of American media and public relations history by providing an account of how one of the most important and influential grassroots communication campaigns in the nation's history used public relations to help accomplish many of the goals of a massive human-rights mission.

Scholars who have examined the role of the media in the civil rights movement generally neglect the idea that much of the publicity was the direct or indirect result of public relations efforts taking place within a particular organization, such as SNCC. The most notable example is Todd Gitlin's *The Whole World is Watching: Mass Media in the Making and Unmaking of the new Left*. Gitlin's thoughtful analysis traces how CBS and the *New York Times* covered the Students for a Democratic Society and examines how this coverage influenced the organization's strategies, tactics, and overall outlook.[5] In another example, Richard Lentz provides a thorough and meaningful analysis of news coverage of the movement in *Symbols, the News Magazines, and Martin Lither King*. He examines coverage from *Newsweek*, *Time*, and *U.S. News & World Report* and analyzes how the symbolic images and messages in these articles shaped American values.[6]

In an article that does look at the importance of public relations, Linda Childers Hon examines Martin Luther King's Southern Christian Leadership Conference (SCLC) and notes the lack of scholarship on how various non-corporate, non-government audiences use public relations to "force business and government institutions to heed to their demands" and that corporations are only one of the many types of entities that have made significant advancements via public relations.[7]

By examining community-oriented and grassroots communications efforts, such as SNCC's, we get a broader view of how public relations can be used as a tool for social reform and promoting social values. I hope this book will serve as an example of how public relations has been a defining component of social movements in addition to supporting commercial, governmental, educational, and religious values.

From a historical perspective, it's clear that public relations has been important to all social movements. For instance, in *The Politics of Nonviolent Action*, Gene Sharp presents a list of 198 "nonviolent weapons" used in movements throughout world history; and many of these are "textbook" public relations tactics, including leaflets, pamphlets, speeches, symbols, media relations, signs, and advertisements. He goes on to describe how these tools were used in various social movements, including Gandhi's fight for Indian independence in the 1920s and 1930s and colonial resistance to British rule in pre-Revolutionary America. Influenced by the SCLC leadership, SNCC workers studied these strategies and followed many of the examples given by nonviolent resistance movements that preceded them.[8]

Historians have identified three phases of SNCC history; and it is possible to identify a distinct type of communication effort for each phase. During the first, the focus was on using nonviolent protest strategies and creating a beloved community, which essentially meant winning civil rights through a combination of pacifism, direct action, and Christian ideals. The second was marked by political activism—voter registration, party building, and the like. The third entailed an expansion from a rural Southern base to a national focus; a radical shift towards the ideas of Black Power and black consciousness; and a call for white exclusion.[9] As one might expect, the lines between these phases are not always clear, even in hindsight. SNCC's steady growth as a political organization can be traced from its initiation to the end of the 1960s, but direct action remained a primary tool throughout.

Communication also remained central to achieving the Committee's organizational goals regardless of specific tactic or strategy—sit-ins, boycotts, voter registration, freedom rides, forming political parties, or informing the rest of the country about racism and resistance in the South. One could even argue that SNCC was an organization whose essential focus was to manage a national communication campaign for promoting civil rights. As SNCC worker Mary E. King explained in a 2002 interview, communication "goes to the very heart of how a nonviolent struggle works."[10] She described the SNCC communication effort as a continuously evolving process requiring clarification and explanation to internal and national audiences alike.

Since the beginning of Reconstruction, racist whites had used brutal tactics to maintain an economic system from which they reaped the vast majority of benefits. As the civil rights movement became increasingly bold in the 1960s, the white majority responded with tactics that protected their corrupt traditions and economic interests. Consequently, SNCC workers organized under the threatening shadows of covert Klu Klux Klan chapters and overt White Citizens Councils and Sovereignty Commissions. The latter two were government-sponsored racist organizations designed to use state statutes to circumvent federal discrimination laws and maintain white supremacy. As Mary King recalled, state and local authorities condoned much of the violence inflicted on SNCC workers and local blacks. Although Citizens Councils and Sovereignty Commissions generally avoided direct involvement in these acts of violence, they rarely spoke out against them and often saw to it that perpetrators received protection and sometimes even praise.

The dangerous atmosphere was amplified by the fact that for the most part, racist whites owned and operated local media outlets—an extraordinary obstacle to disseminating a message of civil rights and racial equality to the general public. Thus, King described much of SNCC's communication work as compensatory: "Had the press been doing its job, we would not have needed such an extensive communication shop. We were offering compensation for the deficits of the Southern news media."[11] While national reporters were generally more sympathetic to the movement, they presented different challenges to SNCC communication goals. For instance, King recalled pleading with reporters in 1963 to cover a story involving the bodies of four black men found floating in a river near Natchez, Mississippi. But the reporters were reluctant because they could not elicit any information from local black residents, who lived in fear of white retaliation. "The question of attribution was a huge challenge," King said.[12]

UNSEEN EFFORTS, UNKNOWN RESULTS

Public relations is a behind-the-scenes profession. Its critics often use such terms as "manipulation" to describe what they view as work performed outside of the public eye. In this vein, the historian Scott Cutlip portrays public relations as an "unseen power,"[13] suggesting that transparency is an important aspect of effectiveness. With very few exceptions, public relations practitioners do not call attention to themselves, nor do they publicly promote their individual efforts. SNCC administrators and communications workers understood this, and were more than willing to diminish their individual needs in favor of organizational goals. The same willingness marked the group's community organizing and local leadership strategies.

Accordingly, during the first two SNCC stages (i.e., "beloved community" and "political organization"), the group decentralized leadership goals—that is, instead of promoting a top-down leadership model, the Committee used behind-the-scenes communication tactics to contact the local organizers of sit-ins, to invite them to join the larger organization, and to encourage them to organize more non-violent protests. SNCC communications workers also understood that they could only pitch stories to national media outlets, and that success in gaining access was determined by reporters, editors, and publishers. In the end, it was the reporters and publishers who received the accolades for their civil rights stories, while politicians received credit for promoting legislation or making speeches in support of civil rights causes. The SNCC lobbyists and Friends of SNCC groups who worked in satellite offices, who provided background information to media representatives, and who tirelessly pushed government representatives to take action received their satisfaction from knowing that their efforts had contributed to a growing number of victories.

Today, such public relations success can often be measured in precise terms—reaching specific population segments, increasing brand name or image awareness among a targeted demographic, etc. The measurement tools we now take for granted did not exist in the early 1960s, and even if they did, SNCC did not have the resources required to use them. Within SNCC, measurements of success were simple and straightforward and came in the form of integrated lunch counters, news coverage, money, political change, a growing volunteer base, and registered voters. Identifying cause-and-effect relationships for a major public relations campaign conducted 35 to 45 years ago would be at best a difficult task open to considerable criticism, especially in light of the intense pace of political change taking place in the 1960s. But the correlations of SNCC's communication work and the advancement of civil rights is evident. Simply by organizing and communicating, the group placed their cause on the national agenda. For instance, during the roughly ten years of the group's existence (1960–1970), the *New York Times* index alone indicates over 950 articles about the organization. So in taking a qualitative approach to measuring SNCC communication success, I did what I could to isolate the Committee's efforts from those of the broad range of civil rights and other social change organizations that were active at the same time. Specifically, I looked at the effects of SNCC communication work on the sit-in movement, Freedom Summer, the Mississippi Freedom Democratic Party, the Lowndes County Freedom Organization, the Black Power Movement, and the globalization of the organization in its final years.

SNCC, by and large, was a southern organization with a headquarters office in Atlanta. As the group grew, so did its field offices. By the close of 1963, SNCC would have major projects underway in Selma and Gadsden, Alabama (managed by Worth Long); Pine Bluff, Arkansas (William Hansen); Albany and Americus, Georgia (Charles Sherrod); much of Mississippi, with bases in Batesville, Biloxi, Clarksdale, Cleveland, Columbus, Greenville, Greenwood, Hattiesburg, Holly Springs, Jackson, Laurel, McComb, Meridian, and Vicksburg, (Robert Moses); Raleigh, North Carolina (Reginald Robinson); and Danville and Farmville, Virginia (Avon Rollins). The core staff consisted of ninety-six mostly black field secretaries and field workers, twelve Atlanta-based administrative staff members, and over one hundred full-time volunteers.

A cursory review of the SNCC papers and newsletters reveals that activities were constantly taking place across the South as protests efforts increased. Moreover, workers at all of these sites continually participated in communication and public relations activities. Mississippi, however, had become one of the group's biggest challenges, and consequently much more time and energy went into penetrating that state. Because so much activity took place there, much of the historical evidence regarding communication activity is Mississippi based. This research, therefore, focuses more on those efforts and the efforts of the centralized Atlanta office that served all field workers. All the activists used communications and public relations, but the smaller projects generally adopted strategies and tactics from the larger organization that came from Atlanta and left behind fewer records of their efforts.

These and other examples highlight one important SNCC characteristic: the ability and willingness to experiment with and introduce new communication and public relations strategies when existing strategies were not working fast enough. That characteristic was severely tested in 1964 just after a massive voting campaign in Mississippi, known as Freedom Summer, which attracted about 1,000 white students into the state. SNCC's summer-long effort had established new political programs and campaigns throughout the Deep South, and its growing number of successes in local communities led many members to believe that the organization would emerge as a powerful political force at the 1964 Democratic Party Convention in Atlantic City. The movement did receive unprecedented national exposure when Fannie Lou Hamer, a former Mississippi sharecropper and SNCC volunteer, made an emotional plea for support for the SNCC-organized Mississippi Freedom Democratic Party. President Johnson, however, rejected her appeal and even called a last minute press conference in an effort to detract press attention, once again proving that national politicians had little understanding of or interest in the needs, desires, and expectations of Southern blacks. Despite Johnson's efforts to thwart the live coverage, the television networks embraced Hamer and showed footage of her powerful story repeatedly that evening.

Although this television visibility can be viewed as an effective communications campaign that garnered financial, political, and emotional support, the group failed in their effort, largely because President Johnson and other politicians feared losing the Southern white vote. The convention defeat shattered the hopes of many SNCC workers. Due to the disappointment and bitterness experienced during the Democratic Convention, some workers were receptive to a new operating philosophy. It was at this point that the idea of nonviolent protest began to lose its appeal. It would be more than a year before the transition to a Black Power philosophy began, but national leaders who chose to reject SNCC appeals for recognition in 1964 helped to sow the seeds.

Black Power and its iconic messenger, Stokely Carmichael (SNCC chair in 1966), were frightening and intimidating to many SNCC supporters. Superficially, the promotion of Black Power was a public relations nightmare in that the concept alienated many whites, a significant number of blacks, and a substantial number of SNCC workers. But the Black Power message was based on some essential truths about racism in America, and so it eventually proved to be a powerful tool of persuasion. Whether or not they agreed with Carmichael's ideas, many whites were drawn to his public appearances. His appeal to the mass media—especially television, which was cementing its position as the primary source of public information—was unprecedented in the organization.

Carmichael argued that civil rights workers should use violent means if necessary to defend themselves against the violent tactics used by racist opponents to the movement. As a result, SNCC endured a great deal of condemnation from the mainstream press, which did not understand the organization's attempts to communicate a Black Power message that was much broader than a simple call to violent revolution. Nevertheless, SNCC workers continued to win support from poor blacks, and they continued to use a variety of communication strategies to promote their message of black empowerment and civil rights for all Americans. Despite the combative image presented in most of the white press, SNCC still managed to communicate a message of racial and cultural solidarity. As the decade progressed, the message contained a growing international relations component that promoted unity between American blacks and African nations trying to pull away from the final vestiges of Western colonialism. By creating international partnerships, SNCC forced an international awareness of racial tensions and violence in the United States and of human rights shortcomings throughout the globe.

As the SNCC leadership worked to promote international collaborations, they simultaneously faced their greatest communication challenge: opposing American involvement in Vietnam. Again, a cursory examination might lead one to describe this decision as a sign that SNCC was abandoning its core doctrine of using public relations to achieve civil rights goals. A more prudent review of its communication efforts during this turbulent period shows that the organization was remaining true to its primary mission of promoting human rights. SNCC leaders were aware that they were alienating the white press and white politicians and inflicting damage on their long-term public relations work, yet by this point they were able to use their established communication channels to present a new message and to promote a new image. The message did in fact alienate the white establishment, yet it was transmitted by mainstream media channels, and therefore did much to build support for the anti-war movement.

In a rare example of support from the white press during SNCC's Black Power phase, Bruce Galphin of the *Atlanta Journal* asked readers to consider the organization's achievements before making an across-the-board condemnation of the group and its spokespersons.

> Snick people speak the language of the Negro poor. They communicate. They go into communities seething with frustrations . . . and teach the basic democratic principles that bad conditions will never improve unless you say something about it. . . . Snick has taught them to speak. And though we find the voice raucous and alarming, we at least owe it to ourselves to ponder the lesson in grassroots leadership.[14]

And as we ponder SNCC successes and shortcomings during one of the most contentious periods in American history, we must keep in mind its leadership role in forcing our nation to acknowledge its multiracial composition and its position in American public relations history. SNCC successfully combined community organizing tactics and public relations strategies in a rapidly evolving media environment to build a foundation for educating, liberating, and empowering Southern blacks.

PIECING TOGETHER SNCC COMMUNICATIONS HISTORY

To document SNCC communication activities, I relied on documents and supporting materials held by the University of Southern Mississippi (USM), Mississippi State University (MSU), the Mississippi State Archives in Jackson, the Wisconsin State Historical Society in Madison, a number of biographical and autobiographical accounts,[15] and oral history collections. The Wisconsin archives include the collections of Mary King, Dorothy Miller Zellner, and other long-time members of SNCC. The USM, MSU, and Mississippi State Archives contain SNCC-produced promotional materials, documents pertaining to special events and fundraising, and news articles on SNCC staffers or on topics that were suggested to the media by SNCC workers. Extensive oral history collections on the civil rights movement in general and SNCC in particular are held by USM, the Mississippi Humanities Council, and the Mississippi Department of Archives and History.[16]

Along with the USM collection of oral histories, my research incorporated information garnered from books that contain oral histories from SNCC staff members. For example, *The Eyes on the Prize Civil Rights Reader* contains interviews with Ella Jo Baker, an SCLC leader who organized SNCC and served as an advisor; Robert Zellner, a white Southerner and important SNCC member; Charles Sherrod, a SNCC leader who organized the Albany, Georgia movement; Robert Moses, organizer of the Mississippi voting projects; Hamer; Sally Belfrage, a SNCC organizer who trained volunteers for Freedom Summer and later worked in the Greenwood project; Forman; and Sellers.[17]

Another important collection of oral histories is *Voice of Freedom: An Oral History of the Civil Rights Movement from the 1950s through the 1980s*.[18] This text contains interviews with Diane Nash, a SNCC leader in the Nashville sit-ins; Lewis; Barry; Bond; Sherrod; Moses; Amzi Moore, the NAACP member who encouraged SNCC to organize in Mississippi; and Robert Zellner among others.

Cheryl Lynn Greenberg also composed an important text based on the transcripts of a 1988 SNCC reunion. The text includes commentary from SNCC leaders concerning crucial organizational events such as the founding of SNCC, voter registration drives, the Lowndes County Freedom Organization, and the emergence of Black Power.[19]

The most important source of information, however, was the seventy-three-roll microfilm collection of the organization's papers containing images of thousands of SNCC papers, many of which describe communication and public relations activities. The collection is available at numerous libraries and archives including Tulane University and the University of Southern Mississippi. The originals are housed at the Martin Luther King, Jr., Center in Atlanta. The guide to the collection includes sections devoted to research, photography, printing, special events, education, fundraising, and international affairs, while the reels contains historical sources to document all of these efforts.

Perhaps the most fulfilling component of the research process is the personal interview. I had an opportunity to learn directly from a number of former SNCC workers including: Joan Browning, who worked in the Atlanta offices during SNCC's first year of operations; Dorothy Miller Zellner, a member of the communication section for three years and a primary contributor to many SNCC publications; Robert Zellner, a SNCC field worker and coordinator; Jack Minnis, SNCC research director who worked closely with the communications department; Robert Beyers, director of communication of the Jackson, Mississippi office during the 1964 Freedom Summer; Julian Bond, the SNCC director of communication from 1961 until 1965; and Mary King.

When considering the vast amount of information provided within these sources, it is clear SNCC workers used public relations as a central organizational component. We must, however, also understand that informing, persuading, and educating served as objectives to help achieve their larger mission of advancing civil rights. With that in mind, it is important to note that this is not a comprehensive study of SNCC, but rather it focuses on the communication tools used to advance the movement. The civil rights movement itself was (and still is) a movement of both community and human empowerment encouraged by individuals who understood the need to give their hearts, souls, and sometimes their lives to the cause. The people who made up the movement came together to break down long-standing barriers to individual freedoms, and it is insufficient to simply categorize civil rights as a freestanding public relations campaign. From a larger perspective, the campaign was based upon and fueled by battles for liberty and social justice. But as this research strives to illustrate, the tools and mechanisms that advanced these changes were based on fundamental principles of communication and public relations.

Chapter One
"Peaceful Petitions to the Conscience"

Every time a student picks up a book or newspaper, he visions a written image created by twenty-one million of his brothers who are struggling to break the ties of prejudice and segregation. This is purpose and stimulus enough to create the freedom image.

The Student Voice (Albany Edition)
December 1961

On February 1, 1960, four black college freshmen took seats at the lunch counter of the Greensboro, North Carolina Woolworth's. They sat for almost an hour, despite employee demands that they vacate the white seating section. The next day thirty students sat for almost two hours at the same counter; the following day an even larger group joined them. National news organizations picked up the story, which filled front pages across the country including the front page of the *Atlanta Daily World*, a black-owned community newspaper. Lonnie King, a student at Morehouse College, found his classmate Horace Julian Bond sitting in the Yates and Milton Drugstore near their campus and insisted that he read the article. The two students, with help from classmate Joe Pierce, organized a noontime meeting that very day, during which the Atlanta student movement was born. Within weeks, seventy-seven of the Atlanta students were arrested and charged with violating Jim Crow laws at lunch counters throughout the South. In the following two months students followed suit around the country and organized fifty-four sit-ins in nine states. These students propelled the civil rights movement and would usher in a decade of protest and social change.

Four months later (April 1960), Ella Jo Baker, executive secretary of the Southern Christian Leadership Conference (SCLC), took the first step toward organizing the students who by this time were members of multiple informal communication networks such as the Atlanta group. She invited sit-in leaders to an Easter weekend conference for the purpose of creating a more formal group—the Student Nonviolent Coordinating Committee (SNCC). It was to become a core organization in the civil rights movement. Within a year, the communication efforts of young and inexperienced SNCC workers would galvanize thousands of other students to make huge sacrifices—in many cases putting their lives at risk—to end a southern way of life marked by racial injustice. And almost immediately, SNCC became an important part of the national media's agenda, and therefore public agenda, of the 1960s.

Communication was central to SNCC goals from the very beginning. A few days before the conference that established the organization, Baker told Southern Conference Educational Fund co-director Anne Braden that "Out of this meeting will come some workable machinery for maintaining . . . communication between youth leaders in areas of recent and future protest activities, and a larger degree of coordinated strategy."[1] During the conference, the image of SNCC as a communications organization was a fundamental to its original blueprint. As one work session report described it, there was a "specific concern" for "providing accurate news and helpful information to our constituencies."[2] Accordingly, the group established three administrative sections the next month, May: coordination, communication, and finance. Communication committee duties included the publication of a newsletter and pamphlets, the distribution of press releases, and the creation of a "system of flash news to alert the nation of emergencies and serious developments."[3] Typical of SNCC press releases were three that were issued in June of 1960. One addressed charges of communist infiltration among student activist organizations, and two others described plans to send SNCC representatives to lobby for the inclusion of civil rights goals in the platforms of the Democratic and Republican parties.[4]

During the group's first year, the paid SNCC staff primarily consisted of Jane Stembridge—a theology student, poet, and intellectual whose desk occupied a small corner of the Southern Christian Leadership Conference office in Atlanta. Stembridge had frequent contact with Baker and Martin Luther King, Jr., both of whom were committed to the strategic use of nonviolent tactics. Combined with Stembridge's religious background, these influences shaped the SNCC approach to communication and its efforts to create a "beloved community," based upon Christianity and the nonviolent perspective that defined SNCC's early years. Stembridge later described the group's initial communication activities as "spontaneous" and unplanned, yet effective.[5] Her success in providing a continuous and reliable stream of information to the organization, the national media, and government officials is remarkable in light of her lack of prior communication experience.

Evidence suggests, however, that Stembridge was also a confident public speaker in addition to being a skilled writer. In an August 25, 1960, letter to Robert Moses, who was instrumental in building a civil rights campaign in Mississippi, Stembridge mentioned that a speech she had made in Minneapolis was "well-received" and that she expected it to "net some support for SNCC, financially." In the same letter she applauded Moses for his voter registration efforts and promised that she would "work [her] fingers off" to put together and send such important communication materials as copies of the Constitution, county registration lists, affidavits, and sample ballots.

By October, Stembridge and Baker had refined SNCC's communication strategies. In addition to creating the monthly newsletter (called *The Student Voice*), a promotional pamphlet, and a system for distributing policy statements, Stembridge sent monthly reports to state representatives and assigned volunteer students as reporters in individual protest locations to facilitate the exchange of information among college newspapers. The goal was to keep sit-in participants and future participants abreast of the "inside story" of various sit-ins, boycotts, and demonstrations.[6] But even as the group's communication activities became more organized, Stembridge remembers that they maintained a strong sense of instinctiveness: "The usual categories in which we talk about organizations and communication . . . and relationships have to be suspended when you talk about something that was so raw and spontaneous."[7]

Limited funds, a small inexperienced staff, the potential for violence, and the swift pace of change within the civil rights movement were all challenges to the collection and distribution of information inside and outside the organization. Stembridge recalled that since the sit-in movement took off so quickly and spontaneously, SNCC was hard-pressed to simply keep up with events across the South. "Boom, boom, boom . . . things were happening, happening, happening," she said in an interview. "We were trying to encourage people about the issue of who had been arrested and who was in jail. What could SNCC do about that? What could the NAACP do? What could SCLC do?"[8]

Stembridge explained that in the first few months, SNCC volunteers often had no knowledge of who was organizing a sit-in in a particular town; so they searched local newspapers for names in order to track down participating students and invite them to join the Committee. On occasion, SNCC took advantage of the SCLC's ministerial network in cities where the student sit-ins were taking place and used the older organization to attract attention and organize students.

But the public relations staple that Stembridge and the Atlanta volunteers relied on most was the press release. In October 1960 Stembridge wrote to friend and fellow civil rights advocate David Forbes, "We have been keeping the name of SNCC in the papers constantly with releases and letters to the editors about everything . . . they will KNOW what SNCC is and what the movement is and that WE SHALL OVERCOME!"[9] In another almost four-page letter, she wrote to legislators, she described the organization's purpose and presented "a brief digest of information which . . . Congressmen should know," including SNCC history and philosophy and facts about the sit-in movement.[10]

Whether or not the press releases paid off depended on the recipient. Southern media organizations were mostly owned and managed by wealthy whites who participated in the oppression of blacks and who openly expressed their racist ideas in their news coverage. Stembridge said that most Southern papers only published negative reports on SNCC and other civil rights activities with the Jackson, Mississippi, *Clarion Ledger* being a prime example. Newspapers in larger cities, such as the *Atlanta Constitution* and *New York Times*, offered more objective coverage, but were still sometimes guilty of obscuring the overall views and images of the movement. Austin Long-Scott, a black Associated Press reporter in the 1960s, said in a 1999 essay that "there was much bitter controversy at the time over whether the media should be doing a better job."

> Editors tended to argue that they were doing as much as they should, simply because they were doing as much as they could bring themselves to do. . . . Most media institutions were dragged kicking and screaming into covering civil rights in the South, their hands forced by the pressure of events. And in the North, where The Movement took on the cosmetically less appealing form of an often hostile confrontation over economic injustice, the media seemed at times powerless to come to grips with the basic underlying issues. There were a few insightful stories that raised the level of understanding about what was going on. But there were even more stories that preyed upon fears and played upon fears and reinforced stereotypes and aggressive and opinionated ignorance.[11]

SNCC workers were very aware of which media outlets were open (even if guardedly) to their message, and purposefully avoided sending press releases to those that were resistant. In August of 1960, Stembridge optimistically told Forbes that she had notified all of the "'good' press people" about an upcoming citywide Atlanta kneel-in and that "coverage should be great."[12]

Stembridge also regularly responded to articles about SNCC that appeared in the local and national press. In an August 11, 1960, unsigned letter to the *Atlanta Journal* that was most likely written by Stembridge, the newspaper was strongly criticized for an attack on civil rights workers in an editorial on "Senate maneuverings":

> How dishonest when you leave unnoticed those people who cripple leg-islation for civil rights—the same people who, in fact, refuse Negroes at the school door, no matter how much federal money goes into its construction; the same people who pervert the Negroes' privilege to vote . . . [13]

Another example is a letter sent to the *Augusta Courier*, charging it with neglect by failing to mention SNCC when discussing the sit-in movement. Again, Stembridge was probably the anonymous author who wrote, "For your information, the consolidating body of the entire student movement is a self-directing organization called the Student Nonviolent Coordinating Committee."[14]

CREATING A COMMUNICATIONS STRATEGY: LAWSON, RUSTIN AND GANDHI

The students who bravely entered segregated facilities and drew the nation's attention to their cause were part of one of the most effective public rela-tions campaigns ever launched, one based on communication principles established thousands of miles from Georgia. Two SNCC advisors, James M. Lawson, Jr., and Bayard Rustin, had traveled to India in the 1950s to work with activists who had studied with Mohandas Gandhi. Those activ-ists had created and followed successful communication strategies in the 1920s and 1930s in an attempt to gain Indian independence from Great Britain. In addition to studying Gandhi's writings on nonviolence, Lawson, Rustin, and others who later filled leadership positions in the civil rights movement analyzed Gandhi's strategy of creating a centralized communica-tions force for the purpose of gaining sympathy and building support for Indian independence. Faced with few resources and little time for laying out a long-term communications plan, SNCC workers used this strategy as a foundation for much of their work. So many of SNCC's public rela-tions strategies—including disseminating information and promoting direct action campaigns—were taken from Gandhi's "toolkits" of "persuasion and protest methods."[15] Specific strategies included symbolic public assem-blies, public prayer, picket lines, vigils, demonstrations, marches, musical expositions, parades, and teach-ins—all of them heavily promoted to attract maximum press coverage.

In 1960 and 1961 America, many sit-ins and similar protests were hurriedly organized independently of SNCC, which responded by using its growing communications network to recruit students who were mostly working in isolation. Once these organizers agreed to inform SNCC of planned actions, communications workers were then able to alert the media beforehand and to disseminate information afterwards. SNCC workers also eventually created a system for recording arrests and tracking the whereabouts of protest participants.

Despite a growing amount of strategic planning, early organizational efforts remained haphazard. Limited resources made it impossible to design and implement a detailed communication plan with any degree of effectiveness in an environment where new events and demands for coordinated responses were taking place every day. SNCC workers had little choice but to react to rapidly evolving situations, but their reactions were based on a model that had succeeded thirty years earlier across the world in India.

PRE-SNCC TACTICS

With the writer and publicist Julian Bond serving as one of its leaders, the Atlanta student group that preceded SNCC likely placed greater emphasis on public relations and communications compared to other southern-based protest organizations. Under the leadership of Bond and Lonnie King, the Atlanta students established many of the public relations tactics that SNCC would eventually adopt as Bond's ideas enacted by the Atlanta group were duplicated on a national scale when he joined SNCC as a staff member in 1961.[16]

But before SNCC was established, the Atlanta students experimented with their own strategies, including visits to the presidents of their universities and colleges to explain their goals and plans for peaceful protests. The school administrators could not openly support these activities,[17] but the president of Atlanta University did advise his visitors to write a statement of principles. The result—an Appeal for Human Rights that was published in the *Atlanta Journal*—may be viewed as the first step in the students' public relations campaign. The group convinced the student government presidents at all of Atlanta's black universities to sign the document, which concluded with a pledge that they would "do whatever was necessary" in the interest of civil rights. In 1960, Bond said that the appeal was designed to provoke the conscience of anyone involved in the "immoral practices of refusing to grant to some those guaranteed rights which are due to every member of the human race."[18]

By that spring—1960—Bond had become the communications manager for the Atlanta committee, where he started the practice of sending a stream of news releases to the black press and of working with the local offices of *Time, Newsweek,* the *New York Times,* the *Washington Post,* and other members of the mainstream national press. At the beginning of the fall semester, committee members continued to organize and promote picket lines and boycotts. A typical target was an A&P grocery store in a predominately black neighborhood and supported by black customers but with only one black employee. The store and its parent chain were an important advertising client for the *Atlanta World,* and its managers used their economic leverage to pressure the paper into attacking the student group. In a 1975 interview, Bond remembered viewing the attack as "the final straw." The Atlanta students realized a strong need for their own paper, but of course they did not have the required resources. The potential for such a newspaper, however, was strong enough to attract interest from a group of local black businessmen, who asked Bond for assistance. The *Atlanta Inquirer* was born in 1960; with Bond serving as a founding writer and editor, it quickly became an important source of news on the emerging civil rights movement and served as a means for Bond to hone the communication skills that he later shared with SNCC.[19]

ATLANTA STUDENTS BECOME SNCC VOLUNTEERS

During the 1960 spring organizing conference, participants established a temporary committee and elected Marion S. Barry, Jr., as its first chairman. They made plans to establish a more formal organization (one that included sit-in organizers) later that year. Charles Cobb, an early SNCC leader, said that "two SNCCs" were active in the first few months of the organization.[20] First, there was the association of campus groups,[21] each with its own name and affiliation; for instance, the Atlanta group was known as the Committee for the Appeal of Human Rights and Howard University activists called themselves the Nonviolent Action Group. Baker's initial idea was to use SNCC as an umbrella organization to coordinate the activities of these independent groups. From Cobb's perspective, the national SNCC staff and officers were best viewed as employees serving the needs of local organizers. The second SNCC emerged with the creation of a field secretary position in the summer of 1961. The Committee began sending its own people into rural Southern communities, giving it the same status as the action-oriented groups. SNCC, however, never abandoned its self-perceived responsibility of acting as an information, communication, and administrative clearinghouse serving local groups. As the organization expanded, local leaders such as Cobb, Bond, Dianne Nash (a leader in the Nashville movement) and John Lewis became national staff members. When Robert Moses moved to Mississippi in early 1961, it marked the beginning of SNCC's official outreach campaign to cultivate local leaders.[22]

In her position as the Committee's only paid employee, Stembridge worked closely with two advisors to SNCC's executive committee: Constance Curry, who ran the National Student Association (NSA), and Baker. Moreover, Bond, Lonnie King, and A.D. King (the brother of Martin Luther King, Jr.) were frequent visitors to Stembridge's office and assisted in many of the day-to-day tasks.[23] Curry had started her job as director of the NSA Southern Student Human Relations Project in Atlanta in 1959.[24] As part of her collaboration with Stembridge, in March of 1961 she started publishing a newsletter containing information on demonstration locations, numbers of arrests, and priorities in terms of needed assistance; the newsletter was distributed from the national NSA office in Philadelphia.[25] Curry, Stembridge, and Baker formed strong personal bonds that clearly benefited the organizations they represented.[26] The three built the initial foundation for SNCC's administrative and communication projects, and their influence is obvious in many of the organization's later activities.

Stembridge later recalled that the "decision to try and succeed in nonviolence—at least for many years—was the greatest communication message" for the organization to disseminate.[27] For instance, on August 5, 1960, she submitted a "public relations report" describing all communication activities used to promote that message between mid-June and the end of July. For the most part, the report consisted of a list of individuals and organizations who had either contacted SNCC for support or who had received letters describing SNCC activities. Expelled students asking for legal assistance wrote several of the incoming letters; outgoing letters included invitations to other civil rights organizations to send representatives to a national SNCC conference. The report also contains a list of "consistent" financial supporters, including the American Friends Service Committee, the SCLC, the National Student Christian Federation, the Southern Conference Educational Fund, the Brotherhood of Sleeping-Car Porters, and Bayard Rustin.[28]

SNCC leaders and advisors came up with many communication and public relations strategies to ensure that the sit-ins and other demonstrations gained national attention and support for the civil rights movement. For instance, rather than participate in direct action campaigns, Curry served as an official observer whose main task was to disseminate information of special events to other activist groups, the media, and families of arrested protesters or victims of violence. She later recalled standing at a phone booth with a handful of change so that she could report the consequences of direct action activities.[29]

Curry had the full support of the NSA for her SNCC activities, to the point of approving her use of Field Foundation funding earmarked for her NSA work to pay some SNCC bills. Her office was very close to the SNCC office; therefore it was common to find volunteers from both organizations sharing mimeograph machines to produce press releases, fund-raising letters, and the *Student Voice*, SNCC's newsletter.[30] Bond later described Curry as "a bridge between the overwhelming number of black sit-in students and white students who were predisposed to join [the movement]" and "an invaluable resource for recruiting money and political support." Curry also publicized the sit-in movement within the NSA network; according to Bond, she "created an audience . . . that [otherwise] might not have been there."[31]

Slowly, SNCC began sponsoring and organizing its own demonstrations. On July 4, 1960, approximately twenty students gathered on the steps of the national Capitol "to see that freedom is truly free for all Americans." They sang freedom songs, prayed, and distributed public relations materials promoting SNCC and the civil rights movement. According to participant Edward B. King, Jr., even though it was broken up by local police officers after forty-five minutes, it was successful. The reason: *Jet*, *Afro*, the *Pittsburgh Courier*, and other national publications later reported on the demonstration. As part of the action, King read a prepared statement "beseech[ing] Congress to enact before the forthcoming national elections a law granting Negro American servicemen and veterans immunity from the racial segregation laws of the several Southern States." Published reports also quote King as stating the group's belief that "human rights takes precedence over States Rights, [and] that the American way of life takes precedence over the Southern way of life."[32]

The national recognition that was earned through this and other acts of resistance fueled SNCC's growth. One month after the Capitol demonstration, the organization included representatives from thirteen Southern states and the District of Columbia, and had official ties with civil rights groups across the country.[33] Stembridge used the growing number of volunteers to build a stronger organization, with the guiding principle still being to "act as an information agency" for both the media and for groups working at the grassroots level. Fundraising became increasingly important because of the growing number of students who had lost their jobs, been expelled from college, or needed to pay for bail and court costs. Acts of violence against demonstrators were attracting attention from all over the country, meaning that Stembridge and her volunteer workers had to split their time between helping individual protesters or protest groups and responding to the growing number of letters flooding into the Committee's office. In her words:

> People were writing us from Seattle and God knows where. "What's happening? What can we do?" These letters said, "Please let us know. Can we send this or that or the other?" Somebody had to watch those letters and try to get all these people who cared about these things in touch with each other."[34]

Despite the success of sit-ins, there was a growing sense among Baker, Stembridge, Curry and the SNCC volunteers that their mission was much larger than integrating lunch counters. Baker had declared at the initial conference that their ongoing work was about "more than a hamburger." When looking back on those days, she called integration a "surface goal" attached to a number of "irritants" that needed to be removed.[35]

Sit-ins and other removal tactics required the consistent execution of at least three communication tasks—the first being a combination of investigation, research, and analysis. For example, the SNCC workers gathered information about the community and location and determined how they might best stage a sit in. The second task focused on education using information gathered through the investigation. Participants were briefed on what to expect and trained in standard nonviolent tactics. The third task was negotiations with the opposition to communicate SNCC positions and perhaps reach a solution without having to organize a demonstration. In addition to sit-ins and picket lines, the last task also included such activities as boycotts, work stoppages, and other means of withholding support from a system based on oppression.[36]

POLITICAL INFLUENCE AND ORGANIZATION

Building good relations with elected and appointed government officials was also a means of dissolving "irritants" and achieving the larger goal of engendering swift and significant changes in civil rights. One of Stembridge and Baker's first collaborative tasks was to prepare a statement for presentation by SNCC Chairman Marion Barry to the 1960 Republican and Democratic national conventions. Barry told delegates that his organization represented thousands of black and white American participants in the sit-in movement, which he described as "peaceful petitions to the conscience of our fellow citizens for redress of the old grievances that stem from racial segregation and discrimination." He openly declared the student movement goals as achieving equal rights for all in education, employment, voting, and legal protection.[37] Before and after this address, Stembridge sent individual letters to political leaders, appealing to their consciences when asking for support for civil rights legislation.[38] In a series of post-convention follow-up letters, she asked each and every member of the House and Senate to address the "nature and scope of the student protest movement."[39] Barry, moreover, wrote a letter to Vice President Richard Nixon expressing regret that Nixon did not give support for the "nonviolent direct action techniques" that the students were using. In the letter, Barry argued that lack of support served to maintain the status quo.[40]

At its October conference, the SNCC leadership looked at potential methods for organizing protest groups across the South and for establishing channels to provide support for those groups. There was general consensus that the organization's relationship with local protest groups should remain "suggestive" rather than "directive"—that is, SNCC's responsibilities would entail providing communication channels and information to national and regional groups, occasionally acting as spokespersons for public relations purposes, but making it clear to all concerned that SNCC did not control local organizations.[41] After the conference, Stembridge left her post (and later returned as a Mississippi field secretary); Edward B. King, Jr., filled her Atlanta job. Over the fall and winter, SNCC took on a more formal structure, with Stembridge's former position being re-titled "executive secretary."[42]

Also during this time, SNCC communications workers established their Gandhi-inspired approach to bringing the plight of oppressed blacks to the attention of members of the local and national media, who had been invited to attend the October conference held at Atlanta University.[43] The group planned several special events designed to bring the group's messages of nonviolence and civil rights for all to the attention of the national media. One of the most important events was a mass picketing scheduled for November 2, Election Day. In a *Student Voice* article, supporters were prompted to speak "forcefully" to politicians and to actively engage in local, state, and national races, since it had become "increasingly important and expedient to realize the rights and duties we have as American citizens to exert political force to improve the conditions of those suffering second-class citizenship."[44] In declaring the Election Day protest a success, the *Student Voice* reported that students had "registered their profound dissatisfaction" with both parties and their limited approaches to civil rights issues.[45] But despite efforts to generate media attention, a special edition of the *Student Voice* declared that that the "unseeing press" ignored the events and instead focused on manufactured "Excitement in the election numbers game." The writer (likely Stembridge) noted that the country's "most significant events go unreported" in newspapers "devoted to the pomp and circumstances of the social set and the most trivial pronouncement of politicians . . ."[46] But in an effort to compensate for the lack of media attention, the four-page newsletter outlined the accomplishments of student groups across the country and concluded that the marches and demonstrations "served notice on both parties that the student movement could not be bought off by empty promises . . ."[47]

A separate demonstration in Atlanta, however, may have held greater significance to the overall movement because it involved Martin Luther King, Jr., Bond and the Atlanta students persuaded King to take part in an October sit in at Rich's Department store, where blacks were routinely refused service. Dr. King was one of several protesters who was arrested and jailed; as a nationally known figure, his presence drew considerable media attention and put pressure on national political leaders. John Kennedy telephoned King's wife, Coretta Scott King, to express his concern, and accordingly Robert Kennedy telephoned a local judge to ask for King's release.[48]

Perhaps due to the enormous amount of publicity that this action generated, SNCC leaders put out a call for students throughout the country to picket retail corporations whose Southern stores followed Jim Crow policies. This campaign, entitled "Make True the Truce . . . Free the South," focused on Woolworth's, S.H. Kress, McCrory, Grants, H.L. Green, Newberrys, Lane Rexall, and Walgreens.[49] In a telephone interview, Constance Curry said that the focus on chain establishments was based on the hope that integration at one lunch counter might lead to the integration of many others.[50] The same national approach was taken in December, when SNCC promoted a Christmas shopping boycott of stores with segregated lunch counters. Called the "Christmas Campaign Nation Wide," it was specifically designed to call attention to the fact that no lunch counters had been integrated in South Carolina, Georgia, Alabama, Mississippi, or Louisiana at that time.[51]

As the sit-in movement grew, SNCC organizers sought ways to encourage further expansion, and they began contacting such groups as the Southern Conference Educational Fund (SCEF), an interracial group of Southerners that confronted segregation and racism directed by Carl and Anne Braden. In a letter to the Committee, the Bradens asserted that the "current student movement is the most important thing that has happened in the South in a long time." They offered their assistance, including coverage of SNCC activities in their newspaper, the *Southern Patriot*. Anne Braden also suggested that SNCC leaders keep her informed of planned events and demonstrations so she could offer help to "key people in various areas of some specific project."[52]

SNCC continued its networking and communications work while it evolved into a more politically active and formal organization. It went through a rapid transformation into a field organization when several student leaders dropped out of school and started working full-time for the movement. The new full-time workers accepted fundraising assignments, which allowed them to get a sense of the tremendous mission they had become part of. Consequently, SNCC leaders raised sufficient funds to hold a seminar entitled "Understanding the Nature of Social Change" in Nashville in 1961. The purpose of the symposium was to educate attendees about nonviolence and the centralized communications activities of SNCC and the overall civil rights movement. Charles McDew, SNCC chairman, later described the event—which featured labor leaders, historians, psychiatrists, psychologists, and entertainers—as an important step toward proving SNCC's openness to all types of input:

> We brought in everybody who would talk to us about different aspects of the system that we were about to attack. I think that's important to understand, that once we decided we were going to make our move, we felt we were making it with the widest possible knowledge and information, and as I said, we talked about all sorts of things as being possible and desirable programs.[53]

FREEDOM RIDES BROADEN SNCC AUDIENCE

In its second year of existence, SNCC expanded its successful strategies to build up its political arsenal. On the next-to-last day of 1960, communications workers wrote an open letter to all members of Congress challenging them to immediately wage war on racist practices throughout the South. The letter, in which SNCC's motivation was defined as "ridding America of second class citizenship," called for updating and vigorously enforcing the 1957 Civil Rights Bill, which gave federal prosecutors authority to sue anyone who interfered with voting rights, "without which all campaign promises become hollow mockery."[54]

The new year also brought broader coverage in the national press—one sign of a successful effort by communication workers to distribute periodic news reports. For example, they had plenty to report on: an internal document dated March 3 includes descriptions of demonstrations and violent resistance in Columbia, Rock Hill, and Sumter, South Carolina; Chattanooga, Tennessee; Lynchburg, Virginia; Tallahassee, Florida; Atlanta and

Macon, Georgia; Houston, Dallas, San Antonio, and Austin, Texas; and Louisville, Kentucky. Hundreds of students were arrested, including 188 who sang hymns during an anti-segregation march on the South Carolina state capitol.[55]

Another strategy that garnered considerable publicity was the "jail vs. bail" campaign that Bayard Rustin proposed to the students. The idea was not only simple; it saved protest organizations a considerable amount of money. Protesters chose to stay in jail rather than post bail, which discouraged local authorities from making additional arrests. Local governments lost money housing the protesters, and movement organizations did not have to deplete their bank accounts on bail and related legal fees.[56] The campaign also sent a powerful message to local authorities and the media that civil rights activists constituted a unified force that could not be ignored. SNCC staff wrote up detailed descriptions of these campaigns and distributed them to college students, federal officials, community residents, and reporters.

In April, SNCC started its involvement in an action that resulted in considerable violence, but that also did much to increase awareness of the civil rights movement throughout the nation. It designed a campaign entitled "Drive Against Travel Bias" for the purpose of informing the American public that Southern bus companies and governments were blatantly ignoring a 1955 Interstate Commerce Commission (ICC) ruling against segregated facilities in bus terminals. Participating students requested equal service and to speak to a manager if refused. Afterwards, participants filed reports on their experiences, and SNCC workers sent the files to the Trailways Corporation and the Justice Department.[57]

Later that spring, SNCC promoted an action that was sponsored by the Congress of Racial Equality (CORE), a civil rights organization based in the North.[58] It was to become one of the most attention-getting events of the entire civil rights movement: the first Southern Freedom Ride, which began in Washington, D.C., on May 4. The riders included seven black and six white activists who set out to test the federal provision that outlawed segregation in interstate bus terminal facilities. By the time the group arrived in Atlanta on May 13, three members were in jail and several violent incidents had occurred. An angry mob confronted the riders in Anniston, Alabama, between Atlanta and Birmingham, and firebombed the bus. Most of the riders suffered from smoke inhalation, and several were severely beaten. When the second bus arrived in Birmingham, a group of men attacked five of the riders with lead pipes.[59]

At this point, CORE dropped its sponsorship of the project. Ruby Doris Smith, a SNCC worker who later served as executive secretary, quickly telephoned all of the SNCC campus affiliates and asked for their support to continue the project.[60] Dianne Nash, the Nashville coordinator, also did what she could to ensure that the rides continued, asking CORE director James Farmer to allow SNCC-affiliated students in Nashville to take over the project. She argued that despite the certainty of violence, discontinuing the rides would imply that the young organizers were giving up:

> If the signal was given to the opposition that violence could stop us . . . if we let the Freedom Rides stop, then whenever we tried to do anything in the Movement in the future, we were going to meet with a lot of violence. And we would probably have to get a number of people killed before we could reverse that message.[61]

After accepting responsibility for the project, SNCC sent the buses from Birmingham to Montgomery (where more violence occurred) and Jackson, Mississippi, where police arrested all of the riders and sent them to a state penitentiary for forty-nine days.

The violence attracted national attention and an outpouring of support for the organization and the movement. In late September, Attorney General Robert Kennedy persuaded the ICC to ban segregation in bus terminals—the orders were effective November 1. The ICC edict was a secondary outcome compared to the national publicity that the rides created. As the historian Clayborne Carson noted, the event sparked an awareness of the students' "collective ability . . . [to] provoke a crisis that would attract international publicity and compel federal intervention."[62]

The SNCC administrative staff provided the national media with a non-stop stream of information during the rides. Upon their conclusion, Edward King made an important public relations move by sending a telegram to President Kennedy, which may have influenced the ICC ruling against segregated facilities. His central message was that the violence imposed on the Freedom Riders was unjustifiable and that the federal government had no choice but to "exercise firm and precise leadership" to address the situation. King insisted that Kennedy inform the entire nation that black Americans were "first class citizens" entitled to "all rights and privileges guaranteed by the Constitution of the United States as they seek to use the various modes of inter-state travel."[63]

MOSES JOINS LOCAL BLACKS TO TAKE ON MISSISSIPPI

Perhaps the most important force behind SNCC's transition from an organization focused on sit-ins to one focused on both direct action and voter registration was Robert Moses, a soft-spoken Harlem-born philosophy student and math teacher. Moses, inspired by the sit in demonstrations, left teaching to join Stembridge and the student movement in the summer of 1960. And on August 13, Moses stepped onto a Trailways bus in Atlanta to begin a three-week tour of Alabama, Mississippi, and Louisiana for the purpose of contacting local civil rights leaders and offering assistance for them to "get organized."[64] At the time, Marion Barry described Moses's plan as establishing "a much stronger network of communication throughout the deep South."[65] In an August 14, 1960 letter to David Forbes, Stembridge predicted that "this could prove to be one of the most important ventures we have undertaken, not only for getting people to the [October national] Conference but for the future communication of the movement."[66]

During his tour, Moses met a local NAACP leader in Cleveland, Mississippi named Amzie Moore. Stembridge, who had heard about Moore through the SCLC, sent him a letter describing SNCC's efforts to "improve the system of communication among students" and asking for his help in introducing Moses to local residents.[67] In a report of his activities, Moses wrote "Amzie is the best I've met yet. . . . I would trust him explicitly and implicitly, and contact him frequently."[68] During their time together, Moore persuaded Moses to pursue voter registration as a means of achieving civil rights goals. Charles Cobb, a SNCC activist, later explained that Moore and other NAACP activists were anxious to organize in Mississippi, but their national leaders considered the state too difficult and dangerous to penetrate. According to Cobb, NAACP members such as Moore, Henry Silas, E.W. Steptow, Aaron Henry, C.C. Bryant, and Hartman Turnbow were "ready to move"; and SNCC having recently "washed in on the Freedom Ride," was able to "open the doors" of Mississippi.[69] As the two men visited communities near Cleveland for the purpose of establishing strategic relationships, they planned a voter registration campaign and a communications strategy to support it.[70]

The idea of voter registration did not win immediate approval within SNCC. An important segment of the membership remained focused on sit-ins, which by August of 1961 had involved more than 70,000 protesters and about 3,000 arrests. In August, SNCC workers met at the Highlander School in Tennessee to debate whether they should continue their focus on direct action or refocus their energy on voter registration. McDew recalled that after four days of heated discussion, "the beloved community nearly fell apart because everybody was arguing so passionately for what direction they felt SNCC should go."[71] But each faction agreed to move the organization forward in both directions. Dianne Nash, the architect of numerous Nashville demonstrations, took charge of the direct action wing, and Charles Jones led the voter registration effort. But within weeks, the two divisions realized that they were working toward the same goal, and therefore had no reason for administrative separation.[72]

Many notable changes in personnel occurred in 1961. When Stembridge left the organization in the spring, Edward B. King, Jr. replaced her as executive secretary until September, when he returned to school.[73] James Forman, a former teacher and reporter for the *Chicago Defender*, replaced King as executive secretary in the fall of 1961. Forman's appointment turned out to be one of SNCC's most important personnel decisions. Baker described him as an "excellent strategist under pressure . . . he was effective, and therefore people deferred to him."[74] One of his first actions was to convince Bond to serve as full-time communications director. It was a position that Bond would hold throughout SNCC's most productive and influential years, yet he credits Forman with establishing the foundation for the organization's most successful public relations projects:[75]

> Forman was a master propagandist. He insisted that SNCC develop a publicity apparatus–called Communications–and that it produce materials of the highest quality and unassailable objectivity . . . From him I learned to write brief, punchy press releases, and how to report on movement activity to skeptical journalists in a believable way.[76]

In addition to producing press releases, Forman and Bond acted as ghost writers for statements attributed to the SNCC chairman at that time, Charles McDew, who spent much of his time in fundraising activities away from Atlanta.[77] McDew gave Bond and Forman authority to issue statements using his name for attribution in SNCC publications, and limited authority for statements distributed to the mainstream media. Consequently, the small communications staff helped elevate McDew's status, which made him a more effective fund raiser and spokesperson for the overall civil rights movement.

There were, however, still considerable barriers in terms of day-to-day operations. That fall, there were four people working regularly in the SNCC office: Forman, Bond, Norma Collins who handled clerical tasks, and John Hardy, described as "a jack of all trades."[78] The primitive working conditions made it difficult to transmit messages quickly and efficiently. Forman remembered that "physically it was a nightmare to get out a mailing. We had to go to another office to use its mimeograph machine; we couldn't spread things out, and there was no room to maintain decent files."[79]

The reason, of course, was money. Despite McDew's efforts, there was never enough to adequately fund all of SNCC's varied projects. One source of frustration was the flow of money to other civil rights organizations that contributors wrongly viewed as being SNCC affiliates. In 1975, Bond told researchers Bob Hall and Sue Thrasher:

> I can remember Forman and I going into the bank to deposit two or five dollars, and seeing Wyatt Tee Walker [head of the SCLC] . . . depositing sacks of checks. It was irritating as the devil because we knew we were the people doing things. King was going around making speeches, but that was it; they didn't have anybody in the field hardly. But they were getting all this dough, much of it I'm sure, marked 'To Southern Students, c/o Dr. Martin Luther King.' The Southern civil rights movement was just known as SCLC . . . [80]

In a 1998 speech to the National Press Club, Bond recalled that one of his initial tasks as communications director was "to get reporters to differentiate between SNCC and the [SCLC]—or Snick and Slick, as we put it—and to make sure our story was told."[81] To accomplish this, SNCC communications workers began adding the words "SNCC is an independent student organization" to all of their press releases and publications and following up with reporters who confused the organizations.[82]

THE PROTECTIVE EYE OF THE NATIONAL PRESS

Public recognition grew as a result of SNCC's political organizing activities as well as slogans and press releases. Through the organizing skills of such leaders as Amzie Moore and Robert Moses, SNCC slowly established voter registration projects throughout the South, especially in Mississippi. According to Bond, one reason SNCC succeeded where other organizations failed was that its "more numerous and less transient" workers actually lived in the isolated rural communities they were trying to organize.[83] This characteristic was a SNCC organizational hallmark. The unconventional partnership of young college students and the rural poor made a lasting impression on oppressed black Southerners. The SNCC workers used their growing experience in communications strategies to promote their activities and to show the nation the destitute standard of living that was common among blacks in the rural South.

But while a public relations campaign may have educated the general population, it did not have the desired effect on the Washington establishment, which continued to exert pressure on SNCC to restrict its activities.

Forman later noted that Attorney General Robert Kennedy encouraged SNCC's voter registration campaign, but for the reason that it "would not embarrass the United States government as much."[84] Concerned that the Justice Department might make an attempt to control the student movement, Forman and other leaders turned down a considerable amount of money in the form of federal grants. As a result, they felt no pressure to appease government officials or to redirect their efforts from rural to urban areas.[85] But although the Committee turned down federal money, it maintained important relationships with several federal agencies. This was helpful for the work being performed by rural field secretaries, who pushed for *enforcement* of the 1957 Civil Rights Bill—especially requirements of federal protection for registered voters and those who were working to register new voters. Forman said that SNCC used this statute in the early 1960s "to pressure the federal government to do what it was supposed to do, and that is to protect people in the exercise of their right to vote."[86]

SNCC workers faced new and more arduous challenges in Mississippi. The state's history of violent resistance to the civil rights movement instilled fear in most local residents. Up to the time that Moses and Moore started their registration campaign, Mississippi leaders had largely managed to block "outside agitators" and maintain racial injustice as a way of life. In terms of public relations, McDew knew that it would take an exceptional effort to convince the national press to travel to Mississippi to do some hands-on reporting, yet without the presence of the national news media, SNCC workers would always be in danger of violent retribution for their organizing work:

> When you made a move on Mississippi, one of the things you had to do was come to grips with your own mortality . . . This is not going to be big demonstrations with lots of television cameras with people around watching . . . when we went on those highways in the middle of the night . . . you had to think that you would never live to see your home again.[87]

That August, SNCC organizers bravely selected McComb, Mississippi—one of the most resistant and potentially violent cities in the state—to begin their registration efforts. They chose McComb based on what they perceived as significant local support. Hollis Watkins, a high school student who participated in some of the SNCC-led activities, recalled that the registration efforts were accompanied by lunch counter sit-ins and demonstrations at local bus stations, which in turn led to a boycott of the local high school after several students had been expelled for their participation.

McComb was also the location of SNCC's first Freedom School, designed to provide political and cultural education and modeled after the Highlander School. Established in 1961, it served as a model for schools offering educational opportunities beyond those of Mississippi's sharply segregated schools, which neglected any mention of African American historical, cultural, or economic contributions.[88]

The school boycott encouraged the national media's interest in the plight of civil rights workers in Mississippi. During his first few days as executive secretary, Forman spent much of his time responding to telephone calls from the press regarding the boycott and other McComb activities. Realizing how ill-prepared the office was to manage the constant flow of media inquiries, Forman focused his considerable organizational skills on making SNCC's external communication activities more professional and timely.[89] He soon convinced Bond to leave the *Atlanta Inquirer* and to work for SNCC full-time as the creator and manager of an apparatus for gaining greater media coverage for the organization and the entire civil rights movement.

After two weeks of training in the Freedom School, small numbers of McComb residents attempted to register at the Pike County courthouse. Although they were met with violent resistance and arrests, they served as inspiring examples worthy of press attention. Hollis Watkins later recalled that SNCC workers were successful in their effort to "educate, motivate, and inspire people from different areas to get up and do something and take some initiative upon themselves." Remaining true to the organizational mission promoted by Ella Jo Baker, SNCC workers never ceased in their efforts to find and support local leaders, therefore many Mississippi SNCC staff positions, paid and volunteer, were soon filled with Mississippians.

As SNCC attracted a growing number of field secretaries from all over the South to work with the indigenous Mississippi activists, the appearance of twelve full-time workers in McComb marked the final stage of SNCC's transformation from an administrative umbrella organization for student groups to a field organization. But Forman and Bond continued their efforts to disseminate information throughout the country, with a special focus on reaching students in northern states for purposes of distributing information and fundraising.[90]

ALBANY, GEORGIA

Albany, Georgia, was the site of a separate SNCC effort to organize a voter registration campaign and to gain publicity for the movement. Former Freedom Riders and sit-in activists Cordell Reagon, Charles Jones, and Charles

Sherrod arrived in Albany to ignite local voter registration efforts. They reported their slow progress to the Atlanta office. Their work, however, which began in October of 1961 and lasted until the following summer, did attract national media attention, and therefore raised awareness about the of horrendous acts of oppression in Albany and of civil rights activities throughout the rural South.

Albany SNCC workers produced several communication tools that remained separate from those created in Atlanta, including fact sheets, press releases, and their own edition of the *Student Voice*. In mid-November the group started a campaign to encourage local residents to register by December 1 in order to be eligible to vote in the 1962 elections. Their plans included letter writing, canvassing the entire town block-by-block, and asking for support and funds at local churches. SNCC representatives wrote prepared speeches for local leaders, but they encouraged speakers to use them as guidelines for writing their own personal statements.[91] One anonymous writer, identifying herself as an Albany housewife, issued a plea for fellow blacks to "awaken" and register to vote. In the essay, which SNCC workers distributed throughout the town's black community, she argued that voting was the best method for changing economic conditions. She asked, "[How long can you] sit, sleep, toil and remain at the foot of the ladder when there's room for you and your family at the top?"[92]

Albany SNCC workers also used their arsenal of communication strategies to conduct direct action campaigns. On November 1, nine civil rights workers participated in a bus station sit-in to test compliance with the ICC anti-segregation ruling. As planned, the students left when threatened with arrests, but they later filed affidavits with the federal agency. The bus terminal action led to the formation of the Albany Movement, consisting of representatives from SNCC, the NAACP, and other civil rights organizations.[93] On November 22, five of the sit-in participants were arrested. Three posted $100 bonds and two chose to remain in jail. Bertha Goeber, one of the students who served time, said that she hoped her decision would "dramatically" represent "the evil and inconvenience of segregation" to local and national communities.[94] Members of the Albany Movement responded with mass meetings held in local churches; the songs that were sung during those meetings came to be known as "freedom songs." That music—later performed by a group calling itself the SNCC Freedom Singers—constituted a major public relations contribution from the Albany campaign.

The students' trial was scheduled for November 27. Between 300 and 400 supporters took part in a demonstration to protest the arrests and the expulsion of two of the students from Albany College, a local black institution.[95] Despite the college's status as a local center for black education, SNCC workers and black Albany residents viewed its administrators as collaborators supporting the town's oppressive status quo. In response to the university policy of reprimanding or expelling student activists unless they agreed to permanently cease their protest activities, an anonymous editorial writer declared in the December edition of the Albany *Student Voice* that "the administration will use any childish form of retaliation in hopes of silencing the free-thinking student."[96] Although the writer did not identify the college president by name, the charge was made that he had committed a crime "against humanity":

> He has not only suppressed, by law and contemptible means, any inquiry or active interest in the correction of a morally degenerate situation which internally affects each and every one of his charged, but he has . . . endorsed and supported the bigoted schemes and vile methods of perpetrators of his corruption. Betrayal is the most damning of these atrocities, not only because he betrays himself and his children both present and to come, but because he betrays with his calumny, the inability of the human mind and the precious right of the eternal soul to seek out and replace with good the evil that surrounds it in such infamous abundance.[97]

In response, the national SNCC office issued a call for all groups to protest the arrests and distributed a statement declaring that "unless the Justice Department and the ICC insure the rights of all passengers to use bus and train facilities without being subjected to harassment . . . the Freedom Rides and the . . . ICC ruling will have been in vain."[98] Charles Jones wrote a call for action in which he encouraged Albany's black community to band together and "take the legal guarantees on thin paper and turn [them] into thick action of implementation."[99] On December 10, SNCC and the SCLC organized a Freedom Ride from Atlanta to Albany, this time by train. The ten riders included Forman, Bob Zellner (SNCC's first white field secretary), Norma Collins, and Joan Browning, a volunteer in the Atlanta administrative office. All ten were arrested as they sat together in the Albany waiting room.

Local Southern jails were particularly notorious as dangerous places for civil rights activists, but the ten protesters refused bail in order to clearly communicate their message of nonviolence in response to oppression. This is an example where a communications strategy served two purposes: increasing external awareness of an event and protecting jailed participants. Bond may have saved several lives with his press relations skills. Browning remembers that within hours of her arrest, Bond distributed a press release to dozens of media organizations that described the details surrounding the arrest and included the names of the incarcerated demonstrators.[100] Once the media had these names, local authorities were less likely to physically abuse their prisoners. In Browning's words, "Once your name is out there in public that you are in jail in Albany it is hard for them to 'spirit' you out of the jail and 'disappear' you without someone knowing." Browning also recalls that Bond was able to maintain a "drum beat of media attention in Albany"; the presence of so many reporters in the area could not be ignored.

The arrests of the Freedom Riders triggered mass rallies and demonstrations in Albany on December 14; in all, about 480 protesters were arrested.[101] However, Laurie Pritchett, the Albany police chief, was familiar with the jail-filling strategy, and therefore made arrangements with surrounding counties to accept the vast majority of prisoners. By keeping the Albany jail empty, Pritchett succeeded in reducing the effectiveness of the local action.[102] The SNCC campaign, however, was successful in building local support and in attracting national attention. Albany officials promised to create a biracial committee to address the demands of the civil rights protesters, including the release of prisoners and enforcement of the ICC ruling.

The negotiations broke down almost immediately. After addressing a large group of civil rights activists, Dr. King was arrested along with 250 other rally participants. King announced his intention to spend Christmas in the Albany jail, and the public response that ensued forced local officials back to the negotiating table. Within two days, King announced that an agreement had been reached regarding compliance with the ICC regulations; he was released on bail as part of the settlement.[103] The agreement was considered a victory, but Albany officials failed to keep their promise to desegregate the local bus system. Demonstrations continued for a while, but the Albany movement went into rapid decline.

The events in Albany had given it a prominent location on the civil rights map. The episode also underscored how the strategic use of certain communication techniques could motivate local residents to resist oppression that they had long considered commonplace. In a SNCC document entitled "Report from Albany," Frances Pauley, a SNCC worker in Albany, argued that even though the movement did not "win specific goals," Albany's black population made tremendous progress during the few turbulent weeks of demonstrations. She also emphasized the fact that the demonstrations were not marred by violence or brutality, even toward demonstrators who had been imprisoned. Furthermore, the Albany negotiations marked the first time that black and white leaders had ever sat down "face to face" and "man to man" to work toward solutions to local issues.[104]

SOLIDIFYING A NATIONAL SUPPORT BASE

The tumultuous events in Albany closed out SNCC's second year. Although most acts of resistance were still imperiled by violence and arrests, the group renewed its commitment to direct action and its expanding voter registration campaign. There was plenty of evidence to support the idea that sit-ins worked. For instance, a 1963 study conducted by Martin Oppenheimer noted that in more than 50 percent of all cases, sit-ins resulted in some progress toward desegregating restaurants, theaters, department stores, or public facilities.[105]

Although it is difficult to directly measure the success of the SNCC communication efforts from a cause and effect perspective, evidence suggests that the impact was significant. For example, SNCC's early communication work also has important ramifications for understanding and exploring the construction of news during the sit in years. By distributing their own publications and by working to diligently maintain a strong relationship with the national press, the group helped to set the nation's agenda via the press and via public relations.[106] In many ways, it clearly illustrates the significant role that public relations played in creating civil rights news. Perhaps most relevant to constructing the news, the young activists quickly realized that staging events, such as sit-ins and protests, attracted the national media and created support for their cause. So even without an accurate calculation of printed news releases and successful stories pitched, we can review the national media of the day to see extensive coverage of SNCC events–events specifically designed to attract the national media and consequently the support of the national public.

At the end of December 1961 SNCC was entering its twentieth month as a formal organization. During its brief life, it had not only created, directed, and encouraged direct-action demonstrations, it had also become a fully functioning entity capable of galvanizing large numbers of supporters from all parts of the United States. In a spring 1961 editorial, the *Student Voice* declared that SNCC had combined "natural and spontaneous leadership within the individual protest groups to carry out nonviolent demonstrations against racial segregation throughout the Southland."[107] Because of SNCC-sponsored sit-ins, the civil rights movement had been expanded far beyond the mostly Southern communities that were the primary targets of the demonstrations.

By early 1962, southern sit-ins had a national audience, one that was increasingly aware of the nonviolent character of the civil rights movement and therefore willing to express vocal and financial support. That awareness was in great part due to the public relations efforts of largely inexperienced college students and administrative staff who mimeographed thousands of pages of reports, press releases, internal memos, and letters to government and political leaders. As the national organization and local groups joined forces, communication efforts became more formal and organized. From a single desk in the corner of a sister organization's office, SNCC had grown to become the primary point group in field actions aimed at forcing social change in all parts of the United States, but especially in the South.

Chapter Two
Freedom in the Air: Politics and Community

Ninety-five percent of the time our staff forms the primary link with "the outside world." Whenever there are atrocities committed against the local population, we must assume responsibility for communicating these to the news media and interested groups.[1]

—SNCC Internal Report, July 15, 1963

In early 1962, SNCC transcended its responsibilities of student group coordination and established itself as an activist organization with full-time field secretaries scattered throughout the South. These field secretaries worked with the administrative staff to make SNCC an organization capable of empowering local leadership—precisely the philosophy that Ella Jo Baker tried to instill in the attendees of the 1960 organizing conference. The growing number of workers added political action and voter registration to their short list of primary goals. And in order to confront the racist political system that ran the American South in the early 1960s, SNCC did its best to convince the residents of black communities that they must join the fight for their voting rights, through which they could improve their lives and those of their children.

These two years—1962 and 1963—stand out in SNCC's history as a time of political growth and recognition. By this time, local, state, and federal authorities were aware of the organization and understood that it had become a component of the public agenda. With this expanding power, the SNCC workers delved into sleepy southern communities and began the process of encouraging blacks to register to vote. Achieving these lofty goals required the construction of communication links among poor and isolated rural black communities, SNCC field secretaries, and Atlanta-based workers whose responsibility it was to disseminate a steady stream of supportive information to the media, the public, and political leaders.

The top-down flow of information consisted of nonviolent strategies for field activities and campaigns. Field secretaries and volunteers forged horizontal connections to share success stories to inspire and motivate both internal and external audiences. And all the while, SNCC's guiding mission was to build a sense of community that crossed state borders, a mission requiring the sophisticated use of very basic communication strategies and tools.

By the close of 1963, SNCC would have major field projects underway in Selma and Gadsden, Alabama (managed by Worth Long); Pine Bluff, Arkansas (William Hansen); Albany and Americus, Georgia (Charles Sherrod); much of Mississippi, with bases in Batesville, Biloxi, Clarksdale, Cleveland, Columbus, Greenville, Greenwood, Hattiesburg, Holly Springs, Jackson, Laurel, McComb, Meridian, and Vicksburg, (Robert Moses); Raleigh, North Carolina (Reginald Robinson); and Danville and Farmville, Virginia (Avon Rollins). The core staff consisted of ninety-six field secretaries and field workers, twelve Atlanta-based administrative staff members, and over 100 full-time volunteer workers. James Forman had also established twelve Friends of SNCC groups in the Northeast and West, primarily on college campuses, to help send SNCC's message and gather support for the organization.

To maintain connections among all of these elements, the central office organized annual national meetings and invited the general public and the media. In a November 1962 letter inviting all SNCC workers to a fall conference at Fisk University in Nashville, Forman described planned workshops on nonviolence, politics, voting rights, economics, and communications.[2] He also expressed his optimism that "good will" would flow from this gathering in the same manner it had flowed through previous meetings. He urged field secretaries to prepare detailed reports of their activities for distribution to all attendees.[3] The Atlanta staff organized the conferences while simultaneously running a media campaign consisting of a non-stop stream of newsletters, press releases, fact sheets, employee/volunteer relations material, event notifications, and invitations. As they gained experience, the communications staff became increasingly savvy in meeting the needs of newspaper editors—for instance, surveying them for guidance as to preferred press release formats, timing, and other suggestions for increasing the chances that their messages would be perceived as legitimate.[4]

Fred Powledge, a 1960s journalist who worked for the *Atlanta Journal* and later the *New York Times,* referred to Julian Bond and Dorothy Miller Zellner as "the captains and lieutenants and colonels" of the southern protests and explained that they manned the Atlanta headquarters office to send press information as soon as an event broke out. He described them as the kind of public relations people that served a valid and valuable service by making sure that reporters had access to the facts.

> If SNCC knew something was going to happen . . . let's say Forman was going to march on a Deep South cracker country courthouse, that meant that a dangerous situation was about to occur. They [Bond and Zellner] would tell the FBI, even though they did not trust them for good reason, and they would also tell the press.[5]

Along with managing the flow of information, the communication staff devised strategies to get their news transmitted even when reporters were not receptive. In a critical media relations strategy, SNCC workers, who knew that their news releases were often ignored, learned through wire service contacts that the wire editors took note of stories about telegrams that had been sent to the federal government and affidavits and complaints filed with government agencies. To take advantage of information, the communication staff used a strategy that Forman developed. The Friends of SNCC representatives asked northern reporters to request a story and determine if a particular event had occurred. This strategy pressured southern wire services to present some of the facts.[6] King said the Atlanta wires were then obligated to carry a report. And this, of course, required that they dispatch a reporter to the scene.[7] So, rather than send a news story directly related to an incident, the group first wired a telegram about the incident or a victim's affidavit to either Robert Kennedy, the attorney general, President Kennedy, or another prominent politician. Forman recalled that not only did this strategy "arouse public opinion in favor of our cause," it also put politicians on the spot publicly and played "on the contradictions between the federal government—that was supposedly official American 'democratic' policy—and the state governments of the South and their blatant racism."[8]

When King joined SNCC's staff in the summer of 1963, she recalled that she was amazed at the extent of influence that the two-person, two-telephone SNCC communication office exerted. The organization had recently installed three Wide Area Telephone Service (WATS) lines. "No WATS lines installed by the American Telephone and Telegraph Company ever got more use than SNCC's." Now that field secretaries could telephone reports without concern for long-distance charges, the communications staff could disseminate more news with greater detail and accuracy. King said that she and Bond used the WATS system to "coordinate action, gather information or news stories as they occurred, break those items to the news media, send messages, issue telegrams, call press conference, lessen reprisal, and sometimes save lives." So even in the face of limited staff and funding, King said that she and Bond, "hunched over two telephones in an obscure street in southwest Atlanta," mobilized support groups across the country, concocted media relations strategies that made "it impossible for the wire services to walk away from a story, [roused] the national press corps into action, [and tried] to prod the FBI into doing right."[9]

Still, keeping the SNCC message in the public eye required enormous persistence on the part of communication workers, administrative staff, field secretaries, and volunteers; and SNCC's success in making the organization an accepted part of the national political arena remains one of its major achievements.

OVERCOMING MEDIA COMPLACENCY

In early 1962, SNCC workers set into motion a more structured communications plan for broadening support for the civil rights movement throughout the country. The political action component was clearly building steam in terms of motivating local residents to participate in protest activities and to assume the risks associated with voter registration. Forman later explained that at the beginning of the year, SNCC made a strong commitment to using voter registration as a "tool by which consciousness might be aroused, politicized, and organized."[10] The timing was right—Northern news organizations had assisted the movement by publishing inspiring stories about sit-in organizers and participants and their ability to move forward despite the threat of violence, but as the sit-ins declined, they lost interest. Danny Lyon, a white Northerner who worked for two years as a SNCC photographer, said that in 1962 few Northerners, including reporters, believed that "Southern blacks in Mississippi would rise up and fight for their rights." He added that the Northern press showed little interest in covering the details of the movement, but they were eager to receive trustworthy information and pictures related to beatings and bombings.[11]

Even when relegated to the back pages of white-owned publications, mentions of SNCC and of student-organized sit-ins still had an impact on communities that were not accustomed to press attention. There was a period, however, when front-page stories featuring sit-ins were expected components of local news, and SNCC workers found it much easier to either generate or disseminate newsworthy stories to the mainstream media. In a 1962 article, a SNCC worker named Betty Garman argued that even with its limited coverage of civil rights activity, the Southern white press had "aided coordination." By 1962, however, Garman and her coworkers were faced with an increasingly difficult task of "devising new ways to direct the spirit of protest into action," since media coverage was far less frequent.[12]

RURAL VOTING RIGHTS, URBAN PUBLICITY

Another possible explanation for the national media's decreasing interest in the civil rights movement is its traditional bias toward urban affairs over rural events. In the latter half of 1961, SNCC activity was focused on Southwest Georgia and Mississippi. This was an important strategic decision that served to distinguish SNCC from other civil rights organizations. Garman pointed out that registration numbers were lowest in rural areas and that rural blacks tended be more apathetic—in no small part because of threats of violence in response to any political activity on their part. From a strategic standpoint, these Deep South rural counties—137 with black majorities—were very important because they carried a "balance of voting strength" in state legislative and congressional elections.[13] Forman called the disproportionate representation of whites in state capitols throughout the south a "rotten boroughs" system that encouraged oppression by local white power structures. So by 1962 it was obvious to SNCC and other civil rights organizations that registering rural blacks was the fastest route to their gaining political power.[14] Forman, the ex-newspaper reporter who generally considered the communications aspect of his decisions, believed that white fear over the potential of lost political power could be translated into greater media coverage for the voter registration campaign. He also accepted the fact that such exposure would more likely than not be the result of violent reactions on the part of local white authorities.[15]

A comparison of two events shows how SNCC's grass roots interactions with the rural poor could be combined with sophisticated communications strategies to promote local civil rights campaigns. The first involved Fannie Lou Hamer and other poor black Mississippians. Hamer, a native of Ruleville, Mississippi, and a plantation worker for most of her life will always be remembered for giving a passionate speech at the beginning of the 1964 Democratic National Convention in Atlantic City. She later told an oral historian that she was never exposed to the idea of blacks voting until she attended a SNCC mass meeting:

> They were talking about we could vote out people that we didn't want in office . . . That sounded interesting enough to me that I wanted to try it. I had never heard, until 1962, that black people could register and vote . . . I heard it from Robert Moses and another man named Jim Forman.[16]

Moses was also involved in the other central event: the decision by CBS to produce a documentary on the Mississippi voter registration campaign and to air it to a prime time national audience in September 1962. The film showed Hattiesburg, Mississippi, voter registrar Theron Lynd turning away black voters and intentionally failing them on a literacy test—long one of the most effective methods for keeping blacks off county voting rolls. The test included difficult questions regarding interpretations of the state constitution. Even when blacks answered correctly, registrars had a list of other guidelines that could be used to reject the respondent's application. Whites were generally registered without taking such tests. To the astonishment of millions of viewers, CBS had captured these overt acts of discrimination on film. Those viewers were unaware that Moses had worked closely with the network production team to ensure not only that the message of overt discrimination would be clearly stated, but also that SNCC's organizing efforts would be shown in the best possible light. The *Student Voice* told its readers that the CBS program made it clear that despite "attacks on voters and registration workers, efforts to register Negroes in the State of Mississippi were not halting and would continue."[17]

There were other symbolic and practical organizing campaigns in between these two extremes of national and grass roots organizing successes. For example, Dianne Nash, the direct action proponent and leader in the Nashville area, spent time in Jackson, Mississippi, helping indigenous community organizers build campaigns for black Congressional candidates—a project that relied heavily on the skills of SNCC workers who had become increasingly experienced and sophisticated in public relations operations. Those skills were used to educate black Jackson residents about the election process, including poll tax payments and literacy tests. Residents received newsletters describing the various candidates and the circumstances surrounding the elections. No one expected that a black candidate could win in 1962 Mississippi, but the idea of running an electoral campaign was a public relations success because it proved to residents that the idea of local black political leadership was both legitimate and possible at a future date. Ten years later, Forman described the Jackson campaign as a "forum" for local issues involving racism and a method of "[shaking] loose some of the fear that many blacks in Mississippi had at that time."[18]

Mississippi racists were more vigorous in their use of intimidation tactics compared to anti-integrationists in other states, but their zealousness often worked against them in terms of media notoriety. In one extremely overt action that took place in early February 1962, SNCC tried to integrate the gallery seating area in the Mississippi legislature. Howard Zinn (a white SNCC advisor who was a professor at Spelman College in Atlanta) and one of his white students joined a group of SNCC workers sitting in the section designated for blacks. Both were ejected from the building, and several days later SNCC organized a picket line on the capitol grounds in protest. Most of the protesters were arrested. As Forman explained, such events were helpful in exposing "one more nerve of the festering body of the racist United States."[19]

The events in Mississippi did much to further the cause of the civil rights movement and to put SNCC in a positive light, but not enough to keep the organization or its operations financially solvent. Charles McDew worked non-stop to raise money in Northern states, but he still had trouble maintaining the distinction between SNCC and other activist groups. John Lewis, soon to be SNCC chair, complained that SNCC was taking on all of the risks associated with grass roots organizing in such states as Mississippi, but the bulk of civil rights contributions was still going to groups that sat on the sidelines. To remedy this situation, in January 1962, Moses created an umbrella group known as the Council of Federated Organizations (COFO). The alliance consisted of SNCC, the SCLC, the Congress of Racial Equality, and the NAACP. Hollis Watkins, the McComb student who by this time was serving as a Mississippi field secretary, described COFO as a means of demonstrating a "sense of unity and harmony" among civil rights organizations and to "prevent conflicts in fund raising." Funds sent to individual groups could be directed toward COFO and used specifically for Mississippi projects.[20] Additional funds came from an organization called the Voter Education Project (VEP), which was sponsored by the Southern Regional Council. Forman later described the project as a "tax dodge" for the Democratic Party—that is, a strategy for registering voters using tax-exempt funds. By designating money for SNCC activities, VEP organizers could help register voters, who would very likely vote for Democratic candidates and collect information on registration irregularities. VEP money was considered tax-exempt under Internal Revenue Service rules concerning "educational activity."[21]

Forman and other SNCC leaders knew they were taking a risk by participating in the VEP plan since taking the money could put them in a position of answering to political leaders who might expect a role in determining their future plans. The shared organizational goals of the two groups, however, dictated collaboration: both wanted to register voters, and the VEP had much deeper pockets than SNCC. As such, SNCC leaders believed that they could use the VEP to encourage the enforcement of federal laws meant to combat the voter registration practices of Southern state governments.[22] Forman hoped that federal voting rights statutes passed in 1957 and 1960 would not only further the cause of registration, but also protect the lives of SNCC organizers who worked under the threat of Southern racist violence.[23] Another incentive for joining forces with VEP was a signal from Kennedy administration officials that additional funding would become available if SNCC retained its focus on voter registration rather than projects that might lead to widespread violence or embarrass the national government.[24] SNCC received VEP funds in June; they used the initial $5,000 grant to support local registration efforts throughout Mississippi.[25,26]

MORE SPACE AND A NEW IMAGE

Forman made three pivotal communications decisions at the June 15, 1962, executive committee meeting: Julian Bond was selected as communications director, and John Lewis replaced Charles McDew as SNCC chairman. And to advance the communication efforts even further, the committee also authorized the purchase of a printing press;[27] this coincided with a move from SNCC's one-room office to a warehouse loft at 135 Auburn Avenue in Atlanta.[28]

Lyon, the white SNCC photographer, described Forman as being "singularly aware" of the need for a new organizational image. Forman therefore pushed for Lewis' election as chairman because of his powerful presence, public speaking skills, strong religious background, and his loyalty to the nonviolence ideal despite having been arrested and beaten on several occasions. In his memoir, Lewis wrote that Forman encouraged him to be aware of his position as "a symbol of the student movement." In that same work, Lewis acknowledged his role as "a walking example of the things that SNCC stood for, the things SNCC was trying to do . . . when people saw me, they saw arrests and beatings and nonviolence."[29,30]

Whereas McDew, out of necessity, had to spend much of his time fundraising in the North, Lewis was more of an inspirational force on the front lines of the movement. He used the word "whirlwind" to describe his travel itinerary to various protest sites in order to "take stock, gather information on what was needed, give a speech, take part in a march or demonstration, perhaps talk to a reporter to two . . ."[31] During this period, Bond's responsibility was to ensure that the press was aware of Lewis's activities, whether or not the two were traveling together. Lewis recalled:

> Julian would call me in West Helena or Forrest City, Arkansas, wherever I was on the road, and he'd ask what had happened that day, what we were planning to do tomorrow, how many people would be marching, and then he would pass that information onto the press, who knew they could depend on what he told them.[32]

SNCC's image-making campaign was incorporated into the non-stop stream of press materials, which increased dramatically with the purchase of the printing press. During the same meeting at which Lewis and Bond were hired, the executive committee again addressed the problem of SNCC receiving less media attention than other civil rights organizations, especially the SCLC. From that point forward, the SNCC name would appear in a prominent position on all press releases and publications. According to the meeting minutes, the committee criticized "SNCC staff [for] not speaking up," and accused SCLC executive director Rev. Wyatt T. Walker of "omitting SNCC when giving credit." The meeting minutes also stated that Dr. Martin Luther King was to remain "under scrutiny about his tactics of non-action until a crisis arises."[33]

Bond expanded the communications staff, hiring Dorothy Miller Zellner in the fall of 1962. In October she took over writing and editing responsibilities for the *Student Voice*. She immediately submitted a request to the Atlanta Police Department for a press pass in order to gain better access to sources and photographic opportunities.[34] Ruby Doris Smith, who would later be SNCC executive secretary, split her time between duties as a corresponding secretary and an assistant to Zellner and Bond. Smith frequently included public relations material along with her responses to incoming letters—for example, sending a reprint of a Saturday Evening Post article to the editor of *United Asia*, who had requested information on the movement; in her letter, Smith expressed a wish that the article "would serve to enlighten you somewhat on the situation."[35]

Reprints of articles appearing in newspapers and national magazines became a common SNCC public relations practice. One in particular, published in the October 26, 1963, edition of the *New Republic*, was incorporated into a SNCC fundraising flyer. Zinn, the article's author, described the frightful conditions that civil rights workers faced in Selma, Alabama, and painted a vivid picture of ineffective and unwilling federal authorities:

> Through all that happened on that Monday, while federal law was broken again and again, these law enforcement officials of the federal government stood by and watched. By the time Freedom Day was over in Selma, the Constitution had been violated in a number of its provisions, several statutes of the U.S. Congress had been ignored, and the Civil Rights Acts of 1957 and 1960 had been turned face down on the sidewalk.[36]

Improved relationships with the national press required renewed efforts in terms of internal communications. Accordingly, in December 1962,

SNCC released an "Inter-Staff" newsletter that was designed to keep field workers and other volunteers informed about the organization's activities. The newsletter contained straightforward articles on movement-related violence, organizational activities, meetings, and workshops. In the initial issue, the editors said that while the newsletter was "intended to serve as a secondary means of communication between the Atlanta office and your far-flung efforts . . . the primary means of communication [must be] initiated by you." Field workers were asked to send in weekly (or in some areas, daily) reports, photographs, and newspaper clippings that could be used to transmit information on various campaigns to SNCC-friendly news organizations. The editors asked "all others" (meaning volunteers who were not involved in field projects) to send money, supplies, cars, and typewriters; to write letters to elected officials; and to openly express their support to SNCC workers scattered throughout the South.[37]

Dorothy Miller Zellner later recalled that obtaining such information from field workers was essential for communicating the SNCC message. "Their job was to call us about what they were doing and all the atrocities that were that were happening. And then we took it from there." Zellner said she and Bond used this incoming information in three ways: they disseminated the information to the press; they used reports of violence contained in affidavits as a foundation for complaints to the federal government concerning its inactions; and they used the same information for SNCC's fund raising operations. "And so the news of what was going on in the field was never viewed as solely news, it was really . . . the core of what we were doing." [38]

In an effort to expand their support base and inform white Southern students of their messages, Forman hired Robert Zellner, a white student activists and son of a Methodist minister, (who Dorothy married in 1963) for a project that was created to build movement support among liberal and moderate white students. But even so, Zellner is known more for his work in black communities and his stays in southern jails. Zellner, however, addressed his first assignment with professionalism and thoroughness. In an October 30 project proposal, he described his plan to visit the University of Mississippi following the riots that occurred after James Meredith's efforts to enroll as the school's first black student. Zellner's mission was to find supportive white students who might serve as community liaisons and contacts for organizing in the Oxford area. To publicize his effort, Zellner wrote articles for the *Student Voice* and the *Southern Patriot*—a civil rights newspaper published by the Southern Conference Educational Fund.[39] In those articles, he suggested that stories and reports "written by students about students" held potential as a powerful communications tool.[40] Zellner tried to cultivate relationships with the editors of newspapers published on the campuses of the colleges that he visited. He distributed the *Student Voice* and SNCC literature when he believed doing so would not endanger the recipients.

Zellner's activities were not restricted to Mississippi. He spent a good deal of time in his home state of Alabama, meeting with religious and secular student organizations to ask for any form of assistance, but especially financial. He spent several weeks promoting a Miles College (Birmingham) concert featuring Pete Seeger, the civil rights activist who was also a member of a very popular 1950s folk group called The Weavers. The concert was an important tactic for garnering support from Birmingham's white community. Zellner recalled that approximately one-third of the audience consisted of whites, both students and non-students.[41] Seeger continued to appear in many other concerts throughout the South to raise awareness about civil rights and to raise money for SNCC and is known among historians and movement participants for promoting the song "We Shall Overcome" as the civil rights anthem.

FREEDOM *AND* MUSIC IN THE AIR

In Albany, Georgia, Charles Sherrod and other SNCC workers remained committed to their effort despite the decline of local civil rights activity. The location served as a prime example of SNCC perseverance. Once Dr. King was released from the Albany prison in December of 1961, protest activities in that town lost their momentum, as did national media attention. SNCC maintained a core group of workers to support the local civil rights community, but it had to share the spotlight with dozens of other large- and small-scale activities taking place throughout the South. In the case of Albany, it took continually greater effort to maintain a presence.

To address this issue and to raise money for their voter registration/direct action campaign, the Albany organizers came up with one of the more unique fundraising ideas of the civil rights movement: a professionally produced 33–1/3 rpm record documentary of the Albany civil rights battle. Entitled "Freedom in the Air," the record appeared in the fall of 1962. For the LP, musicologist Alan Lomax (noted for his field recordings of indigenous folk and blues music throughout the South) and folksinger and civil rights activists Guy Carawan mixed the testimonies of Albany participants with music from the movement. Copies sold for four dollars each. The project drew critical praise from several newspapers: a San Francisco Chronicle reviewer wrote that the album's spoken message had "the dignity and inevitability of conviction," and that it accurately portrayed the way that SNCC leaders, students, workers, and volunteers had "challenged the conscience of America."[42] *The New York Times* called the project the "most effective documentary recording to grow out of the integration movement."[43]

The fall of 1963 also witnessed the appearance of the SNCC "Freedom Singers," who would soon earn a national reputation for using the power of music to disseminate the movement's message in fundraising concerts across the country. In a 1989 interview Seeger recalled that he told Forman to think about booking the singers across the country to raise money and spread SNCC's message. Soon afterward, Seeger's agent booked the group on a tour of colleges around the North and West Coast that reached thousands of people.[44] Some of their earliest performances were presented in Tuskegee, Nashville, Albany, and Chicago.[45] Seeger introduced them to his Atlanta audience during his SNCC promotional tour, and he used his personal equipment to record the group following their joint November 11 concert.[46] A Freedom Singers promotional pamphlet produced by SNCC communications workers described their music as coming from "the country churches, the stockades, the prisons, the farmers' shacks, and the dusty roads of the South," and claimed that the group's freedom message could raise "the spirits of Americans everywhere, giving them a feeling of what it means to break the bonds of oppression."[47]

Bernice Reagon later recalled that simply attending one of the concerts gave people an opportunity to participate in the movement. "This was an initiating experience for many people. It was an intimate experience . . . It was the first time they had to talk with people who had a day-to-day experience . . . in the movement." Cordell Reagon agreed and said the group members were much more than performers. "We were not just singers . . . all of us were organizers."[48]

SNCC satellite offices and Friends of SNCC groups in Northern states quickly followed the Freedom Singers' lead in using music as a public relations and fund-raising tool, sponsoring concerts to communicate the freedom message to audiences of all sizes. In October 1962 the Chicago office sponsored a "Gospel for Freedom Festival" at the Aire Crown Theatre. The program featured the Freedom Singers, several local gospel groups, a presentation by James Meredith, and speeches by other movement leaders. The six-page program was a powerful means of eliciting support: its center leaf contained emotionally charged photographs of movement events, and the last two pages consisted of a list of individuals and organizations that had made significant financial contributions to SNCC.[49]

In February of the following year, Ella Jo Baker, Joanne Grant (a *National Guardian* reporter), and William Mahoney (who ran the New

York City SNCC office) organized a fund-raising concert at Carnegie Hall. Forman called the concert a starting point for building a large support base consisting of nationally known black artists, black writers, and white liberals. Because of this concert, Lorraine Hansberry, Harry and Julie Belafonte, Diahann Carroll, and Sidney Poitier headed the list of celebrities serving as spokespersons, activists, and sponsors of entertainment/fund-raising events for the next three years.[50] Forman also suggested that the Carnegie Hall concert affirmed the organization's willingness to receive support from individuals representing the entire political spectrum: "By accepting the financial support of radicals and progressives," he argued that SNCC was creating "an atmosphere [that enabled] people scared by McCarthyism to come out of the woodwork and engage once again in active struggle [and to] create a climate for radical thought and action."[51]

Forman continued to use the concert for public relations purposes well after its conclusion. In letters sent to attendees and supporters, he promised that all donations would be used to purchase food, clothing, and shelter for forty-two staff members working in "hard-core rural areas" in Mississippi, Southwest Georgia, South Carolina, Alabama, and Arkansas. In his letter to the comedian Mike Nichols, he asserted that the Committee's existence "depends on the kinds of friends we have throughout the country, and we are very lucky that you consider our work of some significance."[52]

A UNIFYING SENSE OF PURPOSE

SNCC had become a major civil rights organization by the winter of 1963, but its rapid expansion did not interfere with a growing sense of community among volunteers and supporters scattered throughout the United States. Staff members in the central office in Atlanta had established strong bonds with field secretaries in southern states, SNCC satellite offices, and a growing number of Friends of SNCC groups outside the South. The Friends groups were crucial to SNCC's efforts to achieve financial security and political influence. In a February 17 letter to the Chicago Friends of SNCC, Robert Moses thanked the group for "opening new dimensions in the voter registration movement in Mississippi" by providing "direct aid"—food and money—to SNCC workers in that state. In his thank you letter, Moses explained that 1,000 people standing in a food line were open to receiving education and news about how to escape their impoverished living conditions. In his eloquent style, Moses described how the Chicago group's assistance also provided emotional strength to people involved in a dangerous task:

You combat your own fears about beatings, shootings and possible mob violence; you stymie, by your mere physical presence, the anxious fear of the Negro community, seeded across town and blown from paneled pine and white sunken sink to windy kitchen floors and rusty old stoves, that maybe you did come only to boil and bubble and then burst, out of sight and sound; you organize, pound by pound, small bands of people who gradually focus in the eyes of Negroes and whites as people "tied up in that mess"; you create a small striking force capable of moving out when the time comes, which it must.[53]

In addition to sending money and food, a few of the larger Friends of SNCC groups organized their own direct action campaigns that served to expand support for the movement. In a newsletter dated June 15, the Chicago group gave brief descriptions of five successful fundraising and publicity events, including a local "march for freedom," a membership meeting, and a direct action protest against segregated housing policies. The newsletter also noted that Dick Gregory, the nationally known comedian, led a march of over 1,500 people who had attracted the attention of local newspapers and television stations.[54]

The exhilaration resulting from these types of events bolstered the spirits of all civil rights workers, although the actual fieldwork remained arduous and perilous. But as the growing sense of organizational security trickled down to grass roots organizers and workers, it propelled them toward greater accomplishments. It was clear to all that the organization was experiencing a growth spurt: sixty workers and 350 volunteers and supporters attended the April 12–13 staff meeting. Gregory (who contributed considerable amounts of money and time to SNCC) and Moses (who outlined plans for continuing voter registration efforts in Mississippi) were featured speakers.[55] Forman remembered his perception of having "achieved more than a certain sense of organizational security" that was accompanied by an "intense comradeship" and "commitment to the future." Forman's conclusion was that the "band of sisters and brothers, in a circle of trust, felt complete at last."[56]

PUBLIC RELATIONS CHANGES AND EXPANSION

At the center of the small administrative core working in Atlanta were communication workers. Bond and Dorothy Miller Zellner were completely dedicated to communications tasks until the summer of 1963, when Dorothy married Robert Zellner and moved to the Northeast to work as an organizer with the Boston Friends of SNCC group (Robert Zellner returned to Brandeis University). Her replacement was Mary King, a recent graduate of Ohio Wesleyan University, who quickly earned the respect of her co-workers for her organized and creative approach to problem solving and communication. For instance, in an October letter, SCEF co-director Carl Braden praised King as not only a "clear thinker" and a "good writer," but as someone with "guts." He made a blanket offer of help in any situation, based on his desire to work with "people who have their heart in it and know what they are doing."[57]

By November, King was simultaneously working on a number of publications. She designed pamphlets on conditions in Selma, Alabama, and the entire state of Mississippi to "pitch" socioeconomic and political information on local communities to assignment editors in the print and broadcast media.[58] The Selma report included background data on the "story of tyranny in Dallas County," whose population was 57 percent black, but with less than 1 percent of that segment being registered to vote. The pamphlet also described the exploits of Sheriff Jim Clark and his deputized "posse" of untrained law enforcers, who were known for using clubs and cattle prods on demonstrators. King wrote, "100 of these deputies wear old army fatigues and helmets and boots . . . carry weapons and make arrests—one struck 23-year-old Willie Robertson from behind on September 16 as he was leaving a sit-in at Carter-Walgreen's Drug Store in Selma; he required seven stitches."[59] Other pamphlets elicited food and clothing donations and promoted the Selma Project, which Bernard and Colia Lafayette started in February of 1963 as a means of educating black adults and children on voter registration and what they could do to improve their economic and political conditions.[60]

King also developed a file of staff biographies, including photographs. These were distributed to the media and used in SNCC's "Adopt a Field Secretary" fund-raising campaign. In addition to print publications, King worked with other communications staff members to produce and distribute tape-recorded information on civil rights activities to radio stations.[61]

Zinn, the white SNCC advisor who was arrested for sitting in the blacks-only gallery of the Mississippi state legislature, also proved to be a remarkable communications and outreach resource. In a book proposal he sent to Beacon Press in September 1963, he argued that there was a need for a book about SNCC, which he described as standing at "the apex of the whole civil rights movement . . . [and] with the fewest inhibitions in thinking about social change beyond the race question."[62] In a typical act of generosity and commitment to the movement, Zinn proposed that the book be used as a SNCC fundraising device; in a separate letter, Zinn said that he did not "feel right collecting royalties on a book about an organization

whose youngsters risk their lives for ten dollars a week."[63] Beacon approved
the project and published *SNCC: The New Abolitionist*, in 1965.

COMMUNICATING IN SELMA

In February 1963 Bernard and Colia Lafayette opened an office in Selma,
Alabama, to begin a voter registration campaign. Selma was considered
particularly dangerous due to its large White Citizen's Council—a group
of local business leaders willing to use their financial and social resources
to resist integration; similar groups existed throughout the South. Forman
understood that the image of so-called "white trash" being at the center of
racist backlash was misleading, and that middle- and upper-class organizations such as these White Citizen's Councils held positions as "truly powerful forces of intimidation and repression." Moderate and liberal whites
were often forced into supporting these Councils out of fear of economic
reprisals—for instance, losing a job or not being able to secure a bank
loan.[64]

In May, the Layfayettes felt prepared to put together a mass meeting, and thus embarked on the dangerous task of pushing the black Selma
community into taking action. This task entailed confronting not only
racist law enforcement officials but also an entire white community filled
with hatred and fear. The SNCC communications staff had to use all of
its established tactics to provide media-based protection for field workers and community members. Whenever a threatening or violent situation
arose, the Atlanta staff immediately transmitted detailed information to
federal and state government officials and the media. When the threat of
violence subsided, communications workers focused their efforts on contacting supporters throughout the country, asking them to put pressure
on their elected representatives and the Justice Department to "prevent
violence from being inflicted upon the mass of people" participating in
registration activities.[65]

Dallas County segregationists were also well organized and knew
how to use public relations and communications tools, although their
sphere of media influence was considerably more local. The challenge for
the SNCC communications staff was to somehow counteract the messages
that racist organizations such as the Dallas County Citizens Council disseminated through media outlets, which, in many cases, Council members
controlled. An example of a SNCC response was a flyer featuring a powerful photograph of two small black children, accompanied by the message
that the actions of the Citizen's Council directly affected the lives of the
two children as well as the reader's. The flier asked for contributions for

SNCC's efforts to support Selma blacks as they "continue to try to become real American citizens."[66]

Tensions in Selma increased dramatically following the bombing of the Sixteenth Street Baptist Church in Birmingham on September 15, in which three young black girls were killed. During nightly mass meetings, segregationists countered with surveillance measures and intimidation by armed deputies in groups referred to as "citizen's posses"; many of these posse members lacked any training whatsoever in law enforcement or crowd control.[67] On September 23, John Lewis participated in a mass meeting and was arrested along with twenty-nine others. The arrests prompted a larger demonstration outside the Dallas County courthouse, during which Lewis carried a sign reading "One man, one vote"—the first appearance of what would become SNCC's official voter registration slogan. Lewis had introduced the phrase a month earlier as part of his "March on Washington" speech; within weeks it appeared on SNCC letterhead, picket signs, buttons, bumper stickers, and publications. It was a slogan that the majority of Americans eventually associated with the civil rights movement in general and the voter registration campaign in particular.[68]

By October, when Lewis was released, the number of arrested activists had grown to more than 300. Lewis and other SNCC leaders created a public relations action called "Freedom Monday"; on one Monday each month, hundreds of Selma blacks attempted to register as voters, creating lines that stretched around the block. That image appeared on the front pages of many newspapers and on the screens of many TV stations around the nation.[69]

DANVILLE, VIRGINIA, APPEARS ON THE NATIONAL AGENDA

A second project that captured national attention in 1963 was an attempt by black residents in Danville, Virginia to expose and protest discriminatory hiring practices by the Danville city government. This was not a SNCC-organized action, but by this time the organization had grown to the point that it could offer many forms of assistance—including training in nonviolent tactics—to local groups such as the Danville Christian Progressive Association (DCPA).[70] Ivanhoe Donaldson, Avon Rollins, and Robert Zellner moved from Atlanta to Danville in the late spring of 1963 and stayed until autumn.[71] Other SNCC staffers spent shorter periods of time helping to organize a mass protest that took place on June 10, 1963—a day that came to be known as "Bloody Monday." Danville authorities used fire hoses and clubs to disperse demonstrators; in all, thirty-eight were arrested. Dorothy Miller Zellner, a witness and participant, wrote a pamphlet describing the event that was later used as a fundraising tool. The pamphlet featured powerful photos taken by Danny Lyon, and contained a long list of names of protesters who had been injured by police and other municipal employees.[72] She wrote:

> Chief McCain bellowed, "Let 'em have it" and firemen turned hoses on the people, many of them women and teen-agers. Nightstick-wielding police and deputized garbage collectors smashed into the group, clubbing Negroes who were bunched for safety against parked cars. Some were washed under the cars; others were clubbed after the water knocked them down. Bodies lay on the street, drenched and bloody. Police and garbage collectors chased those demonstrators who were able to walk for two blocks.[73]

VOTING AND VIOLENCE THROUGHOUT THE SOUTH

Danville and Selma were two important examples of SNCC expansion throughout the South in 1963. By August, SNCC projects were underway in Pine Bluff, Arkansas and locations in Tennessee and Maryland, and new operations were being planned for towns and cities in North Carolina, South Carolina, and Texas.[74] Combined with ongoing activities in Mississippi, the Committee was making another transition, this time into a period that the historian Taylor Branch would name "the firestorm" because of escalating violent resistance to the movement.[75]

In the fall of 1963, Robert Moses and Allard Lowenstein, a white activist from Stanford University, came up with an innovative public relations event to draw attention to SNCC's voter registration campaign: staging mock elections to coincide with actual Mississippi elections that excluded the vast majority of black citizens. The idea was modeled on similar mock elections organized in South Africa. To draw attention to the event, the SNCC administrative staff named it the "Freedom Vote," with candidates representing the "Freedom Party."[76] SNCC workers, COFO staffers, and local organizers created a full-scale election in miniature, complete with candidates and voting venues. Lewis said the mock election was designed as an "exercise to both give black men and women the sense of actually voting and to dramatize to onlookers the exclusion of blacks in the actual political process."[77] Lowenstein brought in approximately 80 white student volunteers from Northern states and the West Coast—a decision that would attract a national media attention.

In September, SNCC and COFO workers printed campaign literature and ballots listing the names of candidates representing the Democratic, Republican, and Freedom parties. Aaron "Doc" Henry, a Clarksdale druggist and chairman of the Mississippi NAACP, ran for governor, with Edward B. King, a white minister at Tougaloo College in Jackson, serving as his running mate. SNCC workers organized political education "clubs" to disseminate information and to serve as forums for discussing issues and candidates.[78] In Lewis's words, the Freedom Vote was "an incredible success." Despite threats of assaults and harassment, more than 90,000 blacks participated in the election. According to Lewis, participants understood that in a real election, their votes would have altered the outcome of the Mississippi gubernatorial race. But even without that official power, participants demonstrated to the national media that "black people could and would actually vote in meaningful numbers."[79] Perhaps more importantly, those blacks who voted in the mock election "were now committed to registering and voting" in real elections—especially the upcoming 1964 national presidential election.[80]

As this first "firestorm" year came to a close, there was plenty of evidence that SNCC's communication efforts had served to break new political ground. But the organization also acknowledged a growing number of new challenges awaiting its attention. The effort to register voters in Mississippi was in its third year, and while the Freedom Vote was a public relations success, few voters were actually registered, and the threat of violence continued. The SNCC communications staff took advantage of this threat to inform the American public about the repressive character of civil rights work in the Deep South. With Forman offering guidance, Bond coming up with fresh ideas, Dorothy Miller Zellner and King writing, and dozens of volunteers printing, folding, and mailing, SNCC communicators brought the most important events of the civil rights movement to the attention of anyone who read a newspaper, listened to a morning newscast on the radio, or watched an evening news program on television. Less obvious was the staff's efforts to maintain clear lines of internal communication among field workers, volunteer support groups, and the Atlanta office. The integration of local communities into the larger organization may have been the most important aspect of SNCC communications work in 1962 and 1963. As Bond noted, SNCC workers were, above all, organizers: "They didn't register voters–they organized the unregistered to register themselves. They didn't integrate lunch counters–they organized a protest that forced the seats open. They didn't integrate America–they showed what an integrated America could be like."[81]

Constance Currie, the SNCC adviser and National Student Association manager, explained in a 2001 interview at the SNCC messages "helped to mobilize students all over the country and lead to not only education and awareness . . . but also . . . to demonstrations, boycotts, and organizing in the rest of the country."[82] Joan Browning, a SNCC volunteer in 1960 and 1961, agreed and recalled that: "The circular nature of leadership recognition, development, growth . . . just seeing their names and pictures encouraged many people to see themselves as valiant, brave, newsworthy. Being written about accurately and admiringly gave people a sense of their importance and their agency to change things."[83]

So amid the immense challenges and in the face of undeniable danger, the SNCC communications staff managed to place the story of the oppression of Southern blacks on the nation's agenda by communicating the events of the civil rights movement to the national media and by communicating the evolving purpose of the organization to local blacks and to civil rights activists and supporters both internally and across the country. These internal and external efforts worked hand-in-hand to promote civil rights and to eventually transform the predicament of Southern blacks.

Chapter Three
Freedom Summer: 1964

You had to bring the country's attention to the state, and the obvious way to do that was to bring the country's children down there.
You make Mississippi a big campaign—you nationalize Mississippi,
essentially, by bringing America's children to Mississippi. Nobody can
ignore the state then.[1]

—Charles Cobb, SNCC worker, October 1996

Local newspapers called it an invasion. But SNCC organizers viewed the
1964 Freedom Summer as an opportunity. Within a three-month period
they would use their public relations skills to expose Americans to the
illegal and immoral activities taking place in the "sovereign state of Mississippi," thereby gaining national support in their battle for civil rights
for citizens of all colors and ethnicities. Although approximately 1,000
volunteers would indeed purposefully try to impose their beliefs upon
white Mississippians during the summer of 1964, their intrusion into the
state's "closed society" would lead to an even greater imposition on the
nation's conscience—bringing into America's living rooms images so horrific and shameful that the country felt compelled to create new laws denying southern racists their long-standing power to deny black citizens their
basic rights.

The Freedom Summer planners had clear intentions from the very
start: to register black Mississippians for the vote, and to educate these
voters on how the electoral process could work to improve their lives. As
the Freedom Summer progressed, SNCC workers expanded their tried-and-
tested communication skills to organize communities, provide political and
cultural education, and to create a political party and convention delegate
selection campaign. The Freedom Summer also represented a period marked
by increasingly proactive communication strategies. Although SNCC plan-

ning tended to look at relatively short time frames, it did allow for the development of new characteristics that would serve the organization well as it followed its path of continuous evolution throughout the decade. Since the organization was gaining national prominence, it was also receiving increasing amounts of cash donations, allowing SNCC leaders and volunteers to carry out more ambitious projects. For the first time, communications work was not limited to the Atlanta headquarters; as procedures became standardized, the group opened communication posts throughout Mississippi.

Many of the white volunteers brought with them experience and knowledge that veteran workers were able to incorporate into the SNCC communications mission. One important contributor was Robert Beyers, who took a leave of absence from his position as public relations director at Stanford University to participate in the Freedom Summer. In the words of communications worker Mary King, Beyers "brought the skills of a technically qualified public relations professional to the staff" for the first time. Although the added financial and human resources allowed SNCC to communicate its message more effectively, King later stated that managing those resources in Mississippi was one of the greatest challenges of the Freedom Summer. Eventually, the human resources would change the appearance of the communications mission. For instance, King organized a telephone bank in Jackson so that reporters could write and file their stories—a task that required the coordination of a larger-than-average number of SNCC workers and volunteers.[2]

The main reason for bringing in about 1,000 college students (mostly white) and other volunteers to Mississippi was to assist in voter registration activities; by the end of the summer, about 1,600 blacks had succeeded in their attempts to register, out of approximately 17,000 who tried.[3] This limited success, however, was secondary to the media coverage that the campaign attracted. The historian Neil R. McMillen wrote that the summer's "triumph" was best "measured in column inches of newsprint" and film footage and that the Freedom Summer was the civil rights movement's most successful effort toward the "nationwide exposure of the iniquities of white supremacy in the deepest of the Deep South states."[4]

MIXED COVERAGE

As expected, coverage in white-owned Mississippi newspapers did not match the more favorable coverage that appeared in national magazines and large urban newspapers published outside the South. Local writers and editors continued to describe voter registration volunteers as "agitators" and "invaders";[5] what little objective coverage did appear was often taken from the national wire services and printed on the back pages.[6] The first black Associated Press reporter Austin Long-Scott was denied the opportunity to cover the Freedom Summer under pressure from Mississippi publishers who had complained to his editor that the AP's coverage "was too favorable to civil rights forces." Long-Scott explained that his editor believed that sending him would only "confirm their accusations."[7]

There were a few notable exceptions. The *Pascagoula Chronicle* was one of the very few papers in Mississippi that supported the movement. Ira B. Harkey, Jr., *Chronicle* editor until 1963, admitted that readers did not want to see news that damaged the reputation of their state or town, therefore the majority of in-state papers rarely printed anything negative about local leaders. Harkey also wrote in his autobiography that until the Freedom Summer, the only times that blacks were mentioned in local newspapers were when they were "in trouble."[8]

Other exceptions were outside of Mississippi. Ralph McGill, editor of the *Atlanta Constitution*, covered many SNCC activities in Georgia, occasionally working with the Atlanta-based SNCC communications staff. He called the young workers "magnificent" and credited them with producing quick change "on the Southern scene." McGill declared that he had "first hand" knowledge of "the inspiration" that SNCC gave to oppressed Southerners. He was also willing to credit SNCC and other civil rights organizations with cracking "the monolith of defiance" that Southern states had perpetuated.[9]

The *New York Times* naturally provided extensive coverage of the Freedom Summer campaign, and Southern Regional Correspondent Claude Sitton traveled throughout Mississippi, writing sympathetic reports of the summer's events.[10] SNCC Communications workers Dorothy Miller Zellner and Mary King both said they had strong working relationships with Sitton and his newspaper.[11] Other national reporters that King described as being especially responsive were Karl Fleming of *Newsweek* and Fred Powledge of the *Atlanta Constitution* (and later, the *New York Times*). She described the two as being "among a small group of Southern white reporters from rural backgrounds who showed discernment and courage in standing up against the prevailing bias."[12]

Powledge later recalled in a 2001 interview that during the 1960s civil rights events, his sense of objective reporting took on a new meaning. "It was hard to adopt that reporters' fake sense of objectivity, of counting oneself as objective . . . because often there was no one on the other side to call and get a quote from. The people on the other side wore sheets over their heads . . . it was so clear as to who the good guys were and who the bad guys were." He credited the SNCC communication workers with providing "reliable" and accurate information. "They never lied to me . . . Their equivalent is almost unheard of today."[13]

Unlike newspapers, some national magazines were more receptive to articles written by SNCC communication workers (e.g., Jerry Demuth, Staughton Lynd, Elizabeth Sutherland, and advisor Howard Zinn) but submitted as the products of freelance writers. When these articles were successfully placed, the communications staff then distributed reprints as a means of attracting emotional and financial support.[14] In other cases, national magazine editors were willing to publish favorable stories from their own writers, many of whom relied on background information supplied by SNCC communications workers. Christopher Jencks, editor of the *New Republic*, who wrote a two-part series about the oppressive conditions in Mississippi and SNCC's efforts to remedy them, made a major contribution.[15] Jencks described SNCC workers as unwilling to accept simple middle-class status in the black community, which was their parents' highest aspiration. Instead, he reported that the young "radicals" sought equality with white citizens and worked to "remake America along more egalitarian and proletarian lines."[16]

As Jenks pointed out, black Mississippians had long endured the weight and magnitude of Southern oppression. The most significant opposition to this oppression began when SNCC organizers sowed the seeds of their laborious and dangerous mission of registering black Mississippi voters in 1961. Robert Moses, who was there from the beginning, created the COFO umbrella organization described in the preceding chapter. While these efforts were laudable in the context of Mississippi's historical resistance to integration, there was a growing sense that they held little or no political significance: by mid-1963, just under six percent of all eligible Mississippi blacks were registered.[17] Jencks's *New Republic* series likely raised awareness about and consequently boosted these efforts. In it, he reported that two-thirds of black Mississippi families had annual per capita incomes of $2,000 or less, acknowledged that family breadwinners could be summarily fired for "displeasing a white employer," and described how creditors could cut off purchasing privileges on a whim. He also gave specific examples of local police officers using force to resist voter registration efforts. Jencks gave a sober account of the type of justice that any Mississippi black who asked for a redress of grievances could expect: "This jury may not be all white, but it will inevitably include enough white supremacists to prevent a Negro's obtaining the unanimous vote in his favor which he would need to get his due from a white man."[18]

MFDP EMERGENCE

Prior to the Freedom Summer campaign, SNCC workers initiated the Freedom Campaign in the winter of 1963, with the assistance of white student volunteers from Yale, Stanford, and other universities outside the South. Many of these volunteers got their first taste of civil rights organizing while working on that year's mock elections. Black or white, workers and volunteers in Mississippi observed that "Negroes in the state were eager for political activity, they wanted to register, they wanted to vote."[19] With the knowledge gained from this success, over the winter of 1963 and 1964, SNCC leaders came up with a plan that they believed neither the federal government nor the national media could ignore.

All these plans came about before a backdrop of racist activity. Although Mississippi's voter registration process was in clear defiance of federal law, national officials—at the behest of influential Southern politicians—largely ignored the illegal activities. Civil rights organizations and local leaders made some progress in penetrating the South's racist political system throughout the 1960s, but it wasn't until the end of John F. Kennedy's abbreviated presidency that a meaningful civil rights bill began making its way through Congress. Southern Senators invoked filibusters to defeat previous efforts, but in November 1963, Lyndon Johnson announced support for the Civil Rights Act 1964 and was able to overcome Southern resistance and push through a version that was signed into law on July 2, 1964.[20] The law called for the integration of all public facilities and the withholding of federal funds to public programs that continued to discriminate against blacks. The law offended many white Mississippi Democrats. When Johnson announced his plans in November, Southern politicians were incensed. In fact, Hayden Campbell, a Mississippi state senator with a large support network, called for state leaders to abandon the Democratic Party and join "white conservative voters" in supporting Barry Goldwater's bid to enter the White House.

The Democratic party's Southern stronghold was clearly threatened.[21] SNCC leaders recognized an important opportunity. According to Robert Moses, the SNCC staff saw in the party's weakness a chance to make political change with lasting effects.[22] The centerpiece of their strategy was legitimizing the Mississippi Freedom Democratic Party (MFDP) as an alternative to the white-controlled Mississippi Democratic Party. SNCC wanted to emphasize local participation in the campaign, which explains why Mary King wrote in 1964 that workers and volunteers in the national organization were deliberately working to "obscure" their role and "emphasize the indigenous nature" of the MFDP.[23] But the plan entailed getting enough blacks registered to ensure MFDP legitimacy at the National Democratic Convention scheduled for August, and therefore they needed far more than the approximately 120 field workers who were active in early 1964.

Because so few Southern blacks could afford the risks or financial burdens associated with the project, it was clear that SNCC needed outside help. Committee leaders knew that having a large contingent of white volunteers would attract substantial attention since their participation during the November 1963 mock elections garnered substantially more media interest than black organizations were accustomed to.[24] Lawrence Guyot, a SNCC field secretary, later explained that his support for increased white participation was largely based on the presence of the FBI in the state, which he believed was tied to white student involvement in the 1963 mock elections. With a larger number of federal agents appearing in Mississippi, organizers believed that federal politicians would eventually feel compelled to acknowledge that federal law was being ignored in the state.[25]

In a 1994 interview, Moses described how these and other factors had come together to create the proper environment for the Freedom Summer project. One was the assassination of Medgar Evers, the Mississippi NAACP president, in June 1963; that single act of violence significantly increased national awareness of the horrific acts of racism taking place throughout the state. Moses called the murder a "touchstone . . . [that] put certain things in motion" for the 1964 project. Allard Lowenstein was so moved by the assassination that he went to Mississippi, where he was a central figure in organizing the 1963 mock elections. Moses also identified the 1963 March on Washington, the aforementioned introduction of a new civil rights bill that same year, and the murder of Louis Allen in January of 1964 as important factors. Allen had witnessed the 1961 killing of Herbert Lee, one of the first Mississippi blacks to register as part of the SNCC campaign. Moses recalled that when the news of Allen's death reached SNCC workers as they were debating the registration project in Hattiesburg, he and others expressed strong feelings of having "gone full circle":

> . . . we came in '61 working in Amite County. . . . [and that] ended
> in Herbert Lee's murder. And the one witness was Louis Allen . . .
> [and he had] been brutalized around that, and so now he is gunned
> down. So . . . you're back where you started but you're in a differ-
> ent place. . . . you've got this whole really national ferment now and
> you've got networks in place and you've got potential strategies lined
> up and you've got some sort of opening to look at in terms of how can
> we respond.[26]

Certain strategies attracted criticism from within SNCC. Some staffers disagreed with the idea of encouraging white volunteers as a means of attracting media attention, since so many blacks had fought, suffered, and died for the cause without proper recognition. As Moses noted, the black-and-white power issue was a never-ending battle.[27] Moses had the support of a large number of SNCC workers who felt a sense of appreciation toward the white volunteers; he felt so strongly about building an integrated organization that he threatened to resign if the opposition prevailed.[28] He stayed, and the summer project proceeded with volunteers from across the country. Charles Cobb, a SNCC activist who openly opposed the involvement of so many whites, conceded in a 1996 interview that the white volunteer proponents had a legitimate argument—that is, bringing the "country's children" to Mississippi would nationalize the issue. Cobb said that despite their reservations, opponents recognized Freedom Summer as "something that was underway," and therefore responded with "programmatic ideas" rather than continuing their resistance.[29] Several of these programmatic ideas—with foundations in basic communication and organizational principles—were immediately enacted. One was the empowerment of Mississippi blacks in the campaign, with life-long Mississippi residents working alongside young, affluent white college students. As SNCC communications worker Casey Hayden pointed out, this was an important accomplishment in that "for the first time in Mississippi, black and white met as equals."[30]

Initial planning discussions took place in November of 1963, and plans were in place by the end of January 1964. In late April, SNCC recruiters began visiting campuses across the country; according to John Lewis, the volunteers were "dying to get involved" and "pouring forth."[31] Recruiters and organizers had media and public relations strategies in mind throughout the process: in addition to personal information, the volunteer application form asked for the names of the applicants' Congressional representatives, the names of their college and hometown newspapers (including frequency of publication and address), organizations they belonged to (and the names and addresses of presiding officers), and ten people who would be interested in receiving information about their activities.[32]

Later, politicians would be contacted as soon as any news surfaced of a constituent being attacked. In one letter, a Pennsylvania congressman was informed that a student in his district who had volunteered for the SNCC campaign had "suffered repeated deprivation of his rights merely because he is a civil rights worker." The letter went on to describe in detail events leading to a physical beating and arrest.[33] In a separate strategy devised by Mike Thelwell (SNCC's Washington, D.C. office manager), church group lobbyists and sympathetic congressmen were asked to immediately contact the Justice Department and FBI whenever a civil rights violation occurred in Mississippi. Thelwell told these participants, "if we end up with 15 Congressional calls and six or seven Senate calls to the [Justice Department] . . . we will have achieved something."[34]

Well-established organizational communication vehicles continued to promote the Freedom Summer campaign, with the entire event being announced in the March issue of the *Student Voice*. In comparing the action to Peace Corps work, the article described such components as voter registration drives, freedom schools, community centers, research projects, law student projects, and white community projects.[35] In a separate *Student Voice* article, Freedom Summer was labeled the "most ambitious project ever undertaken in the civil rights movement."[36] In another example, a Freedom Summer fundraising brochure outlined the Committee's previous Mississippi efforts and asked for financial support to help "SNCC in its commitment to the struggle for justice in . . . Mississippi." The brochure described the state as a place where "individual political life is nonexistent, where the economic condition of a vast majority of the population is appalling, [and] the home of white supremacy . . ."[37]

In May the communications department continued outlining its summer objectives, centered on forcing the press "to reckon with legitimate news sources, actual leadership, and authorized spokesmen," working to avoid "gimmicky news interpretation," and setting up a system for "quick, thorough, and accurate news gathering and dissemination."[38] At the same time, SNCC leaders accepted many public relations responsibilities as natural extensions of their positions. Lewis, Forman, and Moses used their considerable communications skills to ensure that the Committee's project goals were clearly understood by the media. Lewis went on a speaking and lobbying tour promoting Freedom Summer in April 1964. In a speech to the American Society of Newspaper Editors, he explained the details of the summer project, describing it as an opportunity for the federal government to decide clearly if it wanted to extend voting privileges to Southern blacks; he also reminded the group that it was a federal crime to interfere with the voting rights of black citizens.[39]

To better manage the summer project and to prevent acts of violence, SNCC temporarily moved its headquarters from Atlanta to Greenwood, Mississippi. Most news originated from the Greenwood office, but a small number of communications workers remained in Atlanta to assist with disseminating information to national news organizations and support groups outside the South.[40] Bond moved to Greenwood to help coordinate forty-four state projects that were planned for the summer. For the first time,

SNCC staff began to train volunteers as communication workers to ensure that the larger projects would receive adequate attention.[41]

As SNCC leaders had predicted, the national media did indeed show great interest in the Freedom Summer from the onset, including volunteer orientation sessions that were held in Oxford, Ohio.[42] King recalled that 650 students representing 37 states "provided a screen of protection by bringing with them national attention," and that the media attention enabled "local blacks [to] become more assertive and begin to work toward self-determination." She said that she and Bond spent most of their time during the orientation sessions addressing the needs of reporters—for instance, providing them with background information about the status of blacks in Mississippi.[43]

It was the Freedom Summer's darkest moment, however, that generated the most media attention. On June 21, three volunteers disappeared: two affluent white students from New York–Michael Schwerner and Andrew Goodman—and a black Mississippi native named James Chaney. Media coverage escalated during the six weeks that passed before their bodies were found. Mary King, who received news of their disappearance upon her return to Atlanta from the Ohio orientation sessions, immediately started telephoning Mississippi county jails, describing herself as a reporter for the *Atlanta Journal*. When she contacted the Neshoba County jail, where the three men had been held, the local sheriff denied having detained them. King and SNCC workers in Jackson and Meridian also called the FBI, but were told that there was no evidence of a federal law being broken, and therefore they could not initiate an investigation.[44] But by the next day, with pressure from President Johnson's office, on June 22 the Justice Department ordered the FBI to determine whether the three men were in captivity and if their civil rights had been violated.[45]

Emmie Schrader Adams, a volunteer who had just arrived in Jackson to coordinate local communications efforts, later recalled that she and staff members Frances Mitchell, Bill Light, and Bob Weil had left the Oxford orientation session a day early in order to handle simple phone inquiries before the new group of volunteers arrived. Instead of responding to basic questions on the Freedom Summer as they expected, they answered non-stop questions about the missing men. She remembered the "pall of horror" that surrounded the organization and specific instructions that the communications workers "could not officially speak of lynchings or assassinations" before the bodies were found. She also remembered that most of the Mississippi media reported that the incident was a "hoax" designed to attract attention to the state.[46] On July 22, Mississippi Senator James O. Eastland said the same thing, telling the U.S. Senate on the record that the supposed disappearances were likely fraudulent because there was no evidence to suggest otherwise, and because civil rights groups were infiltrated with communists who were part of a "conspiracy to thrust violence" on the people of Mississippi. [47]

Even before the murders, SNCC staff members were well aware of the dangers they would be facing throughout the summer, and they had made every effort to ensure that the volunteers were equally aware.[48] Hollis Watkins, by this time a SNCC staff member, said that volunteers were told in straightforward language during the orientation sessions that they should be prepared to go to jail, to be beaten, and to face death.[49] In another example, in a June 12 statement, John Lewis declared that "the nation is not sufficiently informed, nor the federal government sufficiently aroused, about the possibility of violent reprisal to the summer project."[50]

The murders, which occurred before most of the students arrived in the state, served as the most compelling reminders of how dangerous Mississippi was. But rather than deter participation, the incident reinforced the students' desire to join the movement[51]—in fact, the number of volunteers grew significantly because of the emotions, attention, and publicity generated by the murders. SNCC leaders grew increasingly concerned about having a large disorganized force in the state, and therefore encouraged potential volunteers to organize in their own areas rather than travel to Mississippi. On June 27, Robert Moses sent out an appeal asking potential volunteers to refrain from joining the project, stating that "a wave of untrained and unoriented volunteers . . . [would] disrupt what is now a well-controlled plan."[52]

Because SNCC leaders knew that violence would be unavoidable, they trained communications staff members in proper procedures for responding to reports of violence. Workers received explicit instructions on procedures for filing incident reports, which included calling the Jackson office every two hours and notifying both the Justice Department and the FBI.[53] Robert Beyers recalled that SNCC staffers in Mississippi started the practice of using "incident boards": "We'd put everything regarding a particular incident on that board. Anyone coming in could pick it up and read it. The whole project from a communication standpoint was built on openness and credibility."[54] Along these same lines, communications officers also took on security duties, making sure that safety policies were followed, that phone records were maintained (including incidents of phone line interference), and that FBI notifications were recorded.[55] According to Beyers "We had a whole system set up so that if you were driving from Jackson to Meridian, you left the times and distances. And it was essential that you call even if you were just a few minutes off schedule."[56]

The media attention resulting from the disappearances naturally heightened national awareness of the deplorable state of affairs in Mississippi and even had an immediate effect on the behavior of some local authorities. According to a May 31, 1965, news release issued by the Southern Reporting Services, the influx of reporters, FBI agents, and other federal officials served as a powerful source of control.[57] King wrote that the rush of activity created a "shield of protection" for volunteers and local Mississippi residents, and claimed that "Life would never be as threatening for [Mississippi blacks] again."[58] At the same time, some argued that the attention made the environment even more dangerous for some workers and volunteers.[59] Lewis believed that the media spotlight made volunteers "instant targets," with acts of violence deemed inevitable and additional murders a "distinct possibility."[60]

For a short while, SNCC did not have to tirelessly pursue press coverage of its activities. Robert Beyers, the Stanford public relations manager who served as a communications worker in Jackson that summer, said during a 2000 interview that it was not unusual for nine television news crews to visit the SNCC satellite office in one day, and that he worked with approximately 200 journalists during his two months on the project.[61] A communications report issued later that summer mentioned two to three daily visits or phone calls to the Jackson office by the Associated Press, United Press International, NBC, ABC, and CBS. Major daily newspapers and national magazines that posted reporters in Jackson for the summer included the *New York Times*, *New York Herald Tribune*, *Boston Globe*, *Washington Post*, and *Time*.[62] The contacts made during that summer served the needs of both sides not only in 1964, but also during the rest of the decade, as SNCC expanded and evolved. Ilene Strelitz, a communications worker in Jackson that summer later recalled:

> Many of them have come to identify with us, keep us informed about news throughout the South, etc. Our better correspondents are changing from doubters and observers to understanding educators. The red-baiter and the beat-baiter are increasingly rare, and are usually products of three-day whirlwind tours of the state aimed at making the definite impressionistic report.[63]

Until the bodies were found, SNCC workers performed their communications duties and coordinated numerous press conferences and press releases to explain the circumstances surrounding the missing volunteers. One of several messages that SNCC emphasized was the need for federal protection in Mississippi. When the bodies were found and positively identified in August, Lewis once again demanded federal intervention to protect both SNCC workers and local black Mississippians:

> Now . . . we know without a doubt that Mickey Schwerner, James Chaney and Andrew Goodman—three brave and courageous Freedom Fighters—have been murdered by sick men who are victims of a vicious and evil system . . . America is burning its own cross on the graves of its children because it has not taken the responsibility for enforcing the democratic way of life.[64]

Members of the victims' families joined in the effort to garner federal and public support. Two days following the disappearances, three parents of the white volunteers met with Attorney General Robert Kennedy and petitioned for federal protection and a federal investigation.[65] The parents of other volunteers formed a group for the purpose of visiting approximately fifty congressional offices to inform their representatives about the activities of their constituents in Mississippi. In describing these meetings as especially effective, Mary King stated that "federal authorities were beginning to recognize the unplumbed lawlessness and terrorism than ran rampant in the state and were becoming alarmed at the possibility that the volunteers might be killed."[66] The parents continued their effort throughout the summer, including visits to Mississippi. SNCC field secretary Lawrence Guyot explained that these particular parents traveled to the state to "see what they could do, what kind of data they could get and take back and mobilize around."[67,68]

Rita Schwerner, wife of Michael Schwerner and a COFO worker, collaborated with SNCC to meet with the press, to issue statements, and to push for state and federal assistance in the search. In her June 24 statement, Mrs. Schwerner strongly suggested that the press was only showing interest in the case because two whites were involved:

> It is tragic that white Northerners must be caught in the machinery of Southern injustice before the American people register concern. If Mr. Chaney [the black volunteer] had been alone, I suspect this case would have gone unnoticed.[69]

Mrs. Schwerner and several SNCC leaders did have a meeting with President Johnson, but were unsuccessful in their attempt to meet with Mississippi Governor Paul B. Johnson to ask for assistance in conducting the search. According to Mrs. Schwerner, Governor Johnson said that he and Alabama Governor George Wallace were the only two people who knew where the men were and that they "were not telling." She also claimed that he slammed the door in her face.[70]

But even if the governor ignored these events, the crisis triggered responses from across the country. Friends of SNCC groups in Chicago, New York, San Francisco, and other major cities walked picket lines, held all-night vigils, and made visits to congressional representatives to push for FBI and Justice Department intervention.[71] In Chicago, SNCC leaders Barnard Lafayette, Curtis Hayes, Charles McDew, and Marion Barry announced their intention to issue a statement at the U.S. Attorney's office demanding federal protection for the summer volunteers. Local media representatives visited the picket line outside the federal office building and attempted to cover the story, but according to a WATS (wide area telephone service) report, government employees "locked the group inside, tarpaulined the windows so that press photographers could not take pictures of them, and turned off the electricity so that television crews couldn't shoot film footage."[72]

Throughout the summer, SNCC and its fellow civil rights organizations continued with their planned activities. SNCC workers assigned to MFDP duties remained focused on their main task, which was preparing for the new party's visit to the National Democratic Convention in August with the goal of replacing the traditional segregated party before a national audience. For instance, Casey Hayden and Dona Richards developed instructional pamphlets for organizing precinct and county meetings. Other communications workers produced canvassing materials and organized a speaker's bureau. On July 19, an "emergency memorandum" requested that all summer workers and volunteers focus on the upcoming convention. According to Hayden, volunteers compiled lists of "every county, the status of organizing . . . the number of freedom registrations, the number needed, and specific suggestions for weak areas for getting people to meetings, for keeping records, for feeding us individual contacts in any areas we had not been able to organize."[73]

"THE MANUAL"

The *SNCC Communication Manual* stands as a testament to the planning and training associated with Freedom Summer activities. The first section of the manual consists of a proposal for reorganizing the entire SNCC communications section—that is, assigning workers to perform tasks specific to radio, newspaper, special writing projects, dispatching news from the Atlanta office, and training field personnel in news gathering techniques. In addition to providing instructions on documentation and maintaining accuracy, the *Manual* reminded its readers of their contribution to the civil rights movement's historical record: "Your . . . documentation of events will serve as an important base for what is written about the movement in future years."[74] Information was provided in six areas considered critical to disseminating accurate information on Freedom Summer events: how to access volunteer biographies; achieving "tip of the tongue familiarity" with the political, economic, and social characteristics of a district; working with lists of press contacts; project backgrounds; appropriate sources for media questions; and maintaining a "strong sense of security."[75] The *Manual* also contained descriptions of procedures for managing photographs and conducting research.

The SNCC communications staff maintained an extensive list of names of editors and reporters. One example of a subcategory included the names of reporters who had been based in Mississippi or who had covered the Oxford orientation.[76] To be on this list meant receiving a steady stream of news releases, memos, background brochures, and ideas for feature stories—for example, bios of local residents who were volunteering their time in Mississippi, data on job losses among black citizens, and descriptions of evictions and discriminatory tax policies.[77] Volunteers referred press questions to their project director. If the director was not available, they refrained from argument and exaggeration. Volunteers worked to emphasize the work of Mississippi residents rather than their own activities. As stated in the *Communication Manual*, "This will not be hard to do, or unnatural, if you remember your role in the state."[78,79]

One obscure rule mentioned in some detail in the *Manual* was the Federal Communication Commission (FCC) requirement that broadcast stations offer equal time to opposing viewpoints, including opinions in community service programs that promoted community activities and church services. Communications workers were instructed to obtain program schedules, exhibit them publicly, record offending broadcasts, send letters to the stations asking them to comply with the rule, and submit complaints to the FCC. To facilitate the equal time provision, the Los Angeles Friends of SNCC prepared a fifteen-minute taped radio program containing interviews, letters from volunteers, and reports from SNCC workers and volunteers in Mississippi for use by radio stations.[80]

IN-HOUSE PUBLICATIONS

In terms of describing civil rights activities and the lives of southern blacks, the *Student Voice* was one of the most important communications tools for the Freedom Summer and the entire movement. To maintain a sense of legitimacy in the face of attacks or lack of interest on the part of local media outlets, *Voice* editors made a special effort to give accurate accounts of SNCC/Freedom Summer activities. For example the front page of the June 20 edition featured a photograph of the volunteers' charred station wagon and a second photograph of Mickey Schwerner. The accompanying article referred to the charge that the federal government failed to respond to the needs of those fighting for civil rights and stated that FBI agents did have the authority to intervene in such cases, although agents often used territorial intrusion as an excuse for apathy. In the article, the paper described the following incident: ". . . . [a Justice Department lawyer] said the FBI was not a police force and that he was not sure a Federal offense had occurred. He was told that a provision in the U.S. Code gave the FBI authority to intervene in civil rights cases. He insisted he did not have any authority."[81]

Along with providing details about the missing workers, the paper also included coverage of the MFDP candidates and describes their contributions to the movement as well as their campaign platforms. For example, when describing Victory Gray, a Hattisburg, Mississippi, black woman, who ran against Senator John Stennis, the paper declared, "In opposing Stennis, Mrs. Gray will challenge, 'the whole seniority system."[82]

Many *Student Voice* writers were also responsible for the promotional materials that came out of the Atlanta office—for instance, an eighteen-page booklet on "The General Condition of the Mississippi Negro" and a twenty-six-page booklet describing the Mississippi Freedom Democratic Party, both were published in August of 1964.[83] Other promotional materials were similar to what one might find in any commercially oriented public relations campaign: SNCC "handclasp" pins, "One Man–One Vote" bumper stickers, *We Shall Overcome* songbooks, SNCC posters, a booklet entitled *The Movement*, Howard Zinn's SNCC history entitled *The New Abolitionists*, and fact sheets describing specific projects and individual organizers.[84] The SNCC press also created a steady stream of voting brochures, registration materials and pamphlets, tutorial materials, posters, stationery, education pamphlets, flyers, fact sheets, magazine article reprints, window stickers, and recruitment materials.[85]

SNCC communications workers also produced a number of other newsletters to supplement the *Student Voice*, some of which were published periodically, others that appeared only once or twice. On July 7, 1964, they published the first copy of a staff newsletter that was labeled "unofficial report, strictly confidential, not for public use."[86] The bulk of the newsletter addressed information generated from SNCC WATS line reports[87]–that is, incident reports describing acts of violence against organizers, volunteers, and protestors. The first issue contained this description of an incident involving a white student volunteer:

JACKSON, MISS.—NEW VOLUNTEER BEATEN—June 28. Steven L. Smith, 19, Marion, Iowa, was kicked down on the street and hit on the head by local residents as he prepared to join the summer project. He was knocked to the ground after leaving the Oxford, Ohio—Jackson, Miss. train.[88]

Another internal staff document entitled the *Legal Newsletter* gave a synopses of laws that workers needed to understand in order to protect themselves from local authorities and to promote their cause. The newsletter contained a request for volunteers to report incidents of discrimination in public accommodations and voting registration so that lawsuits could be filed. Volunteers were instructed to carefully observe all Mississippi laws regarding license plates, inspection stickers, and insurance, and warned that minor violations could result in arrest and beatings. The newsletter editors also outlined the four stages of COFO legal policy: challenging all arrests, removing the prosecutions of civil rights workers, phoning the COFO office when arrested, and refusing to stand trial without an attorney.[89]

At least two groups outside of the central SNCC organization created and distributed newsletters. The first included the parents of Freedom Summer student volunteers. Along with providing information about the project and giving advice on how to best support and protect their children, the newsletter gave many suggestions on how to further the cause of civil rights through political action. The August issue contained a report about a meeting held on July 24, at which a decision was made to meet with Democratic convention delegates and to organize a demonstration in Atlantic City. Readers were encouraged to send letters and telegrams to President Johnson demanding federal protection for their children. Instructions were also given on proper procedures in the event that one of their children was arrested, including calling the FBI, the Justice Department, Senators, Representatives, and the press.[90]

The second group of newsletter publishers were Friends of SNCC groups and SNCC chapters in Northern states and California. The *Princeton Freedom Center Newsletter* carried reports "on the violence and accomplishments" written by Princeton University students as well as other Freedom Summer volunteers. The newsletter's purpose was defined as:

> To support the civil rights movement in the South: to raise money for the vital voter education and registration programs being carried on there, to inform the North both of the conditions that exist and of the heroic efforts being made to correct them by such groups as the Student Nonviolent Coordinating Committee (SNCC) and, particularly in Mississippi, by the Council of Federated Organizations (COFO).[91]

Materials published by the central SNCC office complemented these efforts. The Atlanta communications staff sent the names of volunteers, project locations, and work assignments to their hometown newspapers, and let the respective editors know that they would be receiving spot news reports concerning those volunteers.[92] The volunteers themselves wrote down their personal experiences and sent them home for circulation among friends, family, local elected officials, and local media outlets.[93] After the summer, SNCC published and sold a book entitled *Letters from Mississippi* that contained correspondence from summer volunteers.[94]

OTHER SUMMER PROGRAMS

The majority of the student volunteers worked on black voter registration or as teachers in the Freedom Schools. A handful worked on one of two special projects: the white community project or the Law Student Project. The director of the white community project, Ed Hamlett, argued that segregation had enslaved all of Mississippi to the point that most whites in the state failed to see "the lack of jobs, the poverty, the cruelty, and the lack of educational opportunity which exists all around them." SNCC supported this project as a means of forcing white Mississippians to acknowledge the injustices of their racist political system.[95]

In the second project, law students worked on potential lawsuits against officials who violated federal civil rights and desegregation laws.[96] This project spotlighted Mississippi's corrupt legal system, and attracted the attention of federal officials and the media. The law students focused on a body of new laws passed by the Mississippi legislature that were designed to specifically suppress Freedom Summer activities.[97] The new laws doubled the size of the highway patrol, prohibited picketing in public places, outlawed the distribution of boycott literature, and authorized cities to "restrict the movements of individuals and groups" by enforcing curfews.[98]

One of the most unusual Freedom Summer activities involved "forty-eight socially prominent women who kept quiet about the whole thing."[99] These women, the majority from Northern states, were not officially related to either SNCC or COFO, but had gone through SNCC training in Oxford, Ohio before spending two months living in Mississippi homes and working on the self-described mission of "bridging the communication gap between the races." A *Kansas City Star* newspaper article quoted an unidentified source as saying that local Mississippians frequently yelled and jeered at them, but that the women's "high-heeled splendor held them in check."[100] The group included Mrs. Louis G. Cowan, wife of the Director of the Communications Research Center at Brandeis University. Cowan deemed the project a success, claiming that their presence "opened conversations between women of the South who have never before gathered to discuss openly their attitudes toward their problem . . ."[101]

A more standard component of SNCC activism was the Freedom Schools, which also made use of SNCC's growing body of communication techniques to organize local communities and garner support for the movement. The schools helped students overcome a state education system in which white teachers commonly subscribed to the idea that "ignorance is safer than inquiry."[102] COFO promoted the schools as an attempt to inform Mississippi blacks that they had not been "forsaken," and that knowledge and political power were the best avenues to advancement.[103] Freedom School organizers viewed their centers as places where leadership talent could be identified and developed through the teaching of specific skills.

More than 2,000 black children, teenagers, and adults attended 41 Freedom Schools staffed by 175 full-time teachers (including 40 certified professionals).[104] At least three schools printed newsletters. One class wrote a "Freedom" play that the students performed during a tour of several Northern schools that August.[105] Teachers also used newsletter production as a method of teaching the importance of carrying out a project from start to finish, as well as a means of instilling the SNCC messages of black liberation and empowerment in their students and surrounding communities.[106] The newsletters contained factual articles on the movement and the MFDP, school news, creative writing, poetry, inspirational columns, and advertisements from local businesses.

To sustain the schools financially, SNCC leaders and supporters devised an "Adopt-a-Freedom School" campaign. Organizations as disparate as civil rights groups and garden clubs raised the $4,000 required to support one school for the summer. The same organizations and clubs sponsored drives for equipment donations—typewriters, duplicating machines, tape recorders, film projectors, film screens, cameras, and so on.[107]

MFPD DISAPPOINTMENT

The Mississippi Freedom Summer of 1964 was successful in many respects, yet the MFDP failed in its effort to unseat delegates from the entrenched Mississippi Democratic organization at the party's national convention the final week of August. In early August, the state Democratic Party held its convention in Jackson and selected sixty-eight delegates to travel to Atlantic City. Members of the MFDP optimistically approached the Credentials Committee and argued that the state party had illegally barred blacks from voting through the use of violence and intimidation. Despite their powerful presentation, the

MFDP had a powerful opponent: President Johnson, who feared losing all of his southern support and who therefore worked to ensure that the group was not seated.[108] In Dorothy Miller Zellner's words, the national party was "far more interested in trying not to alienate the Southern Democrats—a rabid group of racists—so that they could win their next election."[109] In an attempt at compromise, Joseph Rauh, the MFDP legal counsel, proposed seating both parties. Johnson refused, instead offering two "at large" seats to MFDP delegates. The MFDP rejected the offer, stating that it was insignificant, that it upheld the regular party apparatus, and that it looked the other way at ongoing illegal acts.[110]

Fannie Lou Hamer, the former-sharecropper-turned-SNCC-activist turned MFDP candidate, made her history-rendering speech prior to the decision. Her dramatic and emotion-filled plea illustrated that the denial of voting rights to blacks in Mississippi was linked to economic oppression and violence. Although Johnson called a press conference to keep her off television, the networks loved her and aired the speech repeatedly that evening making Hamer a national symbol for the civil rights movement.

Although the Credential Committee offered a compromise that would give the MFDP two seats, the delegation refused it as a symbolic, but meaningless effort to which Hamer replied: "We didn't come all this way for no two seats when all of us is tired."[111]

This was a classic example of short-term loss for long-term gain. The MFDP challenge permanently altered Mississippi Democratic Party politics. As SNCC staff member Lawrence Guyot described the situation, "We took the regular Democratic Party and turned it on its head."[112] After 1964, segregated delegations were not admitted to the federal convention, and Mississippi blacks began to play pivotal roles in statewide and local elections. In the same manner as the entire Freedom Summer campaign, the MDFP had used public relations and communications tools to present its case to the entire country, leading to dramatic change in the South's most openly racist state.

The failure of the MDFP to unseat white Democrats nevertheless contributed to many positive outcomes, including passage of the 1965 Voting Rights Act. But the failure also served as an important turning point for the SNCC. For many Committee leaders, workers, and volunteers—none of whom had great faith in the national Democratic Party to begin with—their state-level rejection proved that the Party was not to be trusted. Bond later described his feeling "that these people not only don't share our politics but they're . . . removed from the reality of what we're doing." For Bond, the rejection created an "enormous disillusionment, or the solidification of disillusionment, with establishment liberals."[113]

Despite its failure at being seated, the MFDP delegation returned to Mississippi with substantially greater political power and a membership of 75,000.[114] SNCC worker Mendy Samstein noted that "Cracks were finally made in the Mississippi iceberg. For the first time in the state there were literally hundreds of local people who no longer feared to become active workers—not just passive supporters—of the movement."[115]

PERMANENT CHANGE

Though rarely identified as such, in many ways the Freedom Summer of 1964 was a communications campaign embedded within the larger civil rights movement. SNCC leaders used traditional and innovative communication devices to complete a massive, complex campaign with a strong public relations component in less than six months. As part of that campaign, over 3,000 local participants and approximately 1,000 out-of-state volunteers immersed themselves in black Mississippi communities, established about 700 Freedom Schools, and completed a statewide door-to-door voter registration effort. Guyot stated that the primary mission of the project was to "bring the country to Mississippi"—a mission that was clearly accomplished:

> And we did that by bringing the wives, daughters, sons, nephews of the Binghams who were in Congress, the Rockefellers who were elsewhere, into the Freedom Houses of Mississippi. . . . a SNCC volunteer . . . could be seen in the fields of Mississippi by day and in a meeting with people who had congressional contact in the evening, so the national base and the national reaction to atrocities were always spreading.[116]

Using a broad array of communications tools, SNCC empowered black Mississippians and promoted the idea of extending voting and educational rights to black citizens throughout the South. For the first time in its brief history, the Committee extended its communications staff and networks beyond Atlanta, and learned how to personally interact with reporters and film crews on a daily basis. Over a nine-week period, SNCC workers used all of the communication and public relations skills they had practiced in the preceding three years to to expose the final vestiges of the Jim Crow South.

By bringing in the children of America's affluent white majority to Mississippi and sending out a new political party to the national Democratic Convention, SNCC transformed core civil rights issues into issues that touched the lives of citizens throughout the United States. More than any single action, the Freedom Summer made the southern campaign for civil rights a national campaign for human rights.

MEMO

TO: JAMES FORMAN
FROM: JULIAN BOND
RE: JOB DESCRIPTION

As head of the communications department, I oversee
production and distribution of all materials relating to publicity that leave the Atlanta office.

This involves:
                    press releases
                    reprints
                    STUDENT VOICE
                    fund appeals
                    promotional literature
                    leaflets
                    tapes
                    photographs
                    and other materials

Working under my direction are:
                    Mary King
                    Sanford Leigh
                    Mark Suckle
                    Ed Nakawatase

It is my job to:
                    hand out "assignments" for writing press
                    releases, STUDENT VOICE stories, other
                    literature;
                    supervise printing (or mimeographing),
                    layout, distribution and mailing of
                    communications materials;
                    originating press releases and stories
                    for the STUDENT VOICE;
                    correspondence.

A typical week involves:
                    Monday   insure that
                                                    STUDENT VOICE IS
                                                    correct, proof-read
                                                    the last time, make
                                                    sure printing and
                                                    mailing schedules are
                                                    ready and workable;
                    TUESDAY   make sure bulk ship-
                                                    ments of STUDENT VOICE
                                                    are going out;
                    WEDNESDAY   press releases that
                                                    are generally time-
                                                    less (we try to send
                                                    out others as events
                                                     happen);
                    THURSDAY   begin STUDENT VOICE
                    FRIDAY   more STUDENT VOICE
                    SATRUDAY   write STUDENT VOICE
                    SUNDAY   get STUDENT VOICE copy
                                                    set.

Figure 1. SNCC Communication Director's Julian Bond job description. (Used with
permission of the King Library & Archives.)

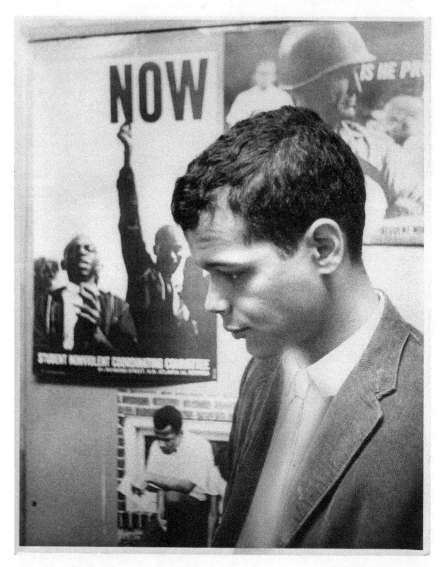

Figure 2. Julian Bond surrounded by images used in many of SNCC's communication materials designed to promote civil rights. (Used with permission of the King Library & Archives.)

NEWS RELEASE   # 52
STUDENT NONVIOLENT COORDINATING COMMITTEE   FOR IMMEDIATE RELEASE
6 Raymond Street, N. W.   May 27, 1964
Atlanta, Georgia 30314

              POLICE CONTINUE HARRASSMENT OF RIGHTS WORKERS

JACKSON, MISSISSIPPI - "Civil rights workers in Mississippi face arrest

almost daily on charges ranging from 'running a stop sign' and 'public

drunkeness' to 'carrying books calculated to incite people to overthrow

the government'", according to John Lewis, Chairman of the Student Non-

violent Coordinating Committee (SNCC).

        During an intensive mock political campaign across the state

last fall, workers from SNCC estimated that police made over 60 arrests

for traffic violations alone during a 21 day period. "Over 100 inci-

dents of official harrassment" were recorded during November, 1963,

when an integrated slate ran in a mock election for the state's two top

offices.

        Civil rights workers here have charged police are stepping up

arrests as the summer approaches. As examples, they cite:

        The overnight jailing in Holly Springs of four workers from
        the Council of Federated Organizations (COFO) for "investi-
        gation";
        The arrest of seven COFO workers in Belzoni on May 14. Po-
        lice said they were arrested "to prevent riots" because the
        group was integrated;
        The arrest in Oxford of six COFO workers May 5. They were
        charged with "suspicion of carrying materials which advo-
        cate the overthrow of the government" when police found
        college textbooks in a trailer behind their car;
        The arrest in Jackson on May 24 of a white COFO worker,
        Dick Jewett, 20, of New York city. Jewett was charged with
        "vagrancy" and "public drunkeness";
        The arrest of two University of Pennsylvania Law School stu-
        dents, Alan Lerner and Charles Woll, and SNCC worker Hunter
        Morey in Jackson May 25. The three, all white, were charged
        with "being fugitives";
        The arrest May 25 of COFO worker Emily Shrader, 20, of Cam-
        bridge, Massachusetts, on "vagrancy" and "public drunkeness"
        charges;
        The arrest that evening, three times, by Pennsylvania law
        student Woll on three different traffic counts;

        SNCC workers expect such arrests to increase when 1,000 sum-

mer workers arrive in Mississippi July 1 to begin work on a COFO-spon-

sored "Summer Project."
                              -30-

Figure 3. The SNCC communications staff continually produced news releases, especially during the 1964 Mississippi Freedom Summer voter registration campaign. These releases frequently recorded police violence directed at civil rights workers. (Used with permission of the King Library & Archives.)

Figure 4. James Forman, a former teacher and reporter for the *Chicago Defender*, became SNCC executive secretary in the fall of 1961 and exhibited a keen sense of the importance of public relations, fund raising, and publicity. (Used with permission of the King Library & Archives.)

STUDENT NONVIOLENT
COORDINATING COMMITTEE
6 RAYMOND STREET, N.W.
ATLANTA, GEORGIA

JAMES FORMAN,
EXECUTIVE SECRETARY

SNCC Executive Secretary James Forman was raised in rural Marshall County, Mississippi. He will spend the summer of 1964 in that state working on the Mississippi Summer Project.

Forman was born in Chicago in 1928 and moved back there from Mississippi. He attended public and private schools there and spent one semester at Wilson Junior College before joining the United States Air Force. He was honorably discharged in September 1951.

He then entered Roosevelt University in Chicago, and was graduated with a degree in public administration in 1957. He attended Boston University on a grant from that school's African Studies Program. He studied there one year while also serving as an assistant in the Government Department. He has done postgraduate study in French and education at Middlebury College in Vermont.

In the fall of 1960, Forman took leave from his school teaching job in Chicago to organize the Fayette County (Tennessee) Relief Program and helped set up Tent City, a stop gap effort to house sharecroppers evicted because they tried to register to vote.

At that time, Forman says, he became concerned that young Negroes must return to the South.

In the fall of 1961 he joined the small staff of the infant SNCC operation, agreeing to serve as executive secretary. He has served in that post since, and has directed SNCC's growth from a 16 man, one room organization to a Southwide group with over 150 staff in seven states.

"Those of us in the Student Nonviolent Coordinating Committee have made our choice," Forman says. "We prefer to work not for money but for the emancipation of our society. We prefer quick death from positive action rather than the slow death that one begins to feel when he learns that he is a Negro in America."

#

Figure 5. The SNCC communication staff provided biographies of organizational leaders to volunteers and reporters. This biography of Executive Secretary James Forman appeared in the 1964 SNCC Communication Manual. (Used with permission of the King Library & Archives.)

Figure 6. Executive Secretary James Forman answers questions from reporters representing national news organizations. (Used with permission of the King Library & Archives.)

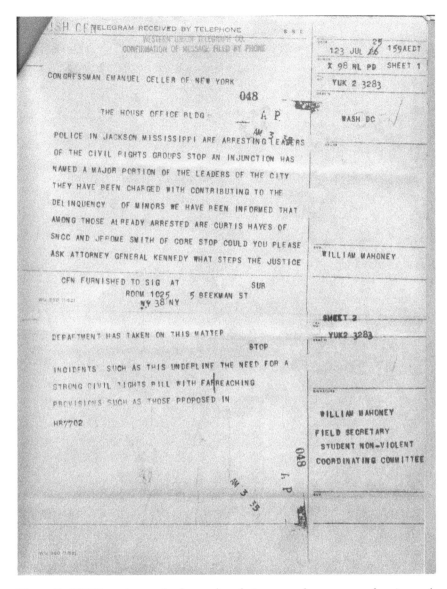

Figure 7. SNCC workers, who knew that their news releases were often ignored, learned through wire service contacts that the wire editors took note of stories about telegrams that had been sent to the federal government. Therefore, they frequently sent telegrams in an effort to generate news and get their stories in the national media. (Used with permission of the King Library & Archives.)

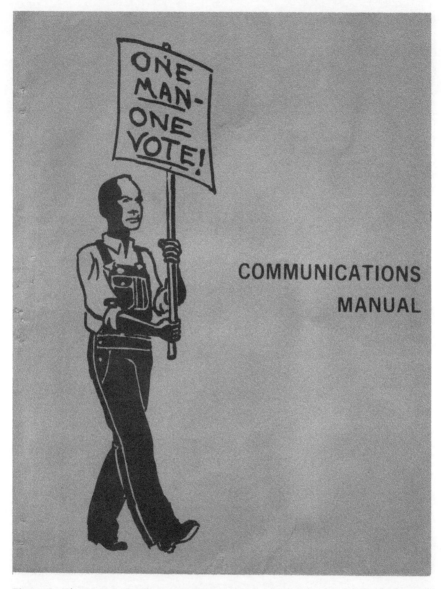

Figure 8. The *SNCC Communication Manual* stands as a testament to the planning and training associated with 1964 Freedom Summer activities. Information was provided in six areas: how to access volunteer biographies; achieving "tip of the tongue familiarity" with the political, economic, and social characteristics of a district; working with lists of press contacts; project backgrounds; appropriate sources for media questions; and maintaining a "strong sense of security." The *Manual* also contained descriptions of procedures for managing photographs and conducting research. (Used with permission of the King Library & Archives.)

Figure 9. SNCC workers had a number of celebrity supporters, including Dick Gregory, who helped raise awareness and change attitudes. (Used with permission of the King Library & Archives.)

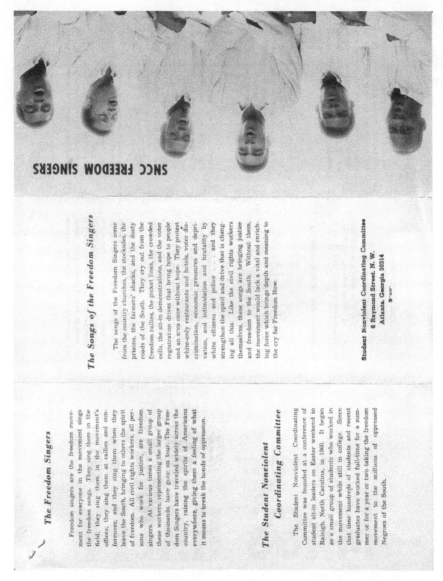

Figure 10a. The SNCC "Freedom Singers" formed in 1963 and later earned a national reputation for using the power of music to disseminate the movement's message in fund raising concerts across the country. (Used with permission of the King Library & Archives.)

The Freedom Singers' New Record

THE FREEDOM SINGERS SING OF FREEDOM NOW!

Mercury Records

The Singers

James Peacock, 23, is a native Mississippian who first became active in voter registration work in South Carolina. He returned to Mississippi and has worked for SNCC in Greenwood, Vicksburg and Jackson. His civil rights work has led to three arrests.

Marshall Jones, 26, is from Knoxville Tennessee. He is a graduate of Florida A. & M. University and became involved in the civil rights movement while studying for his Master's degree at the University of Tennessee. He has been arrested twice for civil rights activity. He was a prize winner at last year's University of Tennessee Folk Festival and has sung with the Knoxville Civic Opera.

Charles "Chuck" Neblett, 22, toured with the first Freedom Singers group, appearing at Carnegie Hall, on television and on campuses throughout the country. Neblett left Southern Illinois University and Missouri in the summer of 1962 and has since worked in Mississippi.

Emory Harris, 20, is from Albany, Georgia. He first came into the movement while still in high school during the time of massive demonstrations in that city. He has worked in SNCC vote drives in Terrell and Lee counties in southwest Georgia, and has been arrested seven times in connection with that work.

Matthew Jones, 28, is from Knoxville Tennessee. He has been arrested 20 times for civil rights participation and was active in SNCC's Danville, Virginia drive in the summer of 1963. A former school teacher, Jones has lost work in Macon, Georgia and Tennessee because of his civil rights work. He has composed many freedom songs.

Rafael Bentham, 21, is from New York. He attended Brooklyn College, New York University and Morehouse College in Atlanta, Georgia. He has been arrested in demonstrations in Atlanta where he was active in the civil rights movement, working with the Committee on Appeal for Human Rights.

Freedom Singers Appearances

If you or your group is interested in obtaining the Freedom Singers for a SNCC rally or benefit please write to:

"FREEDOM SINGERS"
% SNCC
6 Raymond St., N. W.
Atlanta, Georgia 30314

Figure 10b. The SNCC "Freedom Singers" formed in 1963 and later earned a national reputation for using the power of music to disseminate the movement's message in fund raising concerts across the country. (Used with permission of the King Library & Archives.)

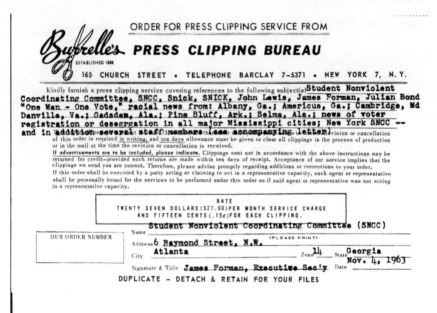

Figure 11. In addition to volunteer and staff efforts, SNCC communication workers used professional press clipping services to survey media accounts of their activities. (Used with permission of the King Library & Archives.)

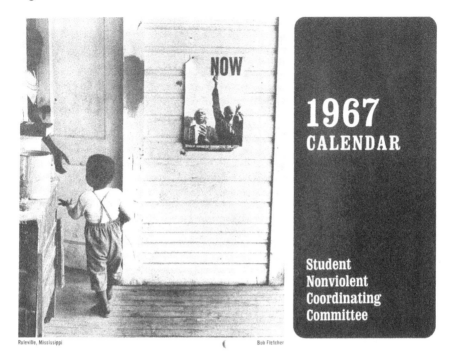

Figure 12. Communication workers used this 1967 calendar to raise awareness about civil rights issues. The calendar notes significant dates in civil rights history. (Used with permission of the King Library & Archives.)

AFRAMERICAN
NEWS
SERVICE

360 NELSON ST.S.W
ATLANTA,GEORGIA
30303
phone (404) 688—0331

WHITE TERRORISM ON THE UPSWING IN TENNESSEE

HAYWOOD COUNTY, TENN. - Nov., 1967

If there's something that makes hunkies mad, its hearing about a "favorable" decision in a school desegregation case. They don't even bother to learn whether the case is harmless to the cause of white supremacy, as is true of "favorable" decisions in the United States courts. What, infact, "favorable" describes is the climate for hunkies to go into their "Klan Act"--demonstrating their displeasure with the court decision.

Such is the case in Haywood County, Tennessee where, on August 4th, the U.S. District Court ruled "favorably" on a school desegregation case. Of course the decision made no provision at all for pupil desegregation in the separate and unequal school system although the government gives them a half million dollars yearly in federal school aid. What the decision did was send ten Negro teachers to "integrate" the faculty in five white schools and correspondingly, some white teachers to go into four Negro faculties.

Not even the most token-minded liberal could miscontrue the decision as "favorable" for school desegregation. But the WPP (White power press) and the hunkies did. So they went into their act. As a result, 29 counted acts of terrorism have been propagated against black people of Haywood County. Terrorism took the usual form of buring and bombing, starting, of course, with homes of the "civil rights activists", but invarialy ending with the homes of black families (one man had 17 children) who had received something "communistic" like an Equal Opportunities Loan to improve their homes.

Most of the fires destroyed entire homes and caused the death of a lady who suffered repeated strokes following the excitemant of the fire bombings. One neighbor described her death:
"When the house burned, she got nervous and couldn't sleep. She had been sick. But she took worse whth heart trouble and had a stroke, it scared her so bad. She was picking cotton and cuttin' off okra that day and she got sick that night. She would scream She couldn't get it off her mind. They took her to the hospital on Thursday and she died the following week.
                    HOW MUCH LONGER WILL THIS HAPPEN?

Figure 13. The *Aframerican News Report*, designed to promote SNCC's international efforts, contained reports of violence against blacks and civil rights news. This November 1967 edition clearly reveals the change in key messages and tone that came with the Black Power period. (Used with permission of the King Library & Archives.)

IS THIS THE PARTY YOU WANT?

DEMOCRATIC PARTY

OF ALABAMA

This is the party of: George Wallace, Al Lingo, Bull Connor, Sheriff James Clark and all the other racists in Alabama.

This is the party of: U. S. Senator John Sparkman and Congressmen G. W. Andrews, A. Selden, R. E. Jones and other racists Alabama sends to Washington.

This is the party of: Tom Coleman, who shot and killed Jonathan Daniels; the grand jury which indicted Coleman for "manslaughter"; Circuit Solicitor Arthur Gamble, who "prosecuted" Coleman; Judge T. Werth Thagard who presided over the "trial"; and the trial jury which acquitted Coleman of "manslaughter".

This is the party of: Lyndon Baines Johnson, President of the United States.

THEY ALL OPERATE TOGETHER, IN ALABAMA AND IN WASHINGTON, UNDER THE BANNER YOU SEE ABOVE

Do you want this party to decide, *for you*, who you can vote for next year in the counties and in the state?

Or do you want to start your own organization, that you will control, that will *not be for white supremacy* that will put on the ballot at next year's general election the candidates of *your choice* for all the County and State Offices?

IF YOU WANT TO BE YOUR OWN MAN IN POLITICS, TURN THIS SHEET OVER AND SEE HOW IT CAN BE DONE

Figure 14a. The Democratic Party of Alabama represented itself with a symbolic white rooster framed by a "white supremacy" banner. In response, the Lowndes County Freedom Organization adopted a black panther for the party's symbol, with Ruth Howard (who worked with Julian Bond in the Atlanta office) modeling the first Black Panther after the mascot of Clark College in Atlanta. (Used with permission of the King Library & Archives.)

ALABAMA LAW SAYS THAT YOU CAN START YOUR OWN POLITICAL PARTY

Title 17, Section 337, Alabama Code: An Assemblage or Organization of Electors which, at the General Election for State and County Officers then next preceding the primary, cast more than twenty percent of the entire vote cast in any county is hereby declared to be a Political Party within the meaning of this chapter within such county; and an assemblage or organization of electors which, at the General Election for State Officers then next preceding the primary, cast more than twenty percent of the entire vote cast in the State, is hereby declared to be a Political Party within the meaning of this chapter for such State.

We all know what happened when the Mississippi Freedom Democratic Party tried to work within the structure of the National Democratic Party (The party of Lyndon Johnson, George Wallace, Bull Connor, James Clark, John Sparkman)--They got the door slammed in their faces.

If Alabama doesn't want to repeat what happened to the Mississippi Freedom Democratic Party then Alabama doesn't have to.

ALABAMA HAS A CHOICE!

Every County in Alabama can begin, now, to organize its own Political Party. Every County in Alabama can have a Political Organization which will hold a nominating convention next May, and nominate *its own candidates* for State and County Offices. Alabama Law says such candidates, nominated in Legal County Conventions, *must be put on the general election ballot next November.*

Alabama SNCC
P. O. Box 672
Selma, Ala.

Figure 14b. The Democratic Party of Alabama represented itself with a symbolic white rooster framed by a "white supremacy" banner. In response, the Lowndes County Freedom Organization adopted a black panther for the party's symbol, with Ruth Howard (who worked with Julian Bond in the Atlanta office) modeling the first Black Panther after the mascot of Clark College in Atlanta. (Used with permission of the King Library & Archives.)

Figure 15a. The illiteracy rate of the Lowndes County, Alabama black population was significant, so SNCC workers often used cartoons and pictures to explain the complicated political processes they were promoting. The eleven-page booklet illustrated here and on the following pages encouraged voter registration. (Used with permission of the King Library & Archives.)

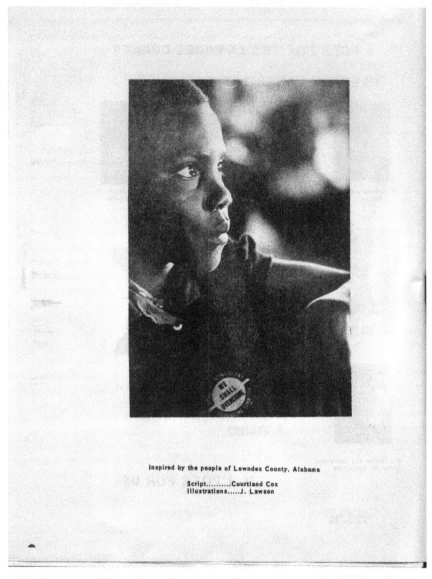

Figure 15b. The illiteracy rate of the Lowndes County, Alabama black population was significant, so SNCC workers often used cartoon and pictures to explain the complicated political processes they were promoting. (Used with permission of the King Library & Archives.)

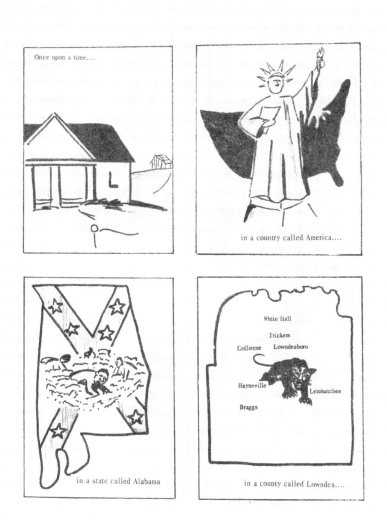

Figure 15c. The illiteracy rate of the Lowndes County, Alabama black population was significant, so SNCC workers often used cartoon and pictures to explain the complicated political processes they were promoting. (Used with permission of the King Library & Archives.)

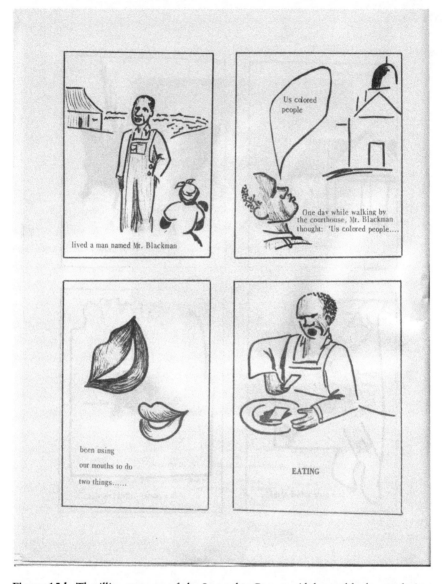

Figure 15d. The illiteracy rate of the Lowndes County, Alabama black population was significant, so SNCC workers often used cartoon and pictures to explain the complicated political processes they were promoting. (Used with permission of the King Library & Archives.)

Figure 15e. The illiteracy rate of the Lowndes County, Alabama black population was significant, so SNCC workers often used cartoon and pictures to explain the complicated political processes they were promoting. (Used with permission of the King Library & Archives.)

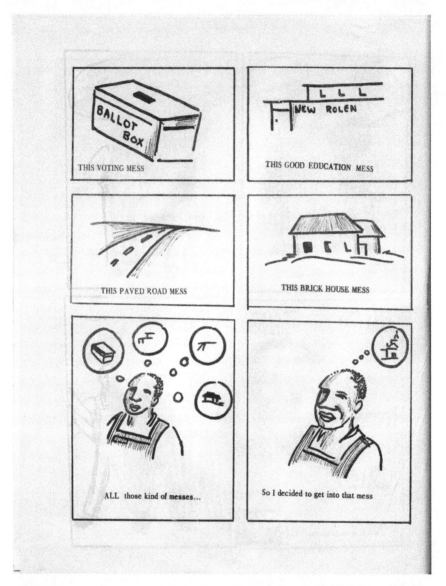

Figure 15f. The illiteracy rate of the Lowndes County, Alabama black population was significant, so SNCC workers often used cartoon and pictures to explain the complicated political processes they were promoting. (Used with permission of the King Library & Archives.)

Figure 15g. The illiteracy rate of the Lowndes County, Alabama black population was significant, so SNCC workers often used cartoon and pictures to explain the complicated political processes they were promoting. (Used with permission of the King Library & Archives.)

Figure 15h. The illiteracy rate of the Lowndes County, Alabama black population was significant, so SNCC workers often used cartoon and pictures to explain the complicated political processes they were promoting. (Used with permission of the King Library & Archives.)

Figure 15i. The illiteracy rate of the Lowndes County, Alabama black population was significant, so SNCC workers often used cartoon and pictures to explain the complicated political processes they were promoting. (Used with permission of the King Library & Archives.)

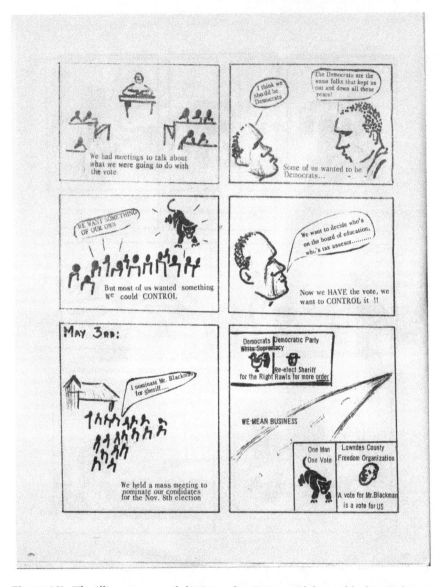

Figure 15j. The illiteracy rate of the Lowndes County, Alabama black population was significant, so SNCC workers often used cartoon and pictures to explain the complicated political processes they were promoting. (Used with permission of the King Library & Archives.)

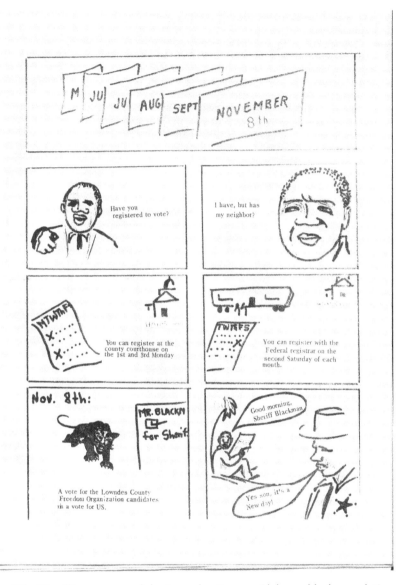

Figure 15k. The illiteracy rate of the Lowndes County, Alabama black population was significant, so SNCC workers often used cartoon and pictures to explain the complicated political processes they were promoting. (Used with permission of the King Library & Archives.)

SPECIAL ISSUE

THE STUDENT VOICE

The Student Voice, Inc.   6 Raymond Street, N.W., Atlanta 14, Ga.   SPRING 1964

SNCC EXPANDING S.W. GEORGIA DRIVE

ALBANY, GA. - The Student Nonviolent Coordinating Committee (SNCC) is expanding its Southwest Georgia voter registration project.

The student group will begin operating in Randolph and Worth Counties. SNCC workers now live and work in four rural counties here.

SNCC work began in Albany, in Nov. 1961, when three SNCC workers came here to begin a voter registration drive.

Local high school students were interested in direct action projects, however, and resulting demonstrations saw over 1,000 people jailed in mass marches.

Direct action proved a stimulus to voter registration, and the SNCC workers moved into rural counties to urge Negroes to register.

As in Mississippi, SNCC workers found much opposition from law enforcement officials here.

Four churches in the area were burned after they were used for voter registration meetings. A vote worker's home was shot into, and two workers injured. The same home was later bombed.

In nearby Americus three SNCC workers were held in jail for 85 days facing the death penalty under an 1867 "insurrection" statute. Others faced police brutality.

CONTINUED ON PAGE 4

SNCC SPEARHEADS ARKANSAS ACTIVITIES

PINE BLUFF, ARK. - SNCC's Arkansas project began with a request from the Arkansas Council of Human Relations to send a worker into the state in the winter of 1962.

Since then, the project has spread into four counties and into direct action protest and voter registration drives.

Project director William Hansen helped reactivate a student group at a Little Rock college, and two days of sit-ins integrated several lunch counters there.

Hansen then moved to Pine Bluff, where he helped to form the Pine Bluff Movement, which has conducted successful vote drives and direct action protest here.

Moving into the Arkansas Delta, SNCC worked with local citizens in Helena on voting and action projects.

Most recently, SNCC workers

CONTINUED ON PAGE 5

PICKETS MARCH IN FRONT of the Forrest County Courthouse during Hattiesburg, Miss. Freedom Day on Jan. 22.

FREEDOM SUMMER PLANNED IN MISS.

JACKSON, MISS. - Plans are underway here for a "Freedom Summer" that will engage 1,000 volunteer workers in Freedom Schools, Freedom Registration, community centers, and voter registration activity.

Three Negroes are running for Congress, and will face white opponents in actual and mock elections.

The summer's activity - sponsored by the Council of Federated Organizations (COFO) - is the most ambitious project even undertaken in the civil rights movement.

The program director for COFO is Robert Moses, who heads the Student Nonviolent Coordinating Committee's voter registration drive here.

Moses began SNCC's first Mississippi project in southwest Mississippi in August, 1961. With a small group of student volunteers, he began a drive which has set a pattern for other civil rights groups. For the first time, vote workers lived and worked with local people in rural areas.

Workers on that first project agreed to sacrifice school and

CONTINUED ON PAGE 3

ALABAMA PROJECT FACES 'POLICE STATE TACTICS'

SELMA, ALA. - A Student Nonviolent Coordinating Committee voter registration drive based here has faced the "tactics common to a police state" SNCC staff coordinator Worth Long said.

Long, who directed the project here, was beaten by police after his arrest during a protest march.

Others were burned with electric cattle prodders. Some local Negroes who tried to register to vote have lost their jobs.

SNCC's work in Alabama began in Gadsden with a direct action voter registration campaign.

SNCC workers participated on

CONTINUED ON PAGE 6

THE TOOLS OF A POLICE STATE are guns and men. Alabama employs both to halt civil rights progress.

Figure 16. From 1960 until 1965, the Student voice, SNCC's official newsletter, provided a forum for the exchange of news about the movement and helped to increase awareness about the organization and its activities. (Used with permission of the King Library & Archives.)

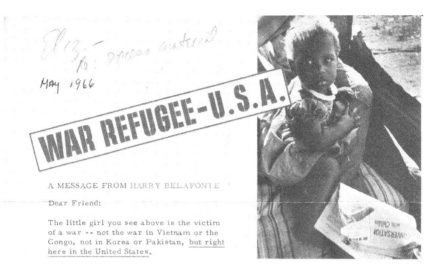

El 13; - appease austria

MAY 1966

WAR REFUGEE-U.S.A.

A MESSAGE FROM HARRY BELAFONTE

Dear Friend:

The little girl you see above is the victim of a war -- not the war in Vietnam or the Congo, not in Korea or Pakistan, but right here in the United States.

She has just been evicted from her home in Lowndes County, Alabama, and is sitting on a mattress waiting to move into a tent with hundreds of families like hers.

She is a victim of the war being waged by Southern segregationists. They are using a weapon more agonizing in a way than the bombings and murders which have oppressed Negroes for a hundred years. That new weapon is starvation. And its victims are everyone.

In Alabama, tenant farmers and sharecroppers are being evicted every day because they dare to register to vote or to run for local office.

Because they try to exercise their citizenship -- just as you and I register and vote -- they are turned off the land without notice, without compensation. And under laws they did not make, the sharecroppers are not eligible for any state or federal welfare program.

WHO WILL HELP THEM?

Who is fighting on their side? For years, I have done whatever I could to help the freedom movement. One of the main ways I have tried to help is by supporting the Student Nonviolent Coordinating Committee (SNCC), a Southern-based organization of courageous young people.

(over please)

Figure 17a. In addition to fund raising concerts, Harry Belafonte made appeals for SNCC support. Other nationally known spokespersons and events sponsors included. Bill Cosby, Lorraine Hansberry, Diahann Carrol, and Sidney Poitier. (Used with permission of the King Library & Archives.)

- 2 -

Today SNCC is fighting alongside the Alabama Negro on two fronts:

> For day-to-day survival, it is providing the
> evicted families with land, tents and food.

> For tomorrow, it is organizing these citizens
> so that they may have a voice in government
> and thus combat oppression.

For months SNCC has been building "freedom parties", with Negroes running
for local office. These new parties are springing up in terror-ridden areas
where Klansmen ride by night <u>and day</u>. They stand for an unheard-of idea:

> That Negroes -- who constitute 80% of the
> population in some Alabama counties -- can
> have a voice in governing their daily lives.

But SNCC cannot wage this battle alone. They need your help.....to put food
in the mouths of these war victims. To put warmth in their bones.....hope in
their hearts.

How much does it cost? More than anyone can give and so much that everyone
must. And that's the point of the enclosed envelope.

Send a contribution today to the workers of the Student Nonviolent Coordinating
Committee. Help them to win the war against starvation.

                                        Yours in freedom,

                                        Harry Belafonte

                                        Harry Belafonte

Figure 17b. In addition to fund raising concerts, Harry Belafonte made appeals
for SNCC support. Other nationally known spokespersons and events sponsors
included. Bill Cosby. Lorraine Hansberry, Diahann Carroll, and Sidney Poitier.
(Used with permission of the King Library & Archives.)

Figure 18. The Black Power concept emerged in June 1966, during James Meredith's "March Against Fear." Here, a marcher wears a version of the Lowndes County Freedom Organization's black panther, which would become symbol of the new movement. (Used with permission of the King Library & Archives.)

Chapter Four

Black Power: Awakening Black Pride and Consciousness

I think Mr. Carmichael—if he weren't where he is, he ought to be on Madison Avenue. He is a public relations man par excellence. He abounds in the provocative phrase.[1]

—Roy Wilkins, August 1966

"Black Power," a slogan that changed the social and racial convictions of an entire nation, was the centerpiece of a passionate communications campaign designed to instill cultural pride and to promote the idea that American blacks should no longer tolerate the unfair and illegal treatment that had been imposed on them for centuries. It marked an about-face in terms of the foundational nonviolent philosophy that supported the 1950s/1960s civil rights movement: suddenly, many blacks began to accept the idea that they had a right to physically defend themselves against injustice.

An examination of SNCC's administrative history, messages, and public relations efforts during these dissident times—the mid-to-late 1960s—reveals how SNCC propelled the Black Power movement and simultaneously made a lasting impression on the social ideologies of the country. Ironically, it was the unification of blacks that panicked many whites and political leaders, which ultimately lead to the organization's demise. But perhaps more importantly, the philosophy led to a new outlook for black Americans—an outlook that served as an influential societal force that would remain an element of black history and pride.

"GOOD, GOOD COPY"

Along with the simultaneous disappointment and empowerment resulting from the Mississippi Freedom Democratic Party efforts discussed in the previous chapter, two additional elements within SNCC helped to propagate the

Black Power movement: the Lowndes County Freedom Organization and Stokely Carmichael—the master of the "provocative phrase," who replaced John Lewis as chairman of the Student Nonviolent Coordinating Committee in May 1966.[2] In fact, by the end of 1966, Carmichael was SNCC to many people. His rhetoric held tremendous appeal to blacks and the media, and he became the representative image of the Committee in the minds of most white Americans.

It was easy to overlook the fact that very little of his message was translated into concrete activities such as lunch counter sit-ins, picket lines, or voter registration campaigns. To many, that didn't matter, since the media was so strongly attracted to the articulate, intelligent, handsome, and confident Carmichael as he described an alternative to the original SNCC ideals of Christianity, nonviolence, and political activism. He presented an aura of controversy. Dorothy Miller Zellner later described him as "good, good copy"—a phrase more closely tied to the print press. What that statement overlooked was Carmichael's charisma, which was perfect for the medium that had gained so much power in the preceding decade—television. This led some SNCC staffers to call their new chairman Stokely "Starmichael."[3]

Carmichael, who had been active in the movement since 1959,[4] joined SNCC full time during the 1964 Mississippi Freedom Summer and was at the organizational forefront when SNCC experienced the disappointing MFDP defeat in Atlantic City. By May 1966, he had replaced longtime chairman John Lewis and was on his way to becoming nationally known as a radical civil rights leader. The authoritative Howard University philosophy graduate offered new and controversial alternatives to the traditional SNCC ideals of Christianity, nonviolence, and political activism. Through his force of personality and ability to shine in front of a camera, Carmichael ensured that the mainstream media kept SNCC in the national spotlight. During his brief twelve-month tenure, Carmichael made hundreds of speeches as SNCC underwent a radical shift from political organizing to promoting Black Power,[5] an idea that combined the right to self-defense against violent resistance with a strong belief in cultural unity, racial pride, and individual and community empowerment. The media was captivated.

Like Zellner, other SNCC leaders, including Carmichael, were well aware of the media's power and range of influence, and they were well aware of Carmichael's appeal. The late civil rights activists and entertainer Nina Simone echoed this idea and recalled that although she first saw Carmichael at a political rally, "politics wasn't what sprung straight to mind" at first sight. "He stood up to speak and I thought he had to be the most handsome man in America . . . . I would have walked into the fires of hell with him and never looked back once."[6]

SNCC workers capitalized on Carmichael's attractiveness and sex appeal that Simone described. They used established public relations tactics such as press releases and conferences, internal and external publications, special events, and speaking engagements to attract much of this attention in the early stages of Carmichael's chairmanship. And as such, the new leader helped to assure that the mainstream media put SNCC's activities high on the media and consequently the public agendas. Although Carmichael seemed perfectly suited to serve as an organizational spokesperson, the turbulent conditions of the mid to late 1960s also propelled his fame. As a *Life* editor wrote almost two years later, the "mood of militancy and exhausted patience was not created by Carmichael: he [was] rather a symptom of it—and its catalyst."[7]

WAVELAND MEETING SIGNALS CHANGE

Although it was not yet articulated as Black Power, the organization was clearly undergoing drastic change as early as the fall of 1964. During the November 1964 meeting held in Waveland, Mississippi, SNCC workers began discussing new strategies, tactics, and organizational changes to support their continued struggle for civil rights. Change seemed certain, and the meeting served as a turning point for the emergence of a new SNCC built on the frustration of the Atlantic City defeat. But despite the impending change, communication remained a central strategy and organizational tool. For instance, Mary King presented a paper reminding meeting attendees that they must maintain their focus on the communications component to ensure future success. She also responded to concerns expressed by some in the organization that SNCC had become unnecessarily bureaucratic, stating that SNCC could reform itself in order to accommodate the evolving goals of the movement and the specific growing pains of the nationally recognized organization:

> We all shun organizations and civil rights groups which seem intent on building the organization and fund raising. We even pride ourselves that other groups do the talking while we do the hard dirty work. Yet SNCC has grown larger and larger and has created its own needs. . . . We can use skills and organization in some areas without letting them *use* us.[8]

King recalled that two factions made their interests known during the Waveland meeting. The one led by Robert Moses advocated the continuation of independent leadership and decision-making, and the one led by James Forman advocated a more centralized management approach.[9]

These competing interests were also evident within the communications department. For the most part, the Atlanta staff had managed the flow of information and produced the bulk of public relations materials up until the Mississippi Freedom Summer, when it began to train communications workers in field offices. After the Atlantic City convention, there was little direction concerning interactions between the field communications workers and the central office.

It seemed to many that the organization was finding it more and more difficult to present unified messages to the media as well as to its external and internal constituents. SNCC communications workers who were scattered throughout the South maintained their focus on community organizing, thus keeping that fundamental objective alive in the face of internal dissension. After the successes of the Freedom Summer, SNCC workers continued their efforts in black communities and their search for indigenous leaders. For instance, in a report dated February 23, 1965, an unnamed field worker wrote that SNCC leaders were "struggling to find better ways . . . of allowing people in the communities to participate more in making decisions affecting their lives."[10] The same report emphasized the importance of rewarding individual workers, suggesting that "people who have less visibility in the organization must be given more responsibility."

In response to this need, the group organized a new executive committee, which would ironically serve as a springboard for Carmichael's rise within the organization. At the age of twenty-four, he was appointed to a committee whose stated purposed was to elevate those SNCC workers who had been denied "visibility."[11] Yet his appointment was tangible evidence that SNCC was moving away from community organizing and local leadership development as its primary organizational missions and into a period of centralized leadership as Forman had proposed.

The shift from nonviolence and political organization to Black Power was both gradual and spontaneous. SNCC's 1964 defeat at Atlantic City is generally considered the stimulus for its giving up faith in the federal government and turning instead to the Black Power movement. The young Southern blacks who had worked so hard to present their case to the Democratic Party and federal authorities returned to their homes feeling defeated and disillusioned. They also had a vision and sense of authority from their important victories during the Freedom Summer, including the simple idea that they had actually participated in national politics. But for many, the idea of returning to nonviolent strategies was unappealing. Arguably, Black Power was the only possible political philosophy and communications strategy for maintaining the hope among Southern blacks that they could someday enjoy the same rights extended to white Americans.

THE LOWNDES COUNTY FREEDOM ORGANIZATION

Although it was Carmichael who appeared in the national media and who served as an iconic leader for the new movement, Black Power began with an important SNCC-affiliated political organization in Lowndes County, Alabama—the Lowndes County Freedom Organization or the LCFO. SNCC workers had been steadily working in Selma, Alabama, since February 1963 to organize local blacks and to promote voter registration. And it was here that SNCC workers, including Carmichael, first cultivated the emerging Black Power movement.

In January 1965, Martin Luther King, Jr.'s organization, the Southern Christian Leadership Conference, sent workers to assist in the SNCC programs.[12] At this time SNCC and SCLC began to plan voting programs for surrounding Black Belt counties where blacks frequently outnumbered whites by nearly five to one.[13] Progress was slow, limited, and dangerous. But on February 18, 1965, when an Alabama state trooper shot twenty-six-year-old civil rights activist Jimmy Lee Jackson, who died nine days later, demonstrations ensued, and nearly three thousand people were soon in the Dallas County jail, including Dr. King. With King at the center of the protest, the national media came to Selma.

SCLC administrators sensed that the public was aroused. In response they planned the now-famous Selma to Montgomery march in honor of Jackson. With the eyes of the country upon them and ensuing violence against civil rights workers, Carmichael and other SNCC workers remained in Alabama and continued with plans to organize their second political party. This new organization—the LCFO—would commence from the seemingly sedate and oppressed communities of Lowndes County. The small county had a population of about 81 percent black people who by and large had never voted in their lives and who generally worked as sharecroppers and domestic help for the white minority.[14]

The opportunity for vast change in Lowndes County presented itself on July 6, 1965, when, after negotiation with the United States Justice Department, the Lowndes County Board of Registrars agreed to remove the literacy test from the voter registration application; this long-standing tool had been used successfully to unjustly and deliberately prevent blacks from voting for many years. Months earlier, on March 15, President Johnson introduced the initiative during a nationally televised announcement that he would sign voting rights legislation. In a tacit acknowledgment of the communications efforts of local and national civil rights organizations, the president noted that their efforts had gained national attention, "summon[ing] into convocation all the majesty of this great government and the greatest nation on earth."[15] In a move that could be described as brazen or daring, the President had directly referred to one of the South's most entrenched procedures for maintaining political power.

Johnson's televised declaration was a strong sign of encouragement, which was bolstered even further by a federal court order against any Alabama state efforts to interfere with a Selma-to-Montgomery march scheduled for March 25; nearly 3,000 participants joined the demonstration.[16] The event, however, was marred by ever-familiar violence: Viola Liuzzo, a white volunteer from Detroit, was shot and killed after driving a group of marchers back to Lowndes County after the march concluded. Thus, media attention came from two sources: the success of the event and yet another act of violent resistance. Moreover, Dr. King's emotionally charged speeches along the way and at a rally held on the capitol grounds never failed to attract attention from the nation's press.

SNCC leaders knew that this national attention and the passage of the Voting Rights Act would provide opportunities for black empowerment, and they urged the Lowndes County blacks to register. But even if they could vote, blacks would still be voting for white candidates, ultimately resulting in little political change. In an effort to incorporate a true change in Alabama politics, Carmichael asked SNCC's research director, former law student Jack Minnis, to find an alternative to black participation in the all-white Democratic Party, whose insignia even included a banner declaring "white supremacy." Minnis succeeded, and found a clause in Alabama's state law that allowed for the formation of independent political parties—a chance to place black candidates on local and statewide ballots.[17, 18]

Armed with national attention, the Civil Rights Act, and news of the Alabama code, SNCC workers soon had the LCFO underway. Because it was started at a time when the national organization was undergoing changes in both its structure and operating philosophy, the new party would embrace both traditional political organizational ideas and the new Black Power concept.

After establishing a plan to form a new party, local SNCC organizers started the slow, laborious process of encouraging participation from the black community, with public relations and communications serving as primary activist tools. SNCC's seasoned community organizers were ideally suited for this task. SNCC worker Courtland Cox noted that the LCFO, like many other SNCC initiatives, focused on developing local leadership and community support. He also noted that organizers stressed the LCFO first, and then tried to teach local residents about their "responsibilities and duties."[19] Gloria House, a SNCC worker in Lowndes County, recalled that residents wanted to participate and were interested in hearing more about "independent organizing," yet it was difficult "to make clear the process by which this kind of operation had to be undertaken." Therefore, communicating that complex message in simple terms was the primary job of SNCC workers.[20] Their tools were educational booklets, fliers, meetings, brochures, posters, and even filmstrips. With clear, powerful messages, these publications and other media served as crucial facilitators of change. For example, one political flier listed six steps to political change: register to vote, pay poll taxes, encourage friends to do the same, drive others to courthouse registration, join Freedom Organizations, and nominate and vote for appropriate representatives.[21] Another flier cited the Alabama law stating that blacks could start their own political party—Title 17, Section 337, Alabama Code: "An . . . Organization of Electors which, at the General Election . . . the next preceding primary, cast more than twenty percent of the entire vote cast in any county is hereby declared to be a Political Party."[22]

Much of this literature featured the ever-powerful symbol of the LCFO—the Black Panther, the precursor to an inspiration for the Black Power movement.[23] On Lowndes County ballots, the Democratic Party candidates had their respective symbol printed next to their names—a white rooster framed by a "white supremacy" banner. This was hardly an invitation for black involvement in the electoral process. The LCFO thus adopted a black panther for the party's symbol, with Ruth Howard (who worked with Julian Bond in the Atlanta office) modeling the first Black Panther after the mascot of Clark College in Atlanta.[24] Some LCFO members later claimed that the original idea of using a panther came from the nickname of SNCC worker Courtland Cox. Alice Moore, a 1966 candidate for Lowndes County tax assessor, said that Cox earned the nickname because of his height, dark color, and angry expression. John Jackson, who would later become the mayor of the county's Whitehall township, recalled that Cox had a reputation for wearing a cape, which strengthened his panther image.[25] Whether or not this story is true, the symbol was quickly adopted by the organization and local blacks. It created a great deal of excitement among workers and volunteers, not only because it represented a legitimate, independent political party, but also because it was immediately perceived as an aid for illiterate voters. According to local black leader John Jackson, "We knew that if a person could not read and write, they sure knew the difference between a cat, an elephant, and a rooster [because] everybody knows how a black cat looks."[26]

John Hulett, the LCFO President who became the first black sheriff of Lowndes County in 1970, said that the panther symbol frightened both blacks and whites because of the power and ferocity that the image evoked, and therefore many came to associate it—and the organization—with violence. But he emphasized that the panther was never intended to incite or condone violence; it was simply a political symbol devised to encourage party support. "It was politically just a symbol . . . that we [were] here to stay and that we were going to do whatever needs to be done."[27] But the symbol did represent the more militant SNCC that was beginning to emerge, and from a communications standpoint, it would also serve as a continuing graphic element for most of the SNCC and LCFO publications and promotional materials. By using this commanding symbol, SNCC workers were able to arouse more enthusiastic support from the black community while creating a powerful identity for themselves. Neither SNCC nor the LCFO, however, initially seemed concerned with the alienating effect that the symbol had on the white community. Alice Moore recalled that the white Lowndes community members interpreted the symbol as meaning that the LCFO and SNCC wanted "to come out fighting."[28]

Accordingly, white residents fought back. Many blacks were beaten or threatened with violence if they were perceived as being associated with efforts to gain civil rights. But black sharecroppers and tenant farmers who were evicted from their homes and jobs formed a tent city and continued to organize themselves.[29] Amid threats of violence, SNCC workers distributed their literature, organized special events, and orchestrated campaigns for black candidates. But they were working with a community in which the illiteracy rate was much lower than in other Southern states. For example, in a request for printed materials, a SNCC worker asked for illustrations and cited such facts as the average educational level for blacks in Lowndes County was the fifth grade and per capita income was less than $1,000 a year. This was the constituency that SNCC and LCFO tried to reach with some very basic political messages:

> Such information would include education about county offices and affairs, stressing the impact of local politics on people's everyday lives. The duties and responsibilities of the sheriff, tax assessor, county commissioners, superintendent of education, and board of education have to be communicated and understood. Therefore, means have to be found and developed to produce information that is relevant to the lives of poor black people in the rural black belt of Alabama.[30]

SNCC workers recognized that rural southerners were "known for storytelling," and used this indigenous talent to design publications describing the electoral process.[31] One particularly effective method was to use a comic book format to explain the responsibilities of elected officials.

Courtland Cox was well aware that simplified drawings and text could be used to explain complex ideas.[32] In one comic that he wrote, a Lowndes County resident named "Mr. Blackman" realizes that he and other "colored people" in his community had "been using [their] mouths to do two things . . . eating and saying yes suh . . ." But Mr. Blackman soon gets involved in voter registration, creating a political party, and winning the local race for county sheriff.[33]

The community-organizing theme was common throughout the LCFO literature. In another simple but powerful example, a flyer featured a pencil drawing of a community meeting below two questions: "Why come together?" and "What can you do when you come together?" The text explained in simple terms that by forming their own political organization, Lowndes County blacks could determine their future rather than continue to have "the people who have been running the show [elect] their own candidate . . . and vote for programs that will benefit them only . . ."[34]

Another brochure showed four panthers aligned with one white rooster, with the text stating, "4 to 1. Negro voting power is 4 times greater in Lowndes County."[35] And yet another used the before-and-after theme with comic book illustrations to explain the power of the vote—under the word "Before" were a white county sheriff, school board member, tax collector, and other officials; the "After" illustration showed the same county offices held by blacks.[36]

Not all publications were this simple. In another comic, a more complex textual message was printed below a prominent drawing of the black panther symbol: "Whenever any form of government becomes destructive . . . [then] it is the right of the people to alter or to abolish it and to institute a new government." Another flyer consisted of a large amount of text next to the white rooster symbol of the Alabama Democratic party, which included the words "White Supremacy . . . For the Right." The text explained that the Democratic Party, its leaders (including George Wallace, then-governor of Alabama) and other racists would continue to make decisions meant to prevent blacks from exercising their civil rights. The document asked readers if they wanted an organization that would "not be for white supremacy, that [would] put on the ballot at next year's general election the candidates of your choice for all the County and State Offices."[37,38]

The election-centered communications campaign combined brochures, leaflets, and booklets containing lots of text with printed materials that had comic book images accompanied by simple sentences or phrases. In both cases, SNCC communication workers emphasized a strong visual component. To educate Lowndes County blacks about the electoral process and why they should participate in it, SNCC and the LCFO distributed a number of traditional informational publications designed to explain the complex process of political party formation and how it might enrich their lives. In several other publications the SNCC staff emphasized the more simple message of a new alternative to the Mississippi Freedom Democratic Party. This would have likely entailed voting for white candidates in black majority counties and which ultimately failed in its initial effort to replace the regular party, warning that "If Alabama doesn't want to repeat what happened to the Mississippi Freedom Democratic Party, then Alabama doesn't have to. Alabama has a Choice!"[39]

On May 3, 1966, approximately nine hundred Lowndes County blacks gathered at the First Baptist Church to vote in a LCFO primary. In the words of LCFO president John Hulett, it was the first time in county history that black people "came together to make a choice of their own candidate for public office." He also said that the number of participants was a clear sign that blacks would soon make important changes in the local political system.[40]

The white minority fought back, forcing many registered blacks to vote for Democratic Party candidates under threats of violence and of being fired. Any participation in LCFO activities was cause for eviction or firing or worse. SNCC worker Gloria House explained that as the number of evicted blacks grew, so did the size of the local tent city, where "whites would drive by and shoot . . . We learned very quickly to hit the ground and wait until the shooting stopped."[41]

The intimidation was enough to cause the defeat of all LCFO candidates in the general election, but in less than five years, blacks would hold prominent elected positions in Lowndes County. The new party instilled a sense of power and community among the black majority. Cleveland Sellers, who would later become SNCC program secretary, wrote in his biography that the 650 people who came together for an inspirational rally the evening before the election were aware that regardless of the next day's outcome, their efforts marked the "beginning of a new epoch."[42]

BLACK POWER EMERGENCE

The transformation of SNCC's central leadership occurred in step with radical changes in Lowndes County and the rest of the South. Lewis, chairman since 1963, was defeated by Carmichael in a controversial late-night vote in May 1966.[43] Within weeks, Carmichael's call for Black Power would permanently alter SNCC's image in the public eye, from a student organization based on non-violent principles to a militant and radical group that disdained passivity as a response to violent attacks. But what the public did not realize was that the organization and its leaders would do much to instill a sense of pride among black Americans.

One month after Carmichael's election, SNCC began to adopt a new communications strategy that encompassed the black empowerment themes suggested by the LCFO campaign and symbol. On June 5, 1966, James Meredith, the first black student at the University of Mississippi, began a one-man march from Memphis to Jackson that he named the "March Against Fear." A sniper's bullet hit him in the leg on the first day. Martin Luther King, Jr., Floyd McKissick of the Congress for Racial Equality, Carmichael, and other civil rights leaders responded by continuing the march while Meredith recuperated. The march gave Carmichael an opportunity to introduce his black power philosophy, and to add detail to the "Black Power for black people" idea that he and the LCFO leadership had introduced earlier in the year. He was not the originator of the phrase—it had already been used by activist groups in African countries and by some American poets and writers. He is, however, credited with creating the two-word version that he would forever be associated with; and from this point forward, "Black Power" would serve as the foundation of the SNCC communications message.[44]

As he walked alongside Dr. King, Carmichael caught the attention of reporters by suggesting alternatives to the nonviolent strategies that the civil rights movement was built on. As King described the march as nonviolent in every respect, Carmichael told the press that he had never viewed nonviolence "as a way of life," and that "no one in this country is asking the white community in the South to be nonviolent—giving them a free license to go ahead and shoot us at will." His argument seemed logical, but the public expression of these ideas clearly intimidated the white community.[45]

Carmichael later said that he planned to introduce the phrase during his speech at Greenwood, Mississippi, where he was well known due to his service there during the 1964 Mississippi Freedom Summer. Willie Ricks, a SNCC worker, was traveling with a small advance group to keep field workers informed of the marcher's arrival time, to make whatever preparations were necessary, and to address local supporters. As part of the planning process, Ricks used "Black Power" in his speech to gauge community reaction, since there was some concern that the slogan might be considered too radical and that poor blacks would avoid taking such a strong stance. Carmichael later said he felt a sense of disbelief when told locals had embraced the term with excitement and enthusiasm.[46]

Upon his arrival in Greenwood, Carmichael began to set up tents on the schoolyard and was arrested and jailed for several hours after refusing to dismantle them. Exhausted and exasperated after six hours of incarceration, Carmichael returned just in time for the rally and during his evening speech, he proclaimed, "What we are going to start saying now is Black Power." To build the momentum, Ricks helped get the crowd into the call-and-response rhetoric, with Carmichael asking, "What do you want?" and the crowd responding "Black Power" with increasing intensity.[47]

As the crowd continued shouting "Black Power," Mississippi state troopers fired tear gas. *Time* reporter Arlee Schwartz compared the scenario to "a scene from hell, with people vomiting, smoke rising . . . choking and crying." The marchers actually adhered to their nonviolent tradition, but the bold resistance marked the beginning of a new movement in which many blacks would no longer tolerate police brutality or economic repression without an empowered response.[48]

The marchers reached Jackson on June 26. During the 22 days of the march that Meredith had designed as a one-man effort to symbolize the erasure of fear among southern Mississippi blacks, approximately 4,000 new voters followed the advice of Carmichael, King, and McKissick and registered at county courthouses throughout the state.[49] Carmichael and his Black Power slogan clearly contributed to this jump, but it had been preceded by the slow, long-term, voter-by-voter organizing efforts of SNCC and local organizations resulting in changes in federal laws. The sharp increase in registered voters may not have been as important as Carmichael's rise in the eyes of the media. By presenting his controversial message to mainstream reporters hungry for good copy, he aroused the interest of the American public as well as support from poor blacks. Cleveland Sellers has suggested that Carmichael's emergence as a national leader was an important milestone for SNCC and that the march generated interest in "independent, black political organizations" and reinvigorated civil rights activities in Mississippi.[50]

Sellers also wrote that the slogan and the philosophy behind it "thrust SNCC to the forefront of the struggle for black liberation," with journalists, intellectuals, politicians, and students responding to "our radical cadence." "Black Power" had special appeal to urban blacks; therefore the idea transformed an Atlanta-based organization with strong ties to the rural South into a nationally known radical group that appealed to blacks from all walks of life in every section of the United States. In ghettos throughout the country, SNCC workers were "hailed as heroes—Young Turks taking it to 'The Man.'"[51]

Many whites viewed the change as an indication of a new wave of urban violence and rebellion, and the news media was more than willing to play on this sense of fear while reporting on the transition taking place in the civil rights movement. McKissick, director of the Congress of Racial Equality, believed that many whites "could not subtract violence from power . . . [they] could only see power as a violent instrument to accompany it."[52] It also seemed that much of white America could not get past the idea of self-defense being practiced by an avowed "nonviolent" committee. In a June 1966 interview, Martin Argonsky of CBS News asked Carmichael to explain his declaration that while blacks intended to take power legally, if they were stopped by white officials they would "take it the way everyone else took it, including the way America took it in the American Revolution." Carmichael responded by describing black-belt Alabama counties with enormous black majorities that had been controlled through the use of violence and "every illegal trick that one can think of." He said that black communities would work to achieve power through the democratic process, but if they continued to be "cheated out of their votes," then they must turn to other methods.[53] In other words, Carmichael did not advocate violence, but he did not rule it out—a fine distinction that captivated the press and appealed to the country's black population.

The sudden appearance of the Black Power philosophy and the black panther symbol gave the impression that SNCC's image had changed overnight, but clues of this impending transformation can be found in structural changes over the preceding year. By the fall of 1965, thirty-five of 129 SNCC staffers were based in large cities in New York, California, Michigan, Pennsylvania, and Massachusetts, as well as Washington, D.C.[54] As SNCC expanded into America's urban centers, many experienced staff members left the organization. Julian Bond resigned as communications director in June 1966 to run for the Georgia State Assembly (discussed in the following chapter).[55] Charles Sherrod, one of SNCC's first field secretaries, resigned in protest after SNCC leaders rejected his plan to bring white student volunteers into Southwest Georgia; he remained in the area, but set up an independent program to achieve his goals. Bill Hansen, who had led many projects in Arkansas, also resigned. By the end of 1966, most of the Alabama SNCC staff had left.[56] In May 1966 Forman resigned as executive secretary but remained active in the organization; he was replaced by Ruby Doris Smith Robinson, with Cleveland Sellers becoming program secretary.

As early as December 1965, John Lewis, then SNCC chair, expressed dissatisfaction with the organization's direction when he was still in the chairman's position. He argued in a memo that the Committee was presenting an unstable image to its supporters, leading to rumors of mismanagement and accusations of communist infiltration. Lewis asked for help from Bond and the communications department in making "a special effort to counter these rumors and attacks . . . and to present the truth about SNCC."[57]

COMMUNICATING A CONTROVERSIAL PHILOSOPHY

The Black Power philosophy represented an organizational turning point, and Carmichael seemed perfectly suited to serve as an organizational spokesperson. But after the emergence of Black Power, SNCC's internal communication strategies would no longer be tailored to appeal to liberal whites—a core SNCC constituency in the preceding years. This exclusionary attitude took time to develop, since many SNCC workers initially believed that white supporters would embrace the Black Power idea. At first, Friends of SNCC groups actively communicated the new message to white supporters and politicians. For instance, the Chicago SNCC office published a pamphlet containing the text of a Carmichael speech and explaining that the group had "moved into the action stage of organizing for Black Power." Monroe Sharp, Chicago SNCC director, asked for support from both blacks and whites but divided their responsibilities, asking blacks to organize communities block-by-block, and asking whites "who cannot get out in the street" to sell buttons and explain the program to people living in white and integrated communities. The pamphlet included a sign-up form and a list of products, including Black Power stickers, buttons, and copies of The Movement, a collection of documentary photographs.[58]

Carmichael also expressed his wish that the media and other audiences, especially politicians, present and acknowledge SNCC accurately and make a special effort to ignore rumors. But his suggestion that blacks should defend themselves and his frequent use of the Black Power slogan had the opposite effect. In a 1990 interview, former Time correspondent Arlie Schardt admitted that reporters tended to "overplay" the Black Power concept and suggested that some of the negative coverage occurred because the new theme was never "clearly articulated," thus allowing for broad interpretation.[59] There is evidence, however, showing that Carmichael did make a special effort to narrowly define the concept to the media in the early months of his chairmanship, going so far as to co-author Black Power: The Politics of Liberation with Charles Hamilton. The authors described the book as "a call for black people in this country to unite . . . to recognize their heritage, to build a sense of community. It is a call for black people to define their own goals, to lead their own organizations."[60] But as time wore on, Carmichael's rhetoric became more militant and accusatory as he criticized longstanding political and economic traditions.

Despite the confusion it created, the Black Power slogan was attractive to many blacks for the same reasons that it offended and frightened whites—its implied message that violence could be condoned as long as it was enacted in response to white violence. Furthermore, the Black Power message included a call for black economic and political independence. Carmichael's impassioned speeches certainly fueled the media's tendency to present him as a symbol of black militancy. In a March 1966 interview published in a Friends of SNCC newsletter, Carmichael declared that his job as chairman was "To organize people to overthrow the governments that are now oppressing them, not to organize them to beg for money from the federal government. If they control these county government offices, they won't have to beg for money. They'll just take it."[61] In another example—a Chicago speech given on July 28, 1966—he argued that blacks should reject being labeled as radical, since "the extremists in this country are the white people" who had worked to oppress blacks. He also said that blacks must now "define [their] own ethic" without apology: "We don't have to . . . obey any law that we didn't have a part to make, especially if that law was made to keep us where we are. We have the right to break it." In the same speech, he accused the press of confusing rebellion with riots, and urged supporters to treat words such as "antiwhite," "hate," "radical," and "militant" in mainstream newspapers as "nonsense."[62]

Other SNCC workers were active in attempts to counteract inaccurate information and rumors that appeared in the media. In a May 24 letter to the editor of the Los Angeles *Herald-Dispatch*, Fay Bellamy, who later served as SNCC secretary and who often contributed to the communications section, wrote, "We in SNCC have complained many times about the way in which white newspapers tend to distort articles about SNCC or anything that Black people have a tendency to do." Her specific target was an article that ran under the headline, "Negroes Regain Control of SNCC." She bluntly claimed that "nothing in the article was true," especially a statement that "Stokely Carmichael and Mrs. Ruby D. Robinson will lead the SNCC back to the road of 'Negro leadership and opinion' under which it was born several years ago"; Bellamy responded by stating that SNCC had always been under Negro leadership and "always will be."[63]

Sellers later acknowledged that the SNCC communication and administrative staff was more concerned—and more successful—in delivering its Black Power message to poor blacks. Ironically, they often did this through the white mainstream media, which Sellers said were "eager to record [Carmichael's] every word." It didn't take long for the new SNCC leadership to understand that Carmichael "could reach millions of people" simply by calling a press conference, and even if the message was distorted, it still aroused interest and support among SNCC's target audience.[64]

Media misinterpretations and misunderstandings, however, created internal problems as external publics grew increasingly concerned and

fearful. In his autobiography, Sellers described Carmichael as a public personality "who attracted attention wherever he went"; unfortunately, there
was a growing public perception that other SNCC workers were his "fol-
lowers."[65] In August, the communications staff responded with a recom-
mendation that Carmichael "step out of the chairmanship by expressing
fear over being isolated as a national leader," arguing that organizational
needs "at this precise moment in history" were not being "served by the
kind of role of external leadership presently practiced." The report went
on to recommend that the organization "define very sharply what leadership articulates for SNCC" and what the "value of the chairman is in
terms of the national role he plays."[66]

The challenge for SNCC communications workers was presenting
SNCC as a complete organization rather than a group built around a single
personality. As the organization went through an intense period of transition, it became increasingly difficult to promote the older SNCC agenda of
black empowerment, cultural unity, and the attainment of civil rights. But
communications workers were willing to take advantage of the many Black
Power supporters outside the organization to give credibility and authority
to their message. In August, the Alabama SNCC staff distributed a detailed
description of Black Power written by black clergymen from the National
Committee of Negro Churchmen. The statement, which was not solicited
by SNCC, first appeared as a full-page advertisement in the July 31 issue
of the *New York Times*.[67] The SNCC staffers distributed the statement to
the press in response "to the undue publicity that SNCC has received in the
past few weeks." According to the cover memo accompanying reprints of
the statement, the press had "blown these two words [Black Power] into
huge proportions and had given the impression that they mean possible
future danger for Whites and Negroes alike, which is not true."[68] The ministers' eloquent statement, which explained the need for black economic
and political independence, also called on the mass media to speak the
truth, as it had during other campaigns:

> During the Southern demonstrations for civil rights, you men of the
> communications industry performed an invaluable service for the entire
> country by revealing plainly to our ears and eyes the ugly truth of a bru-
> talizing system of overt discrimination and segregation . . . You were
> instruments of change and not merely purveyors of unrelated facts.[69]

The ministers reminded reporters that the current task was "more difficult" and that "the truth that needs revealing today is not so clear-cut in its
outlines, nor is there a national consensus to help you form relevant points

of view." To address these challenges, they asked reporters to "look for a variety of sources of truth in order that the limited perspectives of all of us might be corrected."[70]

Carmichael and other SNCC workers were much more direct in expressing their frustration over the SNCC image that was being created in the mainstream press. The repeated efforts of communications workers to present a coherent and unified message to the media were unsuccessful. As Carmichael explained to *Life* reporter Gordon Parks in 1966,[71] the white press continued to equate Black Power with "racism and separatism":

> The stories fail to report the productive dialog taking place in the black community or in the white religious and intellectual areas. As for separatism, what are they talking about? We have no choice . . . They separated us a long time ago. And they sure intend to keep it that way.[72]

Saturday Review television and radio critic Robert Lewis Shayon agreed with Carmichael's contention that the mainstream media had portrayed him as a "monster." Shayon showed how two national networks presented one-sided images, and described how their stories were limited to presentations of Carmichael as a militant with an appeal that was "obviously designed to arouse emotion and courage in his listeners at the rally— and perhaps to induce flutters of fright in white viewers who would see him via the news cameras."[73] Shayon also explained how the mainstream press had reinforced this image by continually using such words and terms as "radical," "hard-core," "racist," and "black nationalists" in their Carmichael stories. After hearing Carmichael speak in a comprehensive interview on a non-commercial radio station, Shayon came away with an impression of a "plausible human being, firm in conviction and purpose, but quietly rational" who did indeed "assert that voters in dominantly Negro areas had the right and intended to take power at the polls."[74]

Despite the misrepresentations, or perhaps because of them, Carmichael took every opportunity to address the media during the early months of his chairmanship. But regardless of how many press conferences he participated in, or how many appearances he made on news shows such as "Face the Nation" and "Meet the Press," the distorted images remained, in no small part due to his steady stream of attacks on established political processes, government officials, and the news media.[75] His appearances on those national network programs provided some of the most defining and controversial images of the entire civil rights movement. In a special ninety-minute version of "Meet the Press" aired on August 21, 1966, Carmichael discussed the Black Power philosophy with Martin Luther King, Jr., Roy

Wilkins (executive director of the NAACP), Whitney Young, Jr. (executive director of the National Urban League), Floyd McKissick (national director of CORE), and James Meredith.[76] The show gave Carmichael a unique forum for correcting the misinformation that surrounded him and the organization he led, an opportunity to win additional support from black communities, and a chance to explain his ideas to white America.

The leaders of the country's major civil rights organizations had long-standing differences, but they had always succeeded in showing a unified front to the press. Interviewer James Kilpatrick immediately challenged the front by asking whether or not Carmichael had called other Negro leaders "Uncle Toms."[77] Carmichael said that he had never publicly criticized any black leader and that he never would. It was on this show that Roy Wilkins made the Madison Avenue statement that begins this chapter. He also argued that no one really believed that black Americans would rebel against white society, even though Carmichael frequently alluded to that potential. "Of course, no one believes that the Negro . . . is going to take up arms and try to rectify every wrong that had been done . . . if somebody doesn't rectify it through the regular channels."[78] Carmichael demonstrated his own patience in his response to Wilkins's remarks, stating simply that he and other blacks were "going to move to get the things that [we] have to get in this country to be able to function as an equal."[79]

Despite signs of disagreement, the black leaders had much in common and were generally supportive of each other. Surprisingly, the job of defining Black Power on the program did not fall to Carmichael, but to CORE's Floyd McKissick, who told viewers:

> When we talk about "Black Power," for instance, and everybody gets excited—two little bitty words in the English language. One, "black"— everybody who has gone through the sixth grade knows what "black" means. "Power"—everybody who has gone through the sixth grade knows what that means, and I get a letter from a professor at Harvard saying, "Explain Black Power." That means putting Black Power in black people's hands. We don't have any and we want some.[80]

ORGANIZATIONAL DECLINE

The appearances on network television were not enough to overcome the distortions presented in the day-to-day news programs and the press. The combination of SNCC's tarnished image in the white press, the volatile self-image that Carmichael sometimes presented, and (as Jack Minnis has suggested) the natural conclusion to an epic period[81] led to SNCC's decline by the end of 1966. The communications staff had failed to maintain a positive image of the organization, and public emotional and financial support diminished. SNCC's vocal opposition to the federal government, especially to its Vietnam policies, resulted in the elimination of government funding for its activities. James Forman later accused the federal government of trying to shut down the organization because of its rhetoric. Support for his contention came in February 2000, when documents released from a Freedom of Information Act lawsuit described how the FBI had infiltrated the organization in 1964 "to establish the extent of communist infiltration"; the documents implied that the FBI had purposefully fed misleading information on SNCC to the national press.[82]

SNCC weathered more changes in personnel and philosophy than it could tolerate without suffering long-term damage. Most SNCC workers admired Carmichael, but he became the target of increasing criticism from within the organization for his non-stop string of public appearances and often non-sanctioned messages; at one point the SNCC staff tried to ban him from speaking to the media. But as SNCC communications worker Dorothy Miller Zellner recalled in a 2000 interview, there was no denying that the press loved Carmichael and his exuberant message. She believed that he was mostly responding to frequent invitations for speaking engagements and interviews in order to explain himself and his organization.[83] Zellner said that when Carmichael "called a commentator or when he called a press conference, they all came. They never knew what he was going to say. He was so witty. He was so smart." She also acknowledged that his press appeal was closely associated with the fear that he incited:

> He was saying something that white America just did not want to hear. They were petrified of what this was going to mean in the end. What would it mean if all the black people actually opted out—everything would grind to a halt. What would they do and how could they possibly promote themselves as kings of democracy when the black people were opting out of the democratic position? This would be a catastrophe for them.[84]

A writer in *I.F. Stone's Weekly* suggested that the main reason for the campaign against SNCC was its stance on the Vietnam War. In June of 1966, SNCC leaders publicly declared their opposition and their belief that they could not "in good conscience meet with the chief policy maker of the Vietnam War to discuss human rights when he violates the human rights of colored people in Vietnam."[85] The communications section was instrumental in constructing the anti-war message. Julian Bond, who won an election for a seat in the Georgia House of Representatives, had to defend his position on the war in front of the U.S. Supreme Court before he could take his seat in the state legislature.

In hindsight, Carmichael's ability to give black Americans a sense of pride and community was remarkable considering the short period that he served as SNCC chairman and the symbolic leader of the Black Power phase of the civil rights movement. But the public perception of his instantaneous appearance was as false as some of their perceptions of the Black Power message. The Lowndes County campaign and the Mississippi "March Against Fear" were the last two examples of SNCC's community organizing and political empowerment approaches to civil rights activism. These were replaced by Carmichael's dynamic use of the media to present symbols and ideas to various constituencies, which came at the expense of grass roots efforts to improve the lives of black Americans. Although Carmichael and the SNCC communications staff alienated the white press, they also managed to build an awareness of the Black Power philosophy and instill a sense of community and cultural pride among blacks in all parts of the country. But the longstanding SNCC message of achieving goals through the principle of nonviolence was permanently lost. In its place was a vaguely defined concept open to wide interpretation. Forman later admitted that SNCC failed to come up with an adequate definition of Black Power, therefore the "door was left open for opportunists to define the term in any manner they chose." But Forman never used this as an excuse to explain SNCC's failures during its Black Power phase. He instead suggested that they were a consequence of "not having our own revolutionary ideology together."[86]

Chapter Five

International Relations, Vietnam Opposition, and Radicalization: SNCC's Final Years

> It is becoming both psychologically and politically impossible for us to continue to raise questions of our own exploitation in this country without also raising the question of American international attitude and policy. We must expand our borrowed cry of "One Man, One Vote" to "Self-determination and Dignity" throughout the world!!![1]
>
> —Dona Richards, SNCC worker

Dona Richards likely started thinking about communicating SNCC ideas to other countries in the weeks following the Mississippi Freedom Democratic Party's rejection at Atlantic City. At that time, SNCC supporter and nationally known black entertainer Harry Belafonte saw a need to inspire and invigorate the frustrated young civil rights workers. He made arrangements for eleven of them to spend three weeks in Africa, meeting with the leaders of newly independent African nations and exploring the possibilities of building networks among various human rights organizations.[2] Two of the eleven—John Lewis and Donald Harris—remained in Africa for a full month after the others returned to the United States, making short visits to Liberia, Ghana, Zambia, Kenya, Ethiopia, and Egypt.

Upon their return, Lewis and Harris proposed that SNCC "establish an international wing . . . [since] "the growing importance of the Afro-Asian countries, their particular political and economic ideologies as well as their increasing influence in world opinion, must be communicated to the people that we work with." With these issues in mind, Lewis and Harris said the main responsibility of the new division would be in the areas of communications and public relations—for instance, sending press information to international contacts and developing relationships with international politicians.[3]

The adoption of the international component was a broad-based goal; and the transition would be slow since for SNCC, the mid and late-1960s were marked by constant change in personnel and ideology. Moreover, the societal turbulence that was occurring throughout the world made the presentation of a unifying message to international and domestic audiences particularly difficult. But SNCC workers still managed to meet some success in reaching an international audience, using the same basic public relations strategies that had served them so well between 1960 and 1964: publications, press releases, media relations, political activism, orchestrating special events, and media relations.

Lewis and Harris used many of the same public relations techniques to address a new international audience and to establish important cross-border relationships during their extended African tour. Examples include the production of a twenty-minute radio program for local stations, the Voice of America broadcasting center in Liberia, and visits to the Liberian Press Union, whose employees introduced Lewis and Harris to reporters willing to interview them. In Ghana they met with leaders of the Afro-American Information Bureau, an organization whose stated purpose was "to keep the Ghanaian people informed about what was going on in the States and to make sure that the information [got into] the press." The Bureau disseminated press releases, background information, and photographs to media outlets throughout Ghana, one of the first African countries to achieve independence in the late 1950s.[4]

Internal and domestic issues kept SNCC workers from fully developing a plan to create an international relations campaign. Nevertheless, in September of 1965, Richards—a member of the first group to visit Africa and a visitor to Ghana with her husband, Robert Moses, in 1965—was a strong advocate of the SNCC African Project, arguing that it was important to "broaden the political concerns" of the Committee. She believed the project would clarify and strengthen the "link between the struggle for self-determination of black people abroad and the struggle of black people in the United States against exploitation." Richards suggested that telling the stories of young Africans involved in liberation activities to blacks in America would give inspiration and strength "from an identification with the African movement toward independence."[5] In an effort to do this, she asked for resources so that the communications staff could produce an African primer for the purpose of teaching black school children and adults with low-level reading skills in the South about their African heritage and the independence and resistance campaigns taking place at that time.[6]

Richards also recommended that SNCC workers send messages describing their work to African countries. In an October letter sent from

Ghana, she described meeting Africans who were eager for information about the civil rights movement in the United States, and asked that SNCC workers continue to send public relations materials to the Bureau of African Affairs. As a result, she initiated an effort to establish an African section in the SNCC Atlanta-based library through subscriptions and donations from the publishers of books about Africa.[7]

But SNCC would wait until June of 1966 to officially respond to Richard's lobbying. At that time it created an International Affairs Committee to be chaired by Lewis, whom Stokely Carmichael had just replaced as SNCC chairman. Lewis traveled to Europe to help establish Friends of SNCC groups in Great Britain, France, Norway, and Sweden. These international chapters performed the same public relations and fundraising functions as their American counterparts, promoting the idea of human rights via local media and government relations, producing and distributing publications, and organizing picket lines and speakers. For instance, Richards encouraged SNCC workers who had traveled to Africa to write about their experience to help transmit SNCC's new message of global independence.[8] In another effort to promote their message of the need for black representation, the group petitioned the United Nations membership for "a permanent group of observers made up of Black people living in America" since few blacks had rights in America and even fewer were represented globally.[9]

Lewis also recruited African students to work in the American South during the summer of 1966 as a means of promoting the movement in Africa and attracting media attention in the United States. He told reporters that student groups in Europe and Africa were "fighting for the same thing that we are" and that SNCC wanted "to link up with them and share techniques, tactics and ideas."[10,11]

While the new international division focused its attention on Europe and Africa, the larger SNCC organization debated and expressed its concerns over another international concern, the American war in Southeast Asia. President Johnson approved the bombing of North Vietnamese villages starting on August 4, 1964 (ironically, the same day that the bodies of Chaney, Goodman, and Schwerner were discovered), ostensibly in response to attacks on U.S. military targets in the Gulf of Tonkin. SNCC workers immediately attacked the validity of the Vietnam War and the paradox of drafting black Southern men who did not have such basic democratic rights as suffrage for the purpose of fighting for the rights of Asians living on the other side of the world. A formal position against the war would not come until January of 1966, but several prominent SNCC members voiced their objections through press releases and other communications tools throughout 1965. For instance, In April 1965, Robert Moses spoke at an antiwar rally sponsored by the Students for a Democratic Society (SDS) in Washington, D.C. During his speech, Moses said that civil rights workers had an intimate understanding of the country's hypocritical portrayal of itself as the world's leader for democracy. Even if individual civil rights workers were not well versed in foreign policy, Moses pointed out that they had endured enormous violence—even murder—before convincing the government to pass civil rights legislation.

SNCC advisor Howard Zinn wrote in an August 30, 1965 *Student Voice* editorial that it was time for SNCC to take a public stance against the war, arguing that the group's civil rights activities in the United States should be accompanied by efforts to support oppressed people in other countries— particularly Vietnam, but also the Dominican Republic, South Africa, and "anywhere else there is a burning issue of injustice." Zinn argued that the time was right for SNCC to publicly declare "freedom now" as an international mission.[12]

Despite this encouragement, the Committee had yet to proclaim an official position on Vietnam when it became a point of controversy for the Mississippi Freedom Democratic Party. The MFDP enclosed a copy of a five-point program opposing the war in its summer, 1965, newsletter after it was initially distributed as a circular in Pike County. The program described opposition to a war and promoted the idea that "no Mississippi Negroes should be fighting in Viet Nam for the white man's freedom until all the Negro people are free in Mississippi." The authors, Joe Martin of McComb, Mississippi, and Clinton Hobson, a law student from New Jersey, produced the document independently and urged Mississippi men to defy the draft or, if already enlisted, to stage hunger strikes.[13]

Although it was not an official MFDP statement, reporters from the mainstream press interpreted it as such, and the party had to endure a great deal of criticism. MFDP leaders responded with a July 31 statement declaring the news media "totally inaccurate" in reporting the position as MFDP endorsed:

> "It is distressing to us that the many activities that the MFDP has initiated and participated in as an organization have been largely ignored by the national press. Yet they have chosen this, not an official MFDP statement, to highlight' and to do so in such a manner as to misrepresent the facts."[14]

The release admonished the press for reporting that the leaflet represented an official MFDP position, especially since they had given so little space to the MFDP's voter-registration drive, its Congressional challenge, various local election campaigns with MFDP candidates, and acts of police brutality during demonstrations in Jackson in June.[15]

Martin and Hobson gave five reasons why "Negroes should not be in any war fighting for America," with the most important being that Mississippi blacks who were not free themselves should not kill other people so that wealthy whites could "get richer."[16] The response from the mainstream press certainly raised awareness of the issue within the MFDP and SNCC. In an interview over thirty years later, an MFDP official named Paul Lauter described the leaflet as the "first public urging of non-cooperation with the military, publicly issued and circulated"[17]

During the SNCC meeting that November, Lewis pushed for a public anti-war position, arguing that SNCC workers were morally obligated to take a stand because they "couldn't talk about what was going on in Mississippi and Alabama and South Georgia and not relate to and identify with the people who were being sent over to Vietnam, as well as the people, American and Vietnamese alike, who were being destroyed there."[18] In the weeks following the meeting, the SNCC leadership accepted the suggestions offered by Moses, Zinn, and Lewis, and started work on drafting an official statement declaring the Committee's opposition to the war. Writing the document and circulating various drafts was a process that lasted through November and December, with Lewis, Forman, and Courtland Cox serving as the primary contributors. The slow progress reflected the concerns of some staff members over potential loss of funding and backlash from the federal government and national press—SNCC's most important institutional audiences.[19]

AN ANTI-WAR ORGANIZATION

Those concerns vanished when SNCC worker and Navy veteran Sammy Younge was murdered in Tuskegee, Alabama, on January 3, 1966. A SNCC press release issued by the Atlanta office described him as a 22-year-old Tuskegee Institute student who had been threatened by a country registrar during black voter registration activities on the day he died. Afterwards, Younge refused to use a segregated restroom at a service station and was shot by Marvin Segrest, the attendant who followed him across the street to the bus station with a gun.[20]

SNCC used press releases once again to accuse the federal government of failing to enforce federal law, claiming that local SNCC workers had reported threats against Younge to the FBI and the Justice Department with no response. The release also included a statement from John Lewis, who called upon President Johnson "to make the presence and the forces of the Federal government visible in . . . Alabama . . . where violence and terror are the order of the day." Despite his reputation for abhorring violence, Lewis made a comment that indicated a move away from SNCC's well-regarded policy of nonviolence:

> If the federal government cannot provide protection for people seeking civil rights guaranteed by the Constitution, then people will have no protection but themselves. We find it increasingly difficult to ask the people of the Black Belt to remain nonviolent. We have asked the President for federal marshals for more than three years. If our plea is not answered, we have no choice.[21]

Younge was buried on January 6. The following day, SNCC communications workers called a press conference at which they announced their official opposition to the Vietnam War. That message helped shape the new organizational foundation that would last until the Committee disbanded. Lewis explained that Younge's murder had triggered SNCC's desire to publicly oppose the war because it was a powerful illustration of the paradox of black men fighting in Vietnam while being denied rights in their own country or protection from their own government as they petitioned for those rights. Lewis later recalled his sense of irony when an American flag was draped over Younge's casket.[22] To what he later described as a "stunned" group of reporters, Lewis expressed a strong belief in the connection between the U.S. government's Vietnam policy and international independence movements:

> We believe the United States government has been deceptive in its claims of concern for the freedom of the Vietnamese people, just as the government has been deceptive in claiming concern for the freedom of colored people in other countries . . . The murder of Samuel Younge in Tuskegee, Alabama is no different than the murder of peasants in Vietnam, for both Younge and the Vietnamese sought, and are seeking, to secure the rights guaranteed them by law . . . We question then, the ability and even the desire of the United States government to guarantee free elections abroad. We maintain that our country's cry of "preserve freedom in the world" is a hypocritical mask behind which it squashes liberation movements which are not bound, and refuse to be bound, by the expediencies of United States cold war policies. [23]

SNCC workers also declared open support for draft resisters since it "would compel them to contribute their lives to United States aggression in Vietnam in the name of 'freedom' we find so false in this country." They emphasized that a disproportionate number of draftees were blacks who had been called to "preserve a 'democracy' which does not exist for them at home."[24]

The statement made headlines in major newspapers across the country the following day; Lewis later recalled "reactions of outrage and alarm." He also believed that the Atlanta office of the FBI forwarded a copy to Washington, and the House Un-American Activities Committee began an investigation. Lewis argued that FBI infiltration helped to ensure the demise of an organization that was already experiencing dissension and change in personnel and operating philosophy.[25]

Lewis and other SNCC administrators put the communications staff to work defending their position and responding to press criticism. Soon after the statement's release on January 26, Lewis explained to the Council for American-Soviet Friendship that the civil rights struggle had led SNCC to recognize the immoral nature of sending armed forces to Vietnam and Santo Domingo to protect "freedom and democracy" in light of the American government's refusal to protect and share those freedoms with its own people. He called for other civil rights organizations to join SNCC to create a "united effort" in garnering public support for their work to "deter our government."[26] Despite these calls, Lewis said that the NAACP and the Urban League "predictably rushed to the side of Lyndon Johnson and Hubert Humphrey." On the other hand, Martin Luther King, Jr. neither supported nor criticized SNCC's position initially; one year later, however, he would publicly express his opposition to the war.[27]

The reaction to SNCC's opposition had a direct effect on Julian Bond, who had just been elected to a one-year term in the Georgia House of Representatives in a special election made necessary by a court-ordered legislative reapportionment of a predominately black district in Atlanta. Bond's campaign had attracted national media attention not only because of his race and youth, but also because he openly endorsed SNCC's anti-Vietnam War statement, which led to the Georgia legislature's refusal to seat him. The outcome was a year of publicity for Bond and the organization, which generated sympathy and support for both and strengthened their anti-Vietnam stance.

The campaign, which began with a $500 SNCC loan, was run by Bond, Charles Cobb, Judy Richardson, Ivanhoe Donaldson, and others based in the Atlanta SNCC office.[28] Its success came from a combination of a savvy communications effort and the favorable redistricting decision that created the downtown electoral district with a large black majority. Bond was criticized by some SNCC staffers for running as a Democrat, but he defended his decision by explaining that Georgia law made an independent candidacy "next to impossible," and that there was too little time before the election to challenge the specific statutes.[29]

When the legislature denied Bond his seat, SNCC workers drafted two official statements—one on the "Georgia attack on SNCC" and the other addressing SNCC's support for Bond's campaign—and scheduled a press conference for January 8 to present their justification. SCLC representative Julius Griffin opened the press conference by reading a short but powerful declaration of support for Bond from Martin Luther King Jr., in which the attempt to unseat Bond was described as "approaching a dangerous totalitarian periphery." The statement also professed support for Bond's "right as a citizen to disagree with our foreign policy because it is an injustice to . . . presume that he is disloyal or that he would fail to support the Constitution . . . solely because he takes issue with the U.S. position on Vietnam."[30] The SCLC also issued a separate press release expressing "indignation" against the legislature's "unconscionable refusal" to seat Bond.[31]

As SNCC chair, John Lewis read the SNCC statement, which called for all "supporters of constitutional rights" to contact the Georgia governor to support Bond's "right to dissent and right to sit in the legislature." After a lengthy debate about press inaccuracies with a reporter attending the conference, Lewis read a second statement, this one addressing the "Georgia attack on SNCC." That statement argued that following the release of the Committee's anti-Vietnam War statement, "the press and Georgia leaders have distorted SNCC's viewpoint in an attempt to destroy the organization." Lewis was asked if he thought recent SNCC policy decisions might destroy the Committee; he disagreed, saying "I think many who support us now will continue to support us, for they know that we are committed to building an interracial democracy."[32]

Although he was officially unqualified to run, Bond quickly announced his candidacy for the special February 23 election to fill the vacancy caused by the state's refusal to seat him. He won that election, but the legislature refused to change its position. Consequently, Bond, Dr. King, and Arel Keyes, (both members of Bond's district) filed suit in federal court charging the Georgia Assembly and the State of Georgia with violating the rights of voters by denying them their elected representation. The suit also contained the charge that Bond's right to freedom of speech had been violated.[33] After rejection from the District Court of Appeals, Bond's attorneys petitioned for a hearing in front of the United States Supreme Court. The ruling would take a full year before being passed down, during which Bond ran for and won the same office a third time. Finally, on December 5, 1966, the Court ruled unanimously in Bond's favor. Chief Justice Earl Warren wrote the decision, which essentially agreed with most of the arguments that were disseminated by the SNCC communications committee: "The interest of the public in hearing all sides of a public issue is hardly advanced by extending more protection to citizen-critics than to legislators . . . legislators have an obligation to take a position on controversial political questions so that their constituents can . . . access their qualification for office."[34]

NEW ALLIANCES AND OUTLOOKS

As SNCC workers branched out beyond their Southern and American roots, they underwent continuous organizational evolution. The changes in leadership and personnel that opened the doors for the Black Power philosophy led to an alliance with the newly formed Black Panther Party in California. The panthers adopted many of Stokely Carmichael's views, most importantly the belief that blacks should take physical means to defend themselves in the face of white violence. Since the panther symbol was shared by the California Party and the Lowndes County Freedom Organization, members of the media (and the general public) often referred to the LCFO and even to SNCC as the Black Panther Party; the two organizations were increasingly viewed as a single entity, although they had no connection beyond their common black panther symbols and some common well-known members.

SNCC communication workers did surprisingly little to resist or rectify this false assumption, and consequently the Committee was frequently criticized for the Black Panther Party's more radical responses to black oppression, such as openly carrying guns. Some SNCC leaders also accepted leadership positions with the Black Panthers, further blurring organizational lines in the minds of the media. The two groups, however, never merged, and for the most part promoted separate programs and objectives.[35]

SNCC's radical messages seemed to become more so by the day and began soon after the Meredith march in 1965. By 1966, Carmichael's rhetoric often contained messages suggesting that the capitalist system was to blame for the economic exploitation that blacks had long suffered. He, however, acknowledged that many in the group preferred reform to dissolution. Toward the end of his tenure as chairman, Carmichael concluded that the reformers (those who believed that "although some aspects of capitalism were unjust," that the problems could be solved) always had the upper hand over the revolutionaries (who believed that the "capitalist system must be totally and completely destroyed").[36]

Whereas SNCC leaders and workers may have understood the fine distinctions that were part of the debate, it is likely that both views added to the distorted and radical public image of the Committee that appeared in the mainstream press. This was a deliberate and marked changed in communication strategy. Fiery rhetoric designed to bring blacks, and only blacks, to action had replaced the more palatable ideals of integration and nonviolence. Arguably a huge public relations mistake, this change, none-theless, did bring about the desired change and created a new more militant attitude among many young urban blacks. It's unlikely that Carmichael or other SNCC leaders considered the long-term consequences of their com-munication efforts. But clearly the fiery passion he expressed would change the attitudes and even the behavior of many blacks throughout the country for many years to come.

Because of the internal dissension and disorganization, the messages emanating from the Committee were not always consistent. For instance, Forman supported the more radical goal of eliminating capitalism entirely, which he believed would result in the elimination of racism and colonial-ism. But he also felt that the organization was ill-equipped to actually enact a radical movement and weather criticism for this viewpoint over the long term. In his autobiography, he said he wanted to use his position and lever-age to "inject" a strong anti-imperialist stance into SNCC and the entire black movement, especially since many of the countries that SNCC leaders were forming alliances with were vocal in their criticism of racism, capi-talism and imperialism. Forman noted that many of those countries were building socialist governments—a movement he supported and believed to be appropriate for the United States. He wrote, "I was never able to get SNCC to declare itself for socialism, but I did not worry about that too much at the time."[37] In contrast to Carmichael's claim that SNCC was not against the complete elimination capitalism, Forman stated that by 1967, most SNCC workers had "achieved a realization that our fight was against racism, capitalism, and imperialism," and that this recognition "represented a major victory in itself."[38]

Despite dissenting and increasingly complex messages, SNCC lead-ers still found a broad forum to present their cause and remained as an influential organization. For instance, in the summer of 1967, Forman and Howard Moore, Jr.—SNCC's legal advisor—were invited to present their ideas at a forum sponsored by the United Nations. A seasoned communica-tor, Forman was skilled at using these types of forums to address complex issues in detail. Entitled an "International Seminar on Apartheid, Racism, and Colonialism in Southern Africa," the meeting was held soon after out-breaks of violence in Newark, Detroit, and fifty-five other cities.[39] Forman argued that what many people in the United States government called riots were actually "rebellions" against years of "forced enslavement."[40] Forman acknowledged that the United Nations did not have any authority to liberate blacks in either America or Africa, but he was determined to use the forum to describe SNCC's role in "shaping public opinion." In a press release following his presentation, Forman wrote:[41]

> There are moments in history when you realize you yourself are making it. Howard Moore and I felt that way as we stepped before the microphone to address the assembled delegates of the United Nations and the liberation fighters
>   . . . there were delegates and liberation fighters around the very large rectangular table who were going to hear and to transmit to their sisters and brothers some of the ideas we would present. Moreover, we were going to raise in this body some of the issues that had confronted us for many years and we had a good chance of drawing more support for our cause.[42]

Forman also used the opportunity to clarify and reinforce SNCC's stance on a variety of issues. And there was at least one important issue that all organizational constituents seemed to agree upon—opposition to the Vietnam War. On the Vietnam question he stated, "It is our firm conviction that American intervention in Vietnam militates against any possible constructive action." He also professed absolute confidence that SNCC's efforts in the United States would "hasten victory in Southern Africa," and argued that it was commonly known that wealthy Americans "derived their positions" from the "sweat and the riches of Africans." The forum allowed the SNCC leaders to make American racism part of an international agenda. By comparing American racism to racism in South Africa, Forman was able to overcome the U.S. government's long-standing effort to keep that subject away from United Nations purview.[43]

AN INCREASING INTERNATIONAL PRESENCE

SNCC leaders continued their efforts to establish international alliances throughout the summer of 1967. Carmichael, still in great demand as a speaker, traveled to London, Algeria, Guinea, Tanzania, Syria, and North Vietnam. But his most historic trip was to Havana to participate in a meeting of the Organization of Latin American States (OLAS) in July, which made him an even greater FBI target after he announced support of the Cuban rebellion and armed revolution.

Forman and other SNCC workers felt that Carmichael seemed to have more of an independent than organizational agenda, and pointed out that SNCC leaders did not officially sanction many of Carmichael's trips, especially after he left the chairmanship. Forman also suggested that Carmichael's messages conflicted with SNCC positions, and that the resulting confusion weakened the organization:

> Much of what Stokely said while abroad was good, but his general attitude represented the zenith of an individualism that has hurt the black struggle in many quarters. His actions indicated that he was more interested in building a cult of personality rather than a strong organization. I felt that he had betrayed his own promise to help strengthen SNCC internally.[44]

Nevertheless, Carmichael remained influential and active in the organization, particularly the international arena in the early part of 1967. For instance, the February 1967 edition of the *New York SNCC Newsletter* contained an article praising him for a "highly successful visit to Puerto Rico"; the article went on to describe Carmichael's participation in demonstrations, meetings, and rallies. Prior to his departure, Carmichael and representatives from two Puerto Rican independence organizations issued a statement "pledging mutual support" in opposing the Vietnam War, resisting the draft, and providing better living and educational conditions for blacks and poor Puerto Ricans. The statement was included in a news release dated January 27 and distributed to publications targeted at black audiences. In the release, SNCC "affirmed the need for a joint struggle against the political, economic, social and cultural oppression inflicted upon Afro-American and Puerto Rican people by the United States . . . [since] black people constitute a colony within the United States . . . [and] Puerto Rico is a colony outside the United States."[45]

Accordingly, SNCC workers spent an increasing amount of time using their communications skills to work to build alliances with civil rights organizations in Africa, Latin America, and Asia. Forman remembers a time when the "cry of 'Black Power' had become an international one."[46] But he also criticized SNCC for missing out on the opportunity to harness what he viewed as a "tremendous upsurge of energy in the black community" in the United States.[47] With few direct action campaigns to promote or report on, SNCC workers in the communications department and Student Voice Press focused on creating support for the organization's new approaches to politics—including Black Power, international involvement, and the avowed destruction of racism, imperialism, and capitalism. In 1967, a *Student Voice* staff meeting report contained this description of the publication department's mission: to "inform, arouse, and educate [black people] to the fact of their oppression and to speak of roads to liberation." As always, the staffers used posters and flyers as part of their arsenal, but the images were very different: for example, Samuel Younge, the Atlanta riots, and Malcolm X.[48]

ARAB-ISRAELI STANCE ADDS TO NATIONAL DEBATE

A new publication named the *SNCC Newsletter* made its debut in the spring of 1967. Its stated goal was to provide information about "black liberation" and Third World struggles that the editors believed were "of concern to all black folks." The editors claimed that the publication gave "political direction" and made the "black community aware of what is happening here in the U.S.A. and abroad."[49] The newsletter, however, was to become the focus of an intense attack on SNCC the following summer. That year's headlines were dominated by the Arab-Israeli War, and while the Committee never took an official position in support of the Palestinian or Arab causes, SNCC workers in Atlanta included a series of pointed questions and cartoons that were clearly critical of Israel in an issue of the *SNCC Newletter*. When contemplating an official stand and speculating about possible reactions, Forman questioned the morality of thinking "that it is enough to know what people are thinking and only to say those things we know will be acceptable"; he also wondered if remaining silent on the Middle East conflict was simply a case of "opportunism."

Reaction to the newsletter text and illustrations was swift and strong. Many Jewish and mainstream liberal organizations withdrew their support of SNCC, describing it as too radical. The Committee tried to remedy the situation by holding a press conference featuring Ralph Featherstone, SNCC program secretary at that time. It did little to soften the criticism. Forman later said that the issue moved the organization "one step further along the road to revolution"—an "inevitable" step if SNCC were to fully accept and promote the view of "racism, capitalism, and imperialism as being indivisible."[50]

The Arab-Israeli issue would close many doors for SNCC and served as yet another public relations mistake, at least superficially. But as Forman argued, the article presented true organizational questions and enabled the group to better define its policies even if do so would create more public controversy and government suppression. The communications section did respond, but rather than continue working to reestablish the organization as a national leader for civil rights as one might expect, the communication staff began to ignore and isolate the organization from many of its previously important constituencies. Ethel Minor, who had replaced Charles Cobb in early 1967 as the communications department director, suggested that communication with the press would be one-way and would consist of only press statements and other prepared information.[51] The issue provided a turning point in the entire communications outlook for the organization. At this point, it seemed that the organization accepted and even encouraged a large degree of isolation from the mainstream press. Since the controversial article appeared in the fully sanctioned *SNCC Newsletter*, the Committee had little chance of regaining support from the moderate left and did not seem to want it. Moreover, it had been under continual government surveillance ever since it officially condemned American policy in Vietnam. And this infiltration made it increasingly difficult to carry on the usual activities. For instance, in April, Minor told readers of the *SNCC Newsletter* in a front-page letter that copies of the first issue had somehow been destroyed in the Atlanta postal distribution center; officials claimed that the newsletters lacked proper postage. Minor interviewed several black postal workers, who said that it was the first time to their knowledge that such an incident had ever occurred. When asked to explain, a government official higher up in the postal agency stood by the insufficient postage claim.[52]

As SNCC's criticism of the Vietnam War escalated, so did concern about the government's efforts to silence the organization. In a May 1967 communications report, Minor warned that "outsiders" had access to confidential SNCC files and that the organization must become more diligent in protecting information.[53] The group's leaders also registered concerned about the organizational records and even entertained such ideas as burying, burning, or shipping the records to Africa.[54] That same month Carmichael reported that because of SNCC's growing international influence, the organization must be "very, very careful" and be aware that black agents would likely infiltrate the group and their job would be to "disrupt and destroy this organization by any means necessary."[55] Forman later wrote in his autobiography that the government "declared SNCC an enemy" in 1966 as the organizational style became more militant. He recalled that agents from the Bureau of Internal Revenue continually harassed him and Ruby Doris Robinson, the executive secretary at that time, for a list of donors and with charges of tax fraud.[56]

But government harassment did little to stop the Committee from using their public relations mechanism to make even more radical and accusatory proclamations regarding American foreign policy in Southeast Asia. An article in the April 6, 1967, edition of the *SNCC Newsletter* accused Massachusetts Senator Edward W. Brooke, a black man, of betraying his race and the peace movement when he stated on national television that volunteering for the military would lead to a "better life" for many poor black men. The editors described Brooke as an "accessory to the fact" in the "murder" of millions of Asians and the "economic exploitation" of his race.[57]

In another example, on April 15, SNCC, the SCLC, and several other civil rights organizations participated in a mass demonstration against the war. As chairman, Carmichael declared that the "real reason" the United States was in Vietnam was "to serve the economic interests of American businessmen" who want to "exploit the tungsten, tin and oil which right-fully belong to the Vietnamese people and to secure strategic bases sur-rounding China."[58] He described the draft as "white people sending black people to make war on yellow people in order to defend the land they stole from red people."[59]

In a move that isolated the group even more, *SNCC Newsletter* articles contained frequent praise for riots that were occurring in ghettos throughout the country, which naturally alienated government officials, conservatives, and former liberal supporters. The April 6 issue included a report on a demonstration that had turned violent at Fisk University in Nashville. The writer described how students "threw bricks, bottles, rocks, and shot at riot cops from dormitory windows with pellet rifles"; three black students were shot and ten policemen were injured that day. Accord-ing to the article, the students had "served notice on this country" that they would no longer respond "under the reigns of the white power structure and their black puppets":

> They are aware of who the enemy is. They will not accept this coun-try's lies about the Vietcong. They know that the white cops are the ones responsible for the deaths of black people throughout the South. They know that white people bomb churches and kill black children, they know that white people are responsible for the deaths, econom-ical and physical of non-white people all over the world. They have defined their own terms and they have found their enemy! They have said "TO HELL WITH THIS COUNTRY AND THE MURDERERS WHO MAKE ITS LAWS."[60]

These and similar messages encouraged further government repres-sion and public rejection, at least from most whites. Accordingly, SNCC workers had to promote their cause with fewer and fewer financial resources. The *SNCC Newsletter* charged a $2/year subscription rate, but its revenues barely covered production costs. The editors complained that their lack of funds were the result of the "increased harassment of SNCC" by federal investigators bent on preventing the organization from "getting the word to black folks."[61] So even if their primary audience of young

urban blacks had thus far been responding to the group's militant communications, it had become increasingly difficult to reach them and to
maintain an organized method for outreach. Without money and with tremendous government resistance, SNCC's communication apparatus was
quickly losing its effectiveness.

The message that these outside government forces were relentlessly
trying to destroy SNCC remained evident in most of the organization's
printed communications in the late spring and summer of 1967 in the few
publications and press releases that the group was able to disseminate. A
June 22 news release (most likely with limited distribution to selected black
media outlets) declared that "white city officials, papers, T.V., radio, and
their black Uncle Toms are trying to kill SNCC, divide our black community, and turn brother against brother." The release disputed claims made by
SNCC opponents that the Committee—especially Carmichael, who continued to make confrontational speeches—was responsible for riots and violence occurring in American cities. The press release writers instead blamed
the white political system, and asked black readers and listeners to consider
if SNCC or Carmichael had ever contributed to their oppression:

> Have SNCC and Stokely Carmichael ever beaten you on the head,
> arrested you on trumped up charges, then carried you to jail for another
> beating? Does SNCC and Stokely Carmichael keep you hemmed up in
> filthy ghettos, send you to bad schools, then refuse to give you a job?
> . . . How long will you believe this very man who messes over us like
> master over slave? How long will you let him turn us around?[62]

As SNCC's message grew increasingly militant, cooperation with or
from the mainstream press, the general public, and national and local governments all but disappeared. Instead of cultivating outside support from these
former sources, SNCC communications workers wrote increasingly aggres-
sive, even warlike messages to encourage the awakening of black consciousness. Those messages also served to inform conservatives and racists that an
important segment of American blacks would no longer tolerate oppression
and were willing to engage in rebellion and violence if it resulted in their liberation. SNCC workers took every opportunity to attack white institutions,
for example, calling the idea of blacks celebrating July 4 as Independence Day
"ridiculous."[63] The writer of this particular news release suggested instead
that blacks adopt August 18, 1965—when the Watts neighborhood in Los
Angeles erupted in violence—as their Independence Day. According to the
release, the date "marks the day the blacks of Watts picked up guns to fight
for their freedom," thus inspiring rebellion in other major American cities:

For 400 years we had begged, pleaded, cried, marched and died for just a little taste of "life, liberty and the pursuit of happiness." The Watts Insurrection signaled the end of begging, crying, marching. . . . On August 18, 1965, blacks stopped moaning "we shall overcome" and started swinging to "Burn, Baby, Burn." That was our Declaration of Independence, and we signed it with Molotov cocktails and rifles.[64]

"LET RAP RAP"

By the spring of 1967, SNCC was clearly a vastly different organization than the one that had organized the Mississippi Freedom Summer. The June 1967 staff meeting in Atlanta signaled yet another personnel change, which resulted in an even more militant and drastic transformation than Carmichael's Black Power movement. Carmichael, who willingly stepped down from the chairmanship because of all the media attention and controversy surrounding him, passed the position on to Hubert "Rap" Brown, a 23-year-old member of the Alabama field staff from Baton Rouge, Louisiana, whose nickname reflected his uncanny ability to communicate with black community members. Brown was a proponent of SNCC's traditional community organizing approach and knew the ropes from his Alabama and Mississippi experiences. As such, he immediately put out a call for organizing all blacks, including "sharecroppers in the South and the ghetto dwellers in the North" so that "all of the institutions within the black community in this country [can be] controlled by black people."[65]

Forman recalled that the group wanted this kind of work to be Brown's primary mission—the development of freedom organizations such as the LCFO with the black panther as a symbol. Brown agreed and soon after the election declared that "SNCC is moving from rhetoric to program."[66] He also cited the need to "encourage young black people to remain in school and to obtain the skills so desperately needed in order to develop our own communities here" as well as in "newly independent African nations."[67]

But despite these intentions, SNCC's organizational structure, including its communications apparatus, had fallen by the wayside; and as Forman described it, many workers were involved in "helter-skelter random activity," so even such familiar organizing activities were no longer possible.[68] Instead a series of speeches and consequent arrests made the new chairman yet another iconic organizational symbol—a symbol of violence, radicalism, and complete distrust of government systems.

Only a few weeks into the election Brown earned his reputation as a violent militant when Carmichael was arrested in Prattville, Alabama, for refusing to stop shouting "Black Power." Local blacks rebelled and exchanged gunshots with whites. More SNCC workers went to jail, and the National Guard took over the black community. Brown immediately called a press conference to warn that SNCC would "no longer sit back and let black people be killed by murderers who hide behind sheets or behind the badge of the law." He called the events a "a declaration of war" by "racist white America" and called for "full retaliation from the blacks across the country. Even though the organization was too disorganized by this time to rally to Brown's call, the event naturally triggered negative and repressive responses from the government, the media, fearful whites, and former black supporters.

Brown held tight to this militant theme throughout most of his speeches. His most controversial incident involved a speech at the Cambridge Action Federation, composed of members of SNCC's former Cambridge affiliate. Brown's July 25 forty-minute speech took place during the same time as some of Detroit's most deadly riots and was the beginning of a series of arrests and legal complications that would define the remainder of his chairmanship.

Although Brown repeated Carmichael's themes of racial pride, he urged blacks to take up arms. "If America don't come around, we are going to burn it down, brother," he declared. No violence occurred immediately, but soon after the speech, police and black residents exchanged gunfire. Seventeen buildings suffered damage or destruction, and the National Guard took control. Although not directly responsible, authorities charged Brown with arson.

Within days of his release, similar charges evolved from an Ohio event. And while out of jail on bond, Brown was again arrested for carrying a weapon across state lines. Forman later recalled that as a result of these events Brown had become a "symbol of resistance" and that the federal government had made him "a scapegoat for the rebellion that black people were mounting."[69] SNCC workers responded using standard public relations mechanisms to explain the predicament and sent numerous letters and explanations to constituents to describe the arrests and the underlying circumstances. Moreover, and perhaps more importantly, they explained that Brown had become a political target and reminded supporters that they must continue their fight despite such illicit federal activities. The theme of much of this material concerned Brown's First Amendment rights. A statement signed by civil rights leaders, including Martin Luther King, Jr., addressed whites and blacks and declared that Brown had never committed a crime and that the government jailed Brown to keep him from speaking:

> As people in organizations committed to social change, we believe
> the goals we work for are crucially threatened when our government
> makes a decision to cope with social problems by using its police power
> to jail its critics and crush its dissenters . . . as critics and dissenters
> ourselves, each of us knows that if one group of dissenters is silent, no
> one is safe. Especially those of us who are white know that if the gov-
> ernment jails and silences and crushes militant black spokesmen, it is
> only a matter of time until white critics of governmental policies will be
> treated in the same way.[70]

Another backgrounder explained that by moving Brown through the
courts and keeping him off the speaking circuit, the government planned to
destroy Brown and SNCC without any "public outcry."[71] And the arrests
and legal actions did indeed keep Brown off the speech circuit. At least nine
schedule changes took place for the October-December schedule indicating
cancellation or replacements for Brown.[72] Nonetheless, Brown continually
issued statements via SNCC that appeared as fliers and fund raising letters. Maintaining his militant stance, Brown declared in a July 26 statement that "we stand on the eve of a black revolution" and called the day's
rioting a "dress rehearsal for real revolution." In another example, under
the heading of "Let Rap Rap," the Committee produced fliers featuring a
photo a Brown and a letter from the Parish Prison in New Orleans dated
February 21, 1968, which declared that "aggression is the order of the
day."[73] The next month, Brown charged "black brothers and sisters . . .
who are caught behind enemy lines" to arm themselves and called America
an "enemy of mankind."[74]

The significance of these messages was crucial to the organization.
Clearly, there was little organization or planning from a communication
standpoint and little discussion of the probable consequences of delivering
such militant messages. The messages created enemies for sure, but they
also brought blacks to action—the desired response of those who created
them. Although SNCC was nearly defunct as an organization and had little
structure, these haphazard communication efforts kept the organization on
the national agenda, resulting in hatred from many whites and rebellion
from many young urban blacks. Changes in attitudes and behavior clearly
resulted from the controversial communication activities. Controversy
meant attention and action, and SNCC got both.

This growing public fear along with escalating tensions with the fed-
eral government and white communities soon almost completely eroded
SNCC's political and financial base. These pressures essentially made 1968
SNCC's final year, although organizational remnants remained. As early as

January 1968, disorganization, frustration, and debt marked SNCC activities. During the June staff meeting, the group chose to elect nine deputy chairmen to replace Brown, who had become too embroiled in is own legal issues and too controversial to continue as chair. One of these deputies— Phil Hutchins—soon became the principal spokesperson, but he never had the widespread appeal of his predecessors. The next month, the remaining group members, who believed Carmichael to be in a power struggle with Forman, expelled him. Ironically, Forman left the organization six months later, a result of exhaustion and frustration. Other longtime SNCC workers such as Cleveland Sellers and Willie Ricks also underwent expulsion resulting from organizational conflicts.

By October, SNCC leaders described their organization as being a "holding operation," surviving on its "reputation" and incapable of bringing together its "scattered projects" into a unified whole.[75] But even then, SNCC leaders were claiming that the Committee played an important role in "liberating people's minds" and "setting up organizational models that challenged new-found radicalism to produce change." To address these goals, the leadership decided to place "less emphasis" on international relations, instead suggesting that their European offices be used to "turn out propaganda," so the department was "decentralized so that interested people around the country could help."[76]

The last SNCC meeting took place in June 1969 in New York City. Brown led a rebellion and demanded control of the organization. At a July 22 press conference, he declared that the organization would become the Student National Coordinating Committee. This group survived for a few years, but only as a holding ground for a few militants. For all intents and purposes, the newly named organization symbolized the end of the Student Nonviolent Coordinating Committee.

One might be hard pressed to argue that SNCC's public relations efforts were successful during the late 1960s. Disorganization and thoughtless decision making defined many of these later efforts. Planning, community organization and political activism, and nonviolent strategy had given way to passion, frustration, iconic leadership, and social unrest. But the impact, positive and negative, of the organizational efforts is undeniable.

The anti-Vietnam messages led to increased opposition to the war and created support for Julian Bond's campaign and ultimately the Supreme Court decision that returned his position in the Georgia legislature. And although it is difficult to draw conclusions regarding the effect of the group's international relations efforts, SNCC workers clearly established a presence, albeit a short-lived one, in other countries, particularly Africa. Rap Brown asked for rebellion, and he got it. And consequently, SNCC earned a respectable place for itself on the agenda of the national media. Although the organization's objectives, particularly Brown and Carmichael's, might have been questionable, they were achieved and had a lasting impact on American society.

SNCC suffered immense criticism for encouraging violence during the late 1960s from many sources, including fellow black Americans, but the organization continued to effectively communicate its message, regardless of the popularity or common acceptance of new Black Power and nationalist philosophies.

Epilogue

SNCC's relatively short life propelled extraordinary change. Beginning with four North Carolina students staging a nonviolent sit in at a Woolworth's lunch counter and ending with H. Rap Brown's calls for violence against the country, the organization continually used communications tactics and strategies to educate their various constituencies, raise awareness, send persuasive messages, change attitudes, influence legislation, and build financial and emotional support for its cause.

SNCC's accomplishments as well as the events leading to the organization's demise had historic and important influences upon American culture. From the modest one-room, one-person office directed by Jane Stembridge, the organization played a role in encouraging the acceptance of civil rights in the South and encouraging a new movement for human rights around the world in a few short and turbulent years during the 1960s. In many ways, the organization's leaders and workers were indeed public relations professionals "par excellence."[1] Despite the tremendous obstacles of racism, violent resistance to the movement, government surveillance, and a generally inhospitable white Southern press, the young and resourceful SNCC workers galvanized the nation with their use of both conventional and unconventional communication campaigns.

As the organization transformed into a powerful political entity, so did the content and magnitude of its communication messages. As demonstrated by the immense public relations efforts of the SNCC communications section, an understanding of the ability to execute a public relations campaign is an inherent aspect of a successful social movement. As the evidence of this study clearly indicates, public relations certainly served as a foundational force for the promotion of civil rights during the 1960s, and to a considerable degree this promotion resulted from the communication efforts of SNCC staff and volunteers as well as the community members they inspired.

The SNCC communications workers were first and foremost civil rights activists. But in order to mobilize a civil rights campaign, they had to become effective public relations practitioners. Therefore, the civil rights movement, even as it appeared beyond SNCC's efforts, was indeed a public relations campaign contained within a larger and history-changing campaign for civil rights. Public relations was not the focus of the movement, but it was the integral tool that pushed it forward. As such, when defining their purpose in the spring of 1960, the young SNCC leaders made it clear that they would organize, coordinate, and communicate. These objectives would remain throughout the organization's history, although the messages sent would change drastically.

Despite the controversial nature of SNCC messages, or perhaps because of them, SNCC workers would repeatedly persuade, educate, and inform a broad range of publics. Through communication, SNCC brought others to action. By effectively using communication and public relations strategies, the small but energized staff opened the doors to vast changes in American society and constructed and generated events and information that would make civil rights a national imperative.

Notes

NOTES TO THE ACKNOWLEDGMENTS

1. Vanessa Murphree, "The Selling of Civil Rights: The Communication Section of the Student Nonviolent Coordinating Committee," *Journalism History*, Spring 2003 (29)1, 21–31; Vanessa Murphree, "The Student Voice: 'Purging the Rabies of Racism,' 1960–1965," *American Journalism*, Winter 2003, (20)1, 73–91; Vanessa Murphree "'Black Power': Public Relations and Social Change in the 1960s," *American Journalism*, Spring 2004, (21)2, 13–32.

NOTES TO THE INTRODUCTION

1. According to a 1963 SNCC brochure, "[SNCC] was born out of the history-making sit-in movement that erupted across the South in the spring of 1960. At Easter of that year, the first South-wide meeting of sit-in leaders was held in Raleigh, North Carolina. Here a temporary committee to promote communication and coordination of activities among protest groups was set up." The brochure is part of the special collections of the Mississippi State University Library, Starkville.
2. A program for the Student Voice, Inc., Student Nonviolent Coordinating Committee Papers, on microfilm, reel 10 (UMI, Ann Arbor, 1994). Hereinafter "SNCC Papers."
3. Thomas Rose and John Greenya, *Black Leaders: Then and Now. A Personal History of Students who Led the Civil Rights Movement in the 1960's—And What Happened to Them* (Garrett Park, Md.: Garrett Park, 1984), 29.
4. Linda Childers Hon has analyzed the public relations efforts behind Martin Luther King, Jr.'s Southern Christian Leadership Conference (SCLC). See Linda Childers Hon, "'To Redeem the Soul of America:' "Public Relations and the Civil Rights Movement," *Journal of Public Relations Research* 9 (3), 1997: 163–212. A loosely related 1992 article addressed Martin Luther King Jr.'s strategies for changing public opinion through Christian

philosophy. See Marilyn Kern-Foxworth, "Martin Luther King Jr.: Minister, Civil Rights Activist, and Public Opinion Leader," *Public Relations Review* 18 (fall 1992): 287–296. I also found two unpublished dissertations on the topic of social movements and public relations: Genevieve Gardner McBride, No *"Season of Silence": Uses of Public Relations in Nineteenth and Early Twentieth Century Reform Movements in Wisconsin.* (Unpublished doctoral dissertation, The University of Wisconsin, 1989) and Margot Opdycke Lamme, "The Campaign Against the Second Edition of Hell: An Examination of the Messages and Methods of the Anti-Saloon League of America Through a Framework of Public Relations History, 1893–1933 (Unpublished doctoral dissertation, The University of Alabama, 2002). Lamme has also published an article: The "Public Sentiment Building Society": The Anti-Saloon League of America, 1895–1910, *Journalism History* 29(3), 2003: 123–132.

5. Todd Gitlin, *The Whole World is Watching: Mass Media in the Making of the New Left* (Berkeley: The University of California, 1980).
6. Richard Lenz, *Symbols, the News Magazines and Martin Luther King* (Baton Rouge: Louisiana State University, 1990).
7. Hon, 164.
8. Gene Sharp, *The Politics of Nonviolent Action,* Vol. 2 (Boston: Porter Sargent, 1973); Mary E. King, *Mahatma Gandhi and Martin Luther King, Jr.: The Power of Nonviolent Action* (Paris: The United Nations Educational, Scientific and Cultural Organization, 1999).
9. Emily Stoper, *The Student Nonviolent Coordinating Committee: The Growth of Radicalism in a Civil Rights Organization* (Brooklyn: Carlson, 1989) and Clayborne Carson, *In Struggle: SNCC and the Black Awakening of the 1960s* (Cambridge: Harvard University, 1981, 1995).
10. Mary E. King, telephone interview with the author, New Orleans and Washington, D.C., 16 February 2002.
11. Ibid.
12. Ibid. King said that Claude Sitton of the *New York Times* finally reported on the bodies but used the phrase "an alleged report from a SNCC spokesman." She also said that Nick von Hoffman of the *Chicago Daily News* traveled to Natchez but could not obtain verification of the story and therefore never reported it.
13. Scott M. Cutlip, *The Unseen Power: Public Relations, A History* (Hillsdale, NJ, Erlbaum, 1994).
14. Bruce Galphin, "Learning from SNCC, Reprint from *Atlanta Constitution* Editorial Page). Aframerican News Service, July 1967 (SNCC papers, reel 17, 236).
15. Some include: James Forman, *The Making of Black Revolutionaries: A Personal Account* (New York: Macmillan 1972); John Lewis with Michael D'Orso, *Walking with the Wind: A Memoir of the Movement* (New York,: Simon & Schuster, 1998); Danny Lyon, *Memories of the Southern Civil Rights Movement* (The University of North Carolina: Chapel Hill, 1992). Cleveland Sellers with Robert Terrell, *The Autobiography of a Black Militant and the Life and Death of SNCC* (Jackson: University Press of

Mississippi, 1990); Stokely Carmichael and Charles Hamilton, *Black Power: The Politics of Liberation* (New York: Vintage, 1967, 1992); Anne Moody, *Coming of Age in Mississippi* (New York: Dell, 1968); Sally Belfrage, *Freedom Summer* (Carter G. Woodson Institute for Black Studies, Charlottesville: University of Virginia, 1990). Scholarly books and article include: Eric R. Burner, *And Gently He Shall Lead Them: Robert Parris Moses and Civil Rights in Mississippi* (New York: New York University, 1994). Joanne Grant, *Ella Baker: Freedom Bound* (New York: John Wiley & Sons, 1998), John Neary, *Julian Bond: Black Rebel*, (New York: William Morrow, 1971). Cynthia Griggs Fleming, *Soon We will not Cry: The Liberation of Ruby Doris Smith Robinson* (Lanham, Md.: Rowman & Littlefield, 1998) Doug McAdam, *Freedom Summer* (New York: Oxford University, 1988); Howard Zinn, *SNCC: The New Abolitionist* (Boston: Beacon, 1964, 1965); Emily Stoper, "The Student Nonviolent Coordinating Committee: Rise and Fall of a Redemptive Organization, " *Journal of Black Studies*, 8 (September 1977), 13–34; Emily Stoper, *The Student Nonviolent Coordinating Committee: The Growth of Radicalism in a Civil Rights Organization* (Brooklyn: Carlson Publishing, 1989); Clayborne Carson, In Struggle: *SNCC and the Black Awakening of the 1960s* (Cambridge: Harvard University, 1981).

16. The University of Southern Mississippi Oral History Civil Rights Documentation Project.

17. Clayborne Carson, David. J. Garrow, Gerald Gill, Vincent Harding, and Darlene Clark Hine, eds., *The Eyes on the Prize Civil Rights Reader: Documents, Speeches, and Firsthand Accounts for the Black Freedom Struggle* (New York: Penguine, 1991).

18. Henry Hampton and Steve Fayer with Sarah Flynn, *Voice of Freedom: An Oral History of the Civil Rights Movement from the 1950s through the 1980s* (New York: Bantam, 1990).

19. Cheryl Lynn Greenberg, ed., *A Circle of Trust: Remembering SNCC* (Rutgers: State University, 1998).

NOTES TO CHAPTER ONE

1. Quoted in JoAnn Grant, *Ella Baker: Freedom Bound* (New York: John Wiley & Sons, 1998), 127. Letter to Anne Braden from Ella Baker, 21 March 1960, MLK Center, Box 32.

2. John Colley reporting for Workout Group #10, Raleigh, N.C.," 16 April 1960 (SNCC papers, reel 1, 1).

3. Ibid.

4. "Resume of the May and June Meeting of the Student Nonviolent Coordinating Committee," 1960 (SNCC papers, reel 1, 197).

5. Jane Stembridge, telephone interview by author, Hattiesburg, Miss., and Arden, N.C., 18 May 2001.

6. "Recommendations of the Temporary Student Nonviolent Coordinating Committee," 14–16 October 1960 (SNCC papers, reel 1, 65).

7. Stembridge.

8. Stembridge.
9. Letter to David Forbes from Jane Stembridge, 14 April 1960 (SNCC papers, reel 4, 810).
10. Letter to Congressmen from the Student Nonviolent Coordinating Committee, 3 August 1960 (SNCC papers, reel 4, 291).
11. Austin Long-Scott, "From Then to Now, A Personal Essay on the Media, the Civil Rights Movement and the Aftermath," *The Caldwell Journals*, the Robert C. Maynard Institute for Journalism Education, Oakland, Calif.
12. Stembridge; Letter to David Forbes from Jane Stembridge, 14 August 1960 (SNCC papers, reel 4, 810).
13. Letter from SNCC to the editors of the *Atlanta Journal* concerning a 10 August 1960 article entitled "Brilliant Tactics," n.d. (SNCC papers, reel 1, 304).
14. Letter from SNCC to Roy V. Harris, editor of the *Augusta Courier*, 16 August 1960 (SNCC papers, reel 1, 306).
15. Mary E. King, "Getting the News Out," draft chapter, *Hands on the Plough: Anthology by Women in the U.S. Civil Rights Movement*, ed. Faith Holsaert, Martha Prescod Norman, Judy Richardson, Betty Garman Robinson, Jean Wheeler, Smith Young, Dorothy Zellner, forthcoming.
16. Bond, King, and other members of the Atlanta group encouraged SNCC to make Atlanta its home base; they also helped to finance the organization. Emily Stoper, *The Student Nonviolent Coordinating Committee: The Growth of Radicalism in a Civil Rights Organization* (Brooklyn: Carlson, 1967), 280.
17. The universities included Morehouse, Morris Brown, and Spelman Colleges, Atlanta University, and the interdenominational Theological Center. "Report from the Committee on the Appeal for Human Rights," n.d. (SNCC papers, reel 4, 966).
18. Julian Bond and Melvin McCaw, "Special Report: Atlanta Story," *The Student Voice*, June 1960, 4.
19. Bob Hall and Sue Thrasher, "Julian Bond: The Movement, Then and Now," *Southern Exposure* (3)4, 1975, 10.
20. Charles Cobb, interview with John Rachal. 21 October 1996, the University of Southern Mississippi Oral History Civil Rights Documentation Project.
21. States where sit-ins occurred included Alabama, Arkansas, Florida, Georgia, Kentucky, Louisiana, Maryland, Mississippi, Missouri, North Carolina, Oklahoma, South Carolina, Tennessee, Texas, and Virginia. For a complete list of sit-in locations and numbers of arrests and convictions, see Martin Oppenheimer, *The Sit In Movement of 1960* (Brooklyn, Carlson: 1989), 90–93.
22. Cobb.
23. Stembridge.
24. The National Student Association, established in 1947, was largely made up of white students at white universities who were interested in promoting civil rights. The group initially received funding from the CIA to monitor international student groups. Public knowledge of this funding

source almost destroyed the organization in 1967, but the group survived by re-organizing.

25. Constance Curry, et. al., 340–341.
26. Curry and Stembridge shared an apartment beginning in the summer of 1960; the three women often spent long hours after work discussing the movement over drinks and dinner.
27. Stembridge.
28. "Public Relations Report: June 13-July 31, 1960: Submitted August 5" (SNCC papers, reel 1, 327).
29. Constance Curry, telephone interview by author, Hattiesburg, Mississippi and Atlanta, 24 June 2001.
30. Quoted in Curry, et. al., 14.
31. Ibid.
32. Letter to Jane Stembridge from Edward B. King, Jr., dated 7 June 1960, but most likely written 7 July 1960 based on dates appearing within the text (SNCC papers, reel 4, 954–955).
33. Unsigned letter to Roy V. Harris, 16 August 1960 (SNCC papers, reel 1, 306).
34. Stembridge telephone interview.
35. Currey, et. al.
36. Ibid.
37. "Statement Submitted by the Student Nonviolent Coordinating Committee to the Platform Committee of the National Democratic Convention Thursday Morning, July 7, 1960, Los Angeles, California," (SNCC papers, reel 13).
38. *The Student Voice*, August 1960, 1.
39. Ibid., 2.
40. Letter from Marion S. Barry, Jr., to Richard M. Nixon, 18 August 1960 (SNCC papers, reel 1, 306).
41. *The Student Voice*, December 1960, 1.
42. Stembridge.
43. "Those invited to conference on "Nonviolence and Achievement of Desegregation: in Atlanta," 14–16 October 1960 (SNCC papers, reel 1, 98). The news organizations included *Life, Time, Newsweek*, the *New York Times*, the *New York Post*, *Afro*, the *Chicago Defender*, the *Courier* (based in Pittsburgh), the *Journal and Guide* (based in Norfolk, Va.), *Nashville News Star*, the *Atlanta Daily World*, the *Atlanta Inquirer*, the *Atlanta Journal*, the *Atlanta Constitution*, the *New York Tribune*, the *Petal Paper* (based in Petal, Miss.,), United Press International, and the Associated Press.
44. *The Student Voice*, August 1962, 7.
45. *The Student Voice*, fall 1960 special edition, 2.
46. Ibid.
47. Ibid.
48. Henry Hampton, *Eyes on the Prize: America's Civil Right Years, 1954–1965* (Alexandria, Va.: Blackside Inc., and the Corporation for Public Broadcasting), video cassette recording.
49. *The Student Voice*, October 1960, 2.

50. Curry, telephone interview.
51. *The Student Voice*, December 1960, 1.
52. Letter to Student Nonviolent Coordinating Committee from Anne Braden, 31 October 1960 (SNCC papers, reel 4, 1090).
53. Quoted in Greenberg, 35.
54. *The Student Voice*, January 1961, 2. The 1957 Civil Rights Act established the Civil Rights Division of the Department of Justice and the Civil Rights Commission. It gave federal prosecutors authority to sue anyone who interfered with voting rights. But since most southern juries did not allow blacks to participate in the judicial system, the Act was essentially ineffectual. Legislators later designed the 1960 Civil Rights Act to allow federal judges to appoint referees to hear voting rights complaints, but with firmly established racist practices in the South, the 1960 Act brought little change. The Civil Rights Act of 1964 would finally bring some change with the prohibition of literacy tests that required ambiguous interpretations of the state constitution and gave registrars a broad opportunity to deny blacks their voting rights. But it was not until 1965, when federal registrars took over the registration process that significant change took place.
55. "News from the Student Nonviolent Coordinating Committee" (SNCC papers, reel 4, 964).
56. *The Student Voice*, April and May 1961, 2.
57. Ibid., 3.
58. The Congress of Racial Equality was founded on the University of Chicago campus in 1942 and was part of the pacifist Fellowship of Reconciliation. CORE leaders embraced nonviolence and worked in northern cities to promote the philosophy as a method of social change. By the early 1960s, CORE had some southern staff members who helped SNCC leaders organize sit ins, freedom riders, and voter registration activity.
59. *The Student Voice*, April and May 1961; 1.
60. Mary E. King, *Freedom Song: A Personal Story of the 1960s Civil Rights Movement* (Morrow: New York, 1987), 317.
61. Quoted in Fred Powledge, *Free at Last?: The Civil Rights Movement and the People Who Made It* (New York: Harper, 1992), 262.
62. Carson, 37.
63. *The Student Voice*, April and May 1961, 1.
64. Letter to David Forbes from Jane Stembridge, 14 August 1960 (SNCC papers, reel 4, 810).
65. Letter to Irving Dent from Marion S. Barry, Jr., 11 August 1960 (SNCC papers, reel 4, 804).
66. Letter to David Forbes from Jane Stembridge.
67. Letter to Amzie Moore from Jane Stembridge, 15 August 1960 (SNCC papers, reel 4, 811).
68. Letter from "Field Representative Bob" n.d. and no address, but based on the tone of their previous correspondence, most likely meant for Stembridge. (SNCC papers, reel 4, 833).

69. Charles Cobb, interview with John Rachal.
70. Letter from "Field Representative Bob."
71. Quoted in Greenberg, 39–40. Myles Horton founded the Highlander Folk School in 1932 as a center for adult education and social change. The school offered leadership courses throughout the 1930s, 1940s, and 1950s focusing on organized labor and civil rights. By the 1960s, the school was largely known as a center for civil rights education.
72. Ibid.
73. For more on Ed King's departure see: Cheryl Lynn Greenberg, ed., *A Circle of Trust: Remembering SNCC* (New Brunswick, Rutgers University, 1998), 48; JoAnne Grant. *Ella Baker: Freedom Bound* (New York: John Wiley , 1998), 142.
74. Quoted in Stoper, 267.
75. Dorothy Miller Zellner agreed with Bond's assessment. She recalled that Forman "pleaded with people to write everything down" so that the information could be used to create both organizational messages and an accurate record of SNCC history. Zellner called Forman a "mastermind of SNCC" who never stopped pushing the communications staff to produce more materials for the movement and the press. Dorothy Miller Zellner, telephone interview by author, Hattiesburg, Mississippi and New York City, 5 May 2001.
76. Julian Bond, Introduction in James Forman, *The Making of Black Revolutionaries* (Seattle: University of Washington, 1985).
77. Forman, 241.
78. Julian Bond, email interview by the author, 13 May 2001.
79. Forman, 241.
80. Bob Hall and Sue Thrasher, "Julian Bond: The Movement, Then and Now," *Southern Exposure* (3)4, 1975, 10.
81. Julian Bond, "Civil Rights: Now and Then," Speech presented to the National Press Club, 27 May 1998.
82. Forman, 244.
83. Bond, Raleigh speech.
84. Quoted in Greenberg, 40–41.
85. Ibid., 41.
86. Ibid., 42.
87. Ibid., 69.
88. Ibid., 62.
89. Ibid.
90. Letter to Madeline Cass from James Forman, 21 November 1961 (SNCC papers, reel 10, 92).
91. "Proposal by the Student Nonviolent Coordinating Committee," n.d., but it contains a reference to a 15 November 1961 meeting. (Personal papers of Joan C. Browning).
92. "The Sleep and the Fearful," authored by "a housewife here in Albany," n.d. (Personal papers of Joan C. Browning).
93. Carson, 59.

94. *The Student Voice*, Albany, Georgia edition, 26 November 1961, 1.
95. Ibid. Black residents boycotted local advertisers after Albany's newspaper editors condemned the march.
96. Ibid.
97. Ibid, 2.
98. SNCC News Release, 7 February 1962 (SNCC papers, reel 14, 654).
99. *The Student Voice*, Albany, Georgia edition, 1 December 1961, 2 (personal papers of Joan C. Browning).
100. Joan C. Browning, telephone interview by author, 20 April 2001, Ronceverte, West Virginia and Hattiesburg, Mississippi.
101. Gordon Roberts, "New Protest Set in Tense Albany," *The Atlanta Journal*, 14 December 1961, 1.
102. Hampton.
103. Carson, 66.
104. Frances Pauley, "Report from Albany: Program Highlights of the Georgia Council on Human Relations." December 1961 (Howard Zinn papers, box 1, folder 3, State Historical Society of Wisconsin, Madison).
105. Martin Oppenheimer, *The Sit In Movement of 1960* (Brooklyn: Carlson, 1989), 178.
106. For more about agenda setting in the news and public relations see: Judy Vanslyke Turk, "Public Relations Influence on the News," chapter in Agenda-Settings: Readings on Media, Public Opinion and Policy Making, Maxwell McCombs and David L. Protess, editors (Lawrence Erlbaum Associates, 1991) 211–222.
107. *The Student Voice*, April and May 1961, 2.

NOTES TO CHAPTER TWO

1. "Explanation of Current Needs," 15 July 1963 (SNCC papers, reel 24, 642). The report called for the recruitment and training of "project reporters" so that SNCC could better communicate with the media and the general public.
2. Other conference workshops addressed community organizing/mobilizing, legal issues, direct action, civil liberties and academic freedom, and the recruitment of white students for the movement. *The Student Voice*, April 1962, 1.
3. Letter from James Forman to "Dear Friend" (SNCC papers, reel 11, 768).
4. Letter from SNCC to "Dear Editor" (SNCC papers, reel 14, 21).
5. Fred Powledge, telephone interview by author, 16 June 2001.
6. James Forman, *The Making of Black Revolutionaries: A Personal Account* (New York: Macmillan, 1972), 264.
7. King, *Freedom Song*, 223.
8. Forman, 242.
9. King, *Freedom Song*, 216, 229.
10. Forman, 264.
11. Danny Lyon, *Memories of the Southern Civil Rights Movement* (The University of North Carolina, Chapel Hill, 1992), 42.
12. Betty Garman, "Students Spearhead Southern Voter Drives," *The Liberal Democrat*, June 1962 (SNCC papers, reel 10, 380).

13. Garman.
14. Forman, 264.
15. Forman, 265.
16. Fannie Lou Hamer, interview with Neil R. McMillen, 14 July 1972, University of Southern Mississippi Oral History Civil Rights Documentation Project.
17. *The Student Voice*, October 1962, 2.
18. Forman, 263.
19. Ibid., 264.
20. Quoted in Greenberg, 64.
21. Forman, 265.
22. Forman, 265.
23. Ibid.
24. Victor Navasky, *Kennedy Justice* (New York: Atheneum, 1971), 118–119.
25. Ibid., 273.
26. While waiting for the VEP funds, SNCC leaders took a "long-range approach to fund raising that would advance SNCC toward financial stability over a long period of time." Strategies included targeting student government and campus Christian associations for annual pledges and asking "wealthy adults" to join a "100 Club" by donating $100. In the summer of 1962, when SNCC was facing a $13,000 debt, Forman suggested that the organization open six offices in cities with large black populations: New York, Washington, D.C., Chicago, Detroit, Philadelphia, and Cleveland. The primary task of these offices would be fundraising, the secondary task building political support. Forman argued, "If people give money, they are performing a political service to the movement. I also reject the popular notion that he who pays the piper calls the tune, for my experience has been that you can put radical policies up front and stick to them and still get financial help." See Forman, 271.
27. Marion S. Barry, Jr., and Claudia Rawles, "Executive Committee Meeting," 15 June 1963 (SNCC papers, reel 3, 814).
28. Forman, 272.
29. Lewis, 210.
30. The combination of Lewis as SNCC symbol and Lyon as photographer combined to create an indelible image in the late summer of 1963. Lewis lead a small demonstration outside of a Cairo, Illinois, segregated public pool. Although the demonstration itself was a minor event, Lyon photographed Lewis and the other participants kneeling in prayer in support of activists who were facing turmoil in Albany, Georgia. The picture, with the caption "Come let us build a new world together," became a widely distributed movement poster. SNCC used its printing press to produce 10,000 copies, which were sold for $1 each. See also Lewis, 192.
31. Lewis, 210.
32. Ibid., 210.
33. Marion S. Barry, Jr., and Claudia Rawles, "Executive Committee Meeting," 15 June 1963 (SNCC papers, reel 3, 814).
34. Letter to the Atlanta Police Chief from Dorothy Miller. 18 October 1962 (SNCC papers, reel 10, 163)

35. SNCC papers, reel 10, 534.
36. Howard Zinn, "Negroes are Dragged off Federal Property as the FBI Looks On," reprinted from *The New Republic*, 26 October 1963 (SNCC papers, reel 25, 6). See also, Burnings, Jailing, Shooting reported in Greenwood, Miss., 14 March 1963, reprinted from *Jet* (SNCC papers, reel 25, 128); James A. Wechsler, Combat Story, 19 March 1963, reprinted from the *New York Post* (SNCC papers, reel 23, 129).
37. *Inter-Staff Newsletter*, Vol. 1, No. 1, 1 December 1962 (SNCC papers, reel 18, 30–35).
38. Zellner, interview by author.
39. The Southern Conference Educational Fund (SCEF), created in 1946, was based in New Orleans. It became one of the most prominent civil rights organizations in the South. Journalists Anne and Carl Braden, who directed the organization beginning in the mid-1960s, developed close ties with SNCC workers.
40. "Prospectus for month of November—White Student Project" (Zellner papers, State Historical Society of Wisconsin, Madison, box 11, folder 59).
41. Ibid.
42. Ralph J. Gleason, *The San Francisco Sunday Chronicle*, 23 September 1962 (SNCC papers, reel 14, 826).
43. *The New York Times*, Sunday, 2 December 1962 (SNCC papers, reel 14, 827).
44. Jim Brown, Ginger Brown, Harold Leventhal, and George Stoney, *We Shall Overcome*, video cassette recording, (San Francisco: California Newsreel, 1989).
45. *The Student Voice*, 19 December 1962, 2. Initially, the group consisted of Cordell Reagon, Bertha Goeber, Bernice Johnson, Dorothy Vils, Rutha Harris, Charles Sherrod, Bernard Lafayette, and Charles Neblett.
46. Ibid., 3.
47. SNCC Freedom Singers (SNCC papers, reel 24, 670).
48. Brown.
49. "Gospel for Freedom Festival program," (Vertical file, State Historical Society of Wisconsin, Madison, Box 47).
50. Forman, 293.
51. Ibid., 294.
52. Letter from James Forman to Mike Nichols, 14 February 1963 (SNCC papers, reel 5, 883).
53. Letter to Chicago Friends of SNCC from Robert Moses, 27 February 1963 (SNCC papers, reel 24, 639).
54. Chicago Area Friends of SNCC Newsletter, 15 June 1963 (SNCC papers, reel 25, 3).
55. Forman, 304.
56. Ibid., 307
57. Letter from Carl Braden to Mary E. King, n.d. (Mary E. King papers, box 3, M82445), State Historical Society of Wisconsin, Madison).

58. Ibid. Braden acknowledged that these kinds of background reports not only served to educate editors, but also encouraged them to read SNCC news releases.
59. "Special Report: Selma, Alabama," 26 September 1963 (SNCC papers, reel 10, 3).
60. *The Student Voice*, April 1963, 4. The Lafayettes held bi-weekly literacy and voter registration classes in Selma, Alabama and traveled to outlying districts in Dallas and Wilcox counties.
61. Mary E. King, "Working Paper," 14 November 1963 (SNCC papers, Reel 3, 815).
62. Letter to Arnold Tovell from Howard Zinn, 17 September 1963 (Howard Zinn papers, box 1, folder 15, State Historical Society of Wisconsin, Madison).
63. Letter to "Louie" from Howard Zinn, 17 September 1963 (Howard Zinn papers, box 1, folder 15), State Historical Society of Wisconsin, Madison.
64. Forman, 347.
65. Ibid., 318.
66. "Ask yourself this important question: What have I personally done to Maintain Segregation?" SNCC flyer based on an advertisement appearing in the *Selma Times Journal*, 9 June 1963 (Howard Zinn papers), State Historical Society of Wisconsin, Madison.
67. Forman, 234.
68. Lewis, 234.
69. Ibid., 234–235.
70. Forman, 327.
71. Ibid., 328.
72. Lyon, 62.
73. Forman, 328.
74. Forman, 344.
75. Taylor Branch, *Parting the Waters, America in the King Years: 1954–1963* (New York: Simon and Schuster, 1988), 803–845.
76. Lewis, 232.
77. Ibid.
78. "News release," October, 1963 (SNCC papers, reel 10, 127).
79. Lewis, 238.
80. Ibid., 238.
81. Lyon, forward by Julian Bond.
82. Constance Curry, telephone interview by author, 23 June 2001.
83. Email interview, Joan Browning, 14 May 2001.

NOTES TO CHAPTER THREE

1. Charles Cobb, interview with John Rachal, 21 October 1996, University of Southern Mississippi Oral History Civil Rights Documentation Project.
2. Mary E. King, telephone interview by author, 16 February 2002, New Orleans and Washington, D.C.

3. Neil R. McMillen, "Black Enfranchisement in Mississippi: Federal Enforcement and Black Protest in the 1960s," *The Journal of Southern History*, 43(3), August 1977, 367. McMillen noted that of the 1,600 or so who successfully registered, most were from Panola County, which was under a federal court order. A COFO report described the order as "an extremely important Circuit Court decision in the spring of 1964 [that] ordered the registrar of Panola County to dispense with both the 'Constitutional Interpretation test' and the 'Duties of a Citizen' section of the form." (SNCC Papers, reel 64, 1198).

4. McMillen.

5. Susan M. Weill, "Mississippi's Daily Press in Three Crises," in *The Press and Race*, ed. David R. Davies (Jackson: University of Mississippi Press, 2001), 38–50.

6. Pi-Yun An, "Coverage of Freedom Summer in Gulf Coast Newspapers," unpublished paper presented at the Southeastern Regional Meeting of the American Journalism Historians Association, Panama City Beach, Fla., February 2001.

7. Austin Long-Scott, "From Then to Now, A Personal Essay on the Media, the Civil Rights Movement and the Aftermath," *The Caldwell Journals* (Oakland, Calif.: Robert C. Maynard Institute for Journalism Education)

8. Ira B. Harkey, Jr., *The Smell of Burning Crosses: An Autobiography of a Mississippi Newspaperman* (Jacksonville, Ill: Harris-Wolfe, 1967), 141.

9. Ralph McGill, "Race, Results Instead of Reasons," 9 January 1965, *The Saturday Review*, 52.

10. Jin Young Kim, "The Coverage of Freedom Summer by the *New York Times*," unpublished paper, June 2000, in author's possession.

11. Dorothy Miller Zellner, telephone interview by author, 5 May 2001, Hattiesburg, Miss., and New York City; Mary E. King, telephone interview.

12. King, *Freedom Song*, 232.

13. Fred Powledge, telephone interview by author, 16 June 2001.

14. "Report from Ben Grinage and Fay Bellamy," 6 March 1965 (SNCC papers, reel 3). Some examples: Howard Zinn, "Battle-scarred youngsters," 5 October 1963, *The Nation*, 193–197; Jerry DeMuth, "Black Belt Alabama," *Commonweal*, 7 August 1964, 536–39; Jerry DuMuth, "Violence in Alabama: The murders of Mrs. Viola Liuzzo and the Rev. James Reeb were part of a pattern that still persists in the most volatile state in the old Confederacy," *The New Republic*, June 1965, 7–10; Elizabeth Sutherland, "Mandate from History: Fourth Leadership Training Conference," *The Nation*, 6 January 1964, 30–33; Staughton Lynd, "Roots of Negro Militancy," *The New Republic*, 22 February 1965, 52; Howard Zinn, Negroes are Dragged off Federal Property as the FBI looks On," *The New Republic*. 26 October 1963.

15. Christopher Jencks, "Mississippi–I–When Law Collides with Custom," *The New Republic*, 25 July 1964, 15–17; "Mississippi–II–From Conversion to Coercion," *The New Republic*, 22 August 1964, 17–21.

16. Jencks, "Mississippi–II–From Conversion to Coercion," 19.

17. "Introduction to COFO Political Programs" (SNCC papers, reel 64, 1198).

18. Jencks, "Mississippi II–From Conversion to Coercion," 18.

19. "Introduction to COFO Political Programs."

20. On November 27, 1963, addressing the Congress and the nation for the first time as president, Johnson called for passage of the civil rights bill to remember Kennedy. "Let us continue," he declared, promising that "the ideas and the ideals which [Kennedy] so nobly represented must and will be translated into effective action." On February 10, 1964, the House of Representatives passed the measure by a 290–130 vote. The senate rule, however, had allowed southerners to mount a filibuster and kill civil rights legislation. In preparation, Johnson encouraged a massive lobbying campaign that encouraged senate passage that June.

21. Connie Field and Marilyn Mumford, *Freedom on My Mind,* (Berkeley, Calif.: Clarity Film, 1994), video cassette recording.

22. Ibid.

23. Mary King to Benjamin T. Spencer, 19 July 1964 (Mary King papers, State Historical Society of Wisconsin, Box 1, M12445).

24. John Lewis with Michael D'Orso, *Walking with the Wind: A Memoir of the Movement.* (New York, Simon & Schuster, 1998), 242–243.

25. Quoted in Cheryl Lynn Greenberg, ed., *A Circle of Trust: Remembering SNCC* (Rutgers: State University, 1998). 80.

26. John Biewen and Kate Cavett interview with Robert Moses, Minnesota Public Radio, "Oh Freedom Over Me," 2001.

27. Ibid.

28. Robert Moses, "Mississippi: 1961–1962," *Liberation,* January 1970 (14) 7.

29. Charles Cobb, interview with John Rachal.

30. Quoted in Curry, et. al., 355.

31. Lewis, 246

32. "Freedom Summer application" (SNCC papers, reel 12).

33. Letter from Mary King to Congressman Robert N.C. Nix, 19 May 1964 (SNCC papers, reel 13).

34. Memo from Mike Thelwell to Julian Bond, Mary King, and other press personnel, Spring 1964 (Howard Zinn papers, State Historical Society of Wisconsin, box 2, folder 6).

35. *The Student Voice,* 3 March 1964, 3.

36. *The Student Voice Special Issue,* Spring 1964, 1.

37. "SNCC Brochure. Available in special collection Mitchell Memorial Library Mississippi State University.

38. Unsigned letter to Bruce Hanson of the National Council of Churches, 18 May 1964 (SNCC papers, reel 13).

39. John Lewis, Text of speech presented to the American Society of Newspaper Editors, Washington, D.C., 16 April 1964 (SNCC papers, reel 2, number 34).

40. "Statement of SNCC Chairman John Lewis, 12 June 1964: SNCC Shifts National Headquarters" (SNCC papers, reel 12, 36).

41. A 3 July 1964 list of "Communications People in Mississippi" included the following: Louise Mermey, Meridian; Zellner, Sayer, Garman, Greenwood; Dorothy Teal, Carthage; Mary McGroarty, Canton; Terry Shaw, Hattiesburg; Cathy Cade, Biloxi; Ron Ridenour, Pascagoula; Paul Cowan, Vicksburg; David Lorens, Columbus; Carl Young, Holly Springs; Dale

Gronemeier, Ruleville; John Sawyer, Greenville; Kathy Amatniak, Batesville; Yvonne Klein, Clarksdale; Willie McGee, Itta Bena; R. Hayes, Tchula; Lester McKinnie, Laurel, and Dennis Flannigan, Cleveland. (Mary King papers, State Historical Society of Wisconsin, Box 1, M82–445).

42. Initially, the sessions were to be in Berea, Kentucky, but Berea College backed out. The president of the National Council of Churches knew the president of Western College for Women in Oxford and helped SNCC leaders arrange the orientation, although some locals opposed the idea. See Richard Momeyer, former SNCC field secretary, personal interview, by Zeke Runyon, 8 May 2001. History in Oxford and Butler County, Ohio. An ongoing project for students of McGuffey Foundation School.
43. King, *Freedom Song*, 377.
44. Ibid., 379.
45. Ibid., 385.
46. Quoted in Curry, et. al.; *The Pascagoula Chronicle*, 25 June 1964, 1.
47. Congressional Record. Proceeding and debates of the 88th Congress, second session, Vol. 110, 22 July 1964, No. 140. Florence Mars, Witness in Philadelphia (Baton Rouge: Louisiana State University, 1977), 85.
48. Lewis, 246
49. Quoted in Greenberg, 64.
50. "Statement of SNCC Chairman John Lewis, 12 June 1964: SNCC Shift National Headquarters," (SNCC papers, reel 12, 36).
51. Field and Mumford.
52. WATS report, 27 June 1964 (SNCC papers, reel 15, 352).
53. Ibid.
54. Beyers.
55. Audio reports complemented written records. The communications office in Atlanta was capable of tape recording telephone reports, which were edited and fed to radio stations. The same system was used to file media reports directly from the field as well as from jails and picket lines. "SNCC Communication Manual" (SNCC papers, reel 10); Zellner.
56. Ibid.
57. "Mississippi Summer Project One Year Later," Southern Reporting Service News Release, 31 May 1965 (SNCC papers, reel 72, 414).
58. King, 390.
59. *Staff Newsletter*, 7 July 1964 (SNCC papers reel 15, 2).
60. Lewis, 246
61. Robert Beyers, telephone interview by author, 30 January 2000, Hattiesburg, Miss., and Oakland, Calif.
62. Ilene Strelitz, "Communications," n.d. (Mary King papers, State Historical Society of Wisconsin, box 1, M82–445).
63. Ibid.
64. *The Student Voice*, 12 August 1 964, 1.
65. King, 386.
66. Ibid.
67. Quoted in Greenberg, 80.

68. King also worked with John Lewis on a telegram that was sent to civil rights ally Walter Reuther of the United Auto Workers, urging him to use his influence to insist that the federal government provide protection to the volunteers. Reuther was specifically asked to "seek an audience with the President, the Justice Department, and other federal agencies to ask for stationing of [federal agents] and whatever other means are necessary to ensure that all Americans have equal value under the law." Quoted in King, 386.

69. "Rita Schwerner's statement to the press in Meridian," WATS Report, 24 June 1964 (SNCC papers, reel 15, 342).

70. "WATS Report from Rita Schwerner taken by Mary King," 25 June 1964 (SNCC papers, reel 15, 346).

71. King, 400–436.

72. WATS report, 24 June 1964 (SNCC papers, reel 15, 342), King, 389.

73. Quoted in Curry, et. al., 357–358.

74. "Communications manual," (SNCC papers, reel 10).

75. Ibid.

76. "List of press contacts to receive mailing of Mississippi Project communication," 31 August 1964 (SNCC papers, reel 13).

77. Memo to communications workers from Francis Mitchell and Mary King, 23 July 1964 (SNCC papers, reel 14, 840).

78. SNCC Communications Manual.

79. Beyers recalled how difficult it was to get big city news organizations to focus on the lives of native Mississippians. "The white volunteers were not the focus. I understood that. But there is no way to tell the New York press that they should focus on someone living in Hattiesburg. They just wouldn't do it." Beyers was one of many SNCC workers and volunteers who recognized how the press focused on the parents of the two white volunteers who were murdered while barely mentioning the mother of the local black victim. Beyers, telephone interview.

80. *Student Voice*, 19 August 1964, 3.

81. *The Student Voice*, 20 June 1964, 1 and 3.

82. *The Student Voice,* 28 April 1964, 2.

83. Ibid.

84. "Literature and material request form," (SNCC papers, reel 38).

85. Suckle (SNCC papers, reel 10).

86. "Staff newsletter," 7 July 1964 (SNCC paper reel 15, 2).

87. The Wide Area Telephone Service (WATS line) was a central resource for security and communications. In the Greenwood summer headquarters there was a national WATS line and a state line. There were other WATS lines in Atlanta and Jackson. All incidents were immediately reported via WATS to the FBI, the press, local movement leaders, and volunteer parents and contacts.

88. Staff newsletter.

89. *Legal Newsletter*, July 1964 (Mary King papers, State Historical Society of Wisconsin, Box 1, M82–45).

90. *Mississippi Project Parents Committee Newsletter*, 1 August 1964 (Carolyn Goodman papers, State Historical Society of Wisconsin, box 1).

91. *Princeton Freedom Center Newsletter*, January 1965 (SNCC papers, reel 34).

92. Letter to editors from communication staff, 15 July 1964 (Robert Beyers personal collection).

93. Ruth Clarke to Julian Bond, 7 June 1964 (SNCC papers, reel 10).

94. Publication list (SNCC papers, reel 72, 396).

95. SNCC news release, 27 June 1964 (SNCC papers, reel 38).

96. "Progress in Mississippi Depends on You: A contribution in any amount will help this project," (SNCC papers, reel 38).

97. An April 20 Associated Press story in the *Jackson Daily News* described lawmakers as "quietly arming the state for an expected invasion." Quoted in *The Student Voice*, 9 June 1964.

98. Ibid.

99. Kuettner, Al. *Kansas City Call*, 14 September 1964, State of Mississippi Sovereignty Commission Files. 2–166–3–21–1–1–1 Document Schwerner, Michael. Pages 1–1–1. Available at state archives in Jackson, Mississippi.

100. Ibid.

101. Ibid.

102. *The Student Voice*, 5 August 1964.

103. "Freedom Summer and violence," n.d. (SNCC papers, reel 56, 198).

104. "Mississippi Summer Project Fact Sheet," 1 August 1964 (Robert Beyers personal collection).

105. *The Student Voice*, 5 August 1964.

106. "Freedom Schools," (SNCC papers, reel 13).

107. "Morning Side Gardens Committee to Support the Mississippi Summer Project," (SNCC papers, reel 38).

108. Field and Mumford.

109. Dorothy Zellner, SNCC list serve posting, 29 June 2001.

110. Ibid.

111. Field and Mumford.

112. Quoted in Greenburg, *Circle of Trust*, 66.

113. Quoted in Fred Powledge, *Free at Last? The Civil Rights Movement and the People Who Made It* (New York: Harper, 1992), 597.

114. Edwin King Memoirs, pts. 4 and 12. Cited in Eric R. Burner, *And Gently He Shall Lead Them: Robert Parris Moses and Civil Rights in Mississippi* (New York: New York University, 1994).

115. Mendy Samstein Papers, 1963–1966, SC 3093 (Civil Rights Workers Miscellaneous Small Collections, State Historical Society of Wisconsin).

116. Quoted in Greenburg, *Circle of Trust*, 80–81.

NOTES TO CHAPTER FOUR

1. Roy Wilkins, president of the NAACP, "Meet the Press," transcript 21, televised August 1966 (SNCC papers, reel 2, 71).

2. After Carmichael's chairmanship, he continued to makes speeches denouncing the U.S. government. After returning from a trip to Cuba in

1967, his passport was confiscated and held for ten months. Once it was returned, he moved with his wife, Miriam Makeba, to Guinea, West Africa and wrote *Stokely Speaks: Black Power Back to Pan-Africanism* (1971). In Africa, Carmichael, adopted the name Kwame Ture in 1978 to honor Kwame Nkrumah and Ahmed Sekou Toure, two African socialist leaders. He helped build the All-African People's Revolutionary and advocated Pan-African ideology for the next thirty years. Party. Carmichael died of cancer in on 15 November 1998 in Conakry, Guinea.

3. Dorothy M. Zellner, telephone interview by author, tape recording, Hattiesburg, Miss., and New York City, 5 May 2001.

4. Carmichael first volunteered in the Youth Marches of 1958 under Bayard Rustin. In 1960, he joined the Nonviolent Action Group (NAG), the Washington, D.C.-based sit-in organization affiliated with Howard University. He was also a Freedom Rider during his college years.

5. Carmichael, a Howard University philosophy graduate who moved to New York City from Trinidad at the age of eleven and soon graduated from the prestigious Bronx High School of Science. After participating in the D.C.-based sit ins and Freedom Rides, he joined SNCC full-time during the 1964 Mississippi Freedom Summer and served as district director of the Second Congressional District in Greenwood.

6. Excerpted from Nina Simone's 1992 autobiography, *I Put a Spell on You*, written with Stephen Cleary, (DeCapo Press), in *The Guardian*, 23 April 2003, online version.

7. Introduction to article by Gordon Parks, "Whip of Black Power," *Life Magazine*, 19 May 1967, 76-A-78 (SNCC papers, reel 20, 873–878). Carmichael, who would later become a national symbol for SNCC and Black Power and who would appear in the mainstream press so frequently that his fellow workers sometimes referred to him as "Stokely Starmichael," recalled that when he first heard about the 1960 sit-ins, he believed the participants were a "bunch of publicity hounds." See previously cited Gordon Parks article.

8. Mary E. King, *Freedom Song: A Personal Story of the 1960s Civil Rights Movement*, (New York: William Morrow, 1987), 443.

9. Ibid., 446.

10. "SNCC Program for 1964," 23 Feb. 1965 (SNCC papers, reel 3, 403.)

11. Ibid.

12. "SNCC Program for 1964," 23 Feb. 1965 (SNCC papers, reel 3, 403).

13. Ibid.

14. For a brief history, see Dwight Cammeron and Tom Rieland, *The Lowndes County Freedom Organization,* 1992 (Tuscaloosa: The University of Alabama Center for Public Television and Radio), video recording.

15. "An Address by the President of the United States, 'We Shall Overcome . . .' Remarks of the President to a Joint Session of Congress, 15 March 1965." Published by the Industrial Union Department of the AFL-CIO, Washington, D.C (SNCC papers, reel 1, 1027).

16. King, 478–479.

17. Title 17, Section 337 of the Alabama Code made it legal to form a political party if its members (in this case, the LCFO) represented at least 20 percent of all eligible voters in the affected district. SNCC papers, reel 14, 419.
18. Jack Minnis, personal interview by author, 12 December 2002, tape recording, New Orleans.
19. Quoted in Greenberg, 108–109.
20. Quoted in Greenberg, 107–108.
21. SNCC papers, reel 18, 756.
22. SNCC papers, reel 14, 419
23. The Black Panther Party, formed in October 1966 in California, was not affiliated with the Lowndes County Freedom Organization. But because of the symbol's popularity, many people (including reporters) erroneously referred to the LCFO as the Black Panther Party. According to James Forman (*The Making of Black Revolutionaries*, 524), by January 1968 there were three different groups using the black panther symbol: the Black Panther Party for Self Defense (led by Bobby Seale and Huey Newton, which became known as the Black Panther Party), the Black Panther Party of Southern California, and the Black Panther Party of Northern California. Nevertheless, Forman, Carmichael, and H. "Rap" Brown, as well as others associated with SNCC, did hold positions in the Black Panther Party. In June, 1968 SNCC agreed to help build the Black Panther Party and formed a short-lived alliance with the California group.
24. Charles Cobb, SNCC listserve. 5 March 2002.
25. Quoted in Cammeron and Rieland.
26. Quoted in *Henry Hampton, Eyes on the Prize II, America at a Racial Crossroad, "Two Societies"* (Alexandria, Va.: Blackside, Inc., 1990).
27. Quoted in Hampton.
28. Quoted in Cammeron and Rieland.
29. Cammeron and Rieland.
30. "Lowndes County Alabama–Voter Education Program: A Proposal for Audio Visual Materials," n.d. (SNCC papers, reel 18, 694).
31. Quoted in Cammeron and Rieland.
32. Greenberg, 108–109.
33. "A Vote for the Lowndes County Freedom Organization . . . Is a Vote for Us," 1966, The Student Voice press, Atlanta (SNCC papers, reel 18, 739).
34. "Why Come Together," n.d. (SNCC papers, reel 18, 690).
35. SNCC papers, n.d., reel 18, 756.
36. SNCC papers, n.d., reel 18, 757.
37. "Is this the party you want?" n.d. (SNCC papers, reel 18, 759).
38. The LCFO offered a slate of qualified black candidates for the 1966 general election. A booklet published during the electoral campaign featured prominent photographs of the candidates next to comic strip illustrations explaining the role of each office. The candidates included Sidney Logan for sheriff, Alice Moore for tax assessor, Frank Miles for tax collector, Emory Ross for coroner, and Robert Logan, "Mr. Hinson," and "Mrs. Strickland" for school board positions. "Voting booklet," 1966, The Student Voice press (SNCC papers, reel 18, 765–778).

39. Flyer produced by Alabama SNCC, n.d., but likely produced in late 1965. The text states that candidates "must be put on the general election ballot next November" (SNCC papers, reel 18, 760).
40. Quoted in Hampton.
41. Quoted in Greenberg, 160–161.
42. Cleveland Sellers, *A River of No Return: The Autobiography of a Black Militant and the Life and Death of SNCC* (Jackson: University of Mississippi, 1990). 152–153.
43. SNCC organizers met in Nashville to elect officers in May 1966, the same time as the LCFO campaign. John Lewis won the election initially. But some powerful members of the group, including Jack Minnis, wanted a new organizational direction and believed that Carmichael could produce it. After most of the voting constituents had gone to bed believing that Lewis would remain as chair, Minnis pointed out a possible election error that reopened the nomination. Those remaining in attendance elected Carmichael. Lewis later recalled that Worth Long challenged the nomination saying that it violated the SNCC constitution. SNCC, however, did not have an approved constitution or by laws. See Lewis' *Walking with the Wind* and Carson's *In Struggle*.
44. Quoted in Hampton.
45. Ibid.
46. Ibid.
47. Quoted in King, 506.
48. Ibid.
49. Ibid.
50. Sellers, 168. Sellers also noted that the march enabled SNCC workers to form a "deep friendship" with Martin Luther King, Jr. and that he since believed King to be a "staunch ally and a true brother," 169.
51. Sellers, 183.
52. Quoted in Hampton.
53. "Face the Nation" as broadcast on the CBS Television Network and the CBS Radio Network, 19 June 1966 (SNCC papers, reel 2, 1152–1165).
54. King, 518.
55. Bond was elected in 1965 to a one-year term in the Georgia House of Representatives. House members, however, refused to seat him because of his public opposition to the Vietnam War. He won a second election in 1966, and was again denied membership. In November of 1966 he won a third election for a two-year term. This time the U.S. Supreme Court ruled that the Georgia House had denied him his rights, and he served his term. He was later elected to the Georgia Senate in 1975 and nominated for Vice President at the 1968 Democratic National Convention.
56. King, 508.
57. John Lewis, "Memo," December 1965 (SNCC papers, reel 2, 25).
58. "Black Power. Notes and comment."
59. Quoted in Hampton.
60. Stokely Carmichael and Charles Hamilton, *Black Power: The Politics of Liberation* (New York: Vintage), 1967, 1992.

61. "Interview with Stokely Carmichael, 'It's very simple: We intend to take over Lowndes County,'" *The Movement*, March 1966, published by the Student Nonviolent Coordinating Committee of California (SNCC papers, reel 56, 220).

62. "Black Power: Notes and Comment," The Student Nonviolent Coordinating Committee, Chicago, Illinois. Pamphlet containing transcript of speech by Stokely Carmichael delivered 28 July 1966, Chicago, Illinois (SNCC papers, reel 20, 859–863).

63. Fay D. Bellamy to the Editor of the *Herald-Dispatch*, Los Angeles, 24 May 1966 (SNCC papers, reel 2, 453).

64. Quoted in Sellers, 184.

65. Ibid.

66. "Report of the Communications Section of the Atlanta Office," (SNCC papers, reel 3, 482).

67. Sellers, 172.

68. Memo to "addressee" from the Alabama staff, 2 August 1966 (SNCC papers, reel 20, 831).

69. Gayraud Wilmore, Executive Commission on Race, New York; Isaiah Pogue, pastor, St. Mark's Presbyterian Church, Cleveland; Leroy Patrick, pastor, Bethesda United Presbyterian Church, Pittsburgh; Elder Hawkins, pastor, St. Augustine Presbyterian Church, New York; and Bryant George, staff, Board of National Missions, New York. Presbyterian delegation's report on Black Power, 1 August 1966 (SNCC papers, reel 20, 828–830)

70. Ibid.

71. Parks (a black writer who traveled with Carmichael for two months) wrote a favorable feature story, in which Carmichael was given a national forum for explaining Black Power.

72. Gordon Parks, "Whip of Black Power." *Life Magazine*, 1967, 76A (SNCC papers, reel 20, 873–878).

73. Robert Lewis Shayon, "The Real Stokely Carmichael," The Saturday Review, 9 July 1966 (SNCC papers, reel 20, 897).

74. Ibid.

75. "Summary of a statement by Stokely Carmichael, chairman of the Student Nonviolent Coordinating Committee, on the Civil Rights Bill of 1966, at a press conference in Washington, D.C.," 1 July 1966 (SNCC papers, reel 3, 68–69).

76. Reporters on the panel included Lawrence E. Spivak, permanent panel member of "Meet the Press"; Carl T. Rowan of the *Chicago Daily News*; James Kilpatrick of the *Richmond News Leader*; Rowland Evans of the Publishers Newspaper Syndicate, and Richard Valerriani of NBC News. Transcript of 21 August 1966 "Meet the Press" production, Merkle Press, Inc. (SNCC papers, reel 2, 1256–1274).

77. Many moderate black leaders publicly registered opposition to the Black Power philosophy. A. Philip Randolph, Bayard Rustin, Roy Wilkins, and Whitney Young, Jr., issued a 1966 manifesto entitled "Crisis and Commitment" that denounced Black Power. Martin Luther King, Jr. initially

opposed the strategy and even took out a full-page *New York Times* ad condemning the slogan just after the Meredith march. He did not sign the 1966 manifesto, but he gave signs of increasing support up until his death in 1968.

78. "Meet the Press," 26. By this time, the organization had been infiltrated with federal agents who were investigating the organization based on concerns that its leaders and workers had Communist interests. SNCC reports suggest that these infiltrators passed along information from private meetings to the mainstream press.

79. Ibid.

80. "Meet the press," 27.

81. Minnis.

82. Gregory Lewis, "60s Activists Look Back and Ahead," *The San Francisco Examiner*. "FBI-Freedom of Information Act–Student Nonviolent Coordinating Committee."

83. Zellner.

84. Zellner.

85. "Behind the hostile press campaign unleashed by the election of Stokely Carmichael: SNCC does not wish to become a new version of the white man's burden," *I.F. Stone's Weekly*, 6 June 1966 (SNCC papers, reel 20, 924)

86. Forman, 459.

NOTES TO CHAPTER FIVE

1. Memo to SNCC staff from Dona Richards regarding "A SNCC African Project," n.d., but most likely written in September of 1965, just before the establishment of the International Affairs Division (SNCC papers, reel 16, 385).

2. Participants included James Forman, John Lewis, Robert Moses, Dona Richards Moses, Prathia Hall, Julian Bond, Ruby Doris Robinson, Bill Hansen, Donald Harris, Mathew Jones, and Fannie Lou Hamer.

3. John Lewis and Donald Harris, "The Trip," 14 December 1964, 13. (SNCC papers, reel 1, 1045).

4. Lewis and Harris, "The Trip."

5. Memo to SNCC staff from Dona Richards regarding "A SNCC African Project."

6. Dona Richards to "SNCC People," 10 October 1965 (SNCC papers, reel 17).

7. Ibid.

8. To SNCC staff from Dona Richards, n.d., but Richards indicated the proposal was written in September 1967, (SNCC papers, reel 17, 384).

9. Petition of Africans (descendants of African Nationals) living in the United States of America, August 1967, (SNCC papers, reel 17, 380).

10. "SNCC Stand Presented by John Lewis," *The New York Post*, 3 June 1966.

11. Lewis resigned his post as Director of the International Affairs division and from the organization in August of 1966 after Merdith's March Against Fear and the consequent explosion of the Black Power philosophy; his post would remain empty until the following May, when James Forman was appointed as new Director. Forman's appointment marked a renewed interest in and a stronger commitment to establishing and maintaining international relationships. The SNCC New York office was chosen to serve as the division's headquarters, and four "desks" were established—one each for Africa, the Caribbean, Latin America, and Asia. Each desk created and distributed public relations material designed to bolster SNCC's international image. The African desk published the *African Alert*, a newsletter containing announcements of events and calls to action that was distributed to campus SNCC groups, and the *Afro-American Report*. A separate publication named the *Aframerican News Report*, edited by Fay Bellamy, contained longer and more detailed articles. "Campus program meeting," 16 February 1967 (SNCC papers, reel 3, 1096). Reference to Fay Bellamy's editorship found in "Student Voice Prospectus 1967," n.d. (SNCC papers, reel 3, 1115).

12. *The Student Voice*, 30 August 1965, 3.

13. William L. Chaze, "FDP Draft Dodging Investigation Set," *Jackson Clarion Ledger*, 1 August 1965.

14. MFDP and Vietnam," Mississippi Freedom Democratic Party press release, 31 July 1965 (Howard Zinn papers, State Historical Society of Wisconsin, box 3, folder 5).

15. "MFDP and Vietnam," Mississippi Freedom Democratic Party press release, 31 July 1965 (Howard Zinn papers, State Historical Society of Wisconsin, box 3, folder 5). According to a MFDP press release the leaflet was written in response to the death of John D. Shaw, a twenty-three-year-old McComb, Mississippi native and former civil rights activist who was killed in Vietnam.

16. The remaining points stated that no Mississippi blacks should be fighting in Vietnam until all blacks are free in the state; Mothers of draftees "should encourage their sons not to go; Mississippi blacks should force the government to "take our sons away" protecting themselves at home; and those blacks already in Vietnam should consider hunger strikes since such an effort had recently been successful for a New Jersey white soldier. See: Mississippi Freedom Democratic Party. "The War on Vietnam: A McComb Mississippi Protest." In Joanne Grant (ed.) *Black Protest: History, Documents, and Analyses, 1619 to the Present*. 2nd ed. (Greenwich, Connecticut: Fawcett, 1974), 415–416.

17. Quoted in Greenberg, Cheryl Lynn, ed. *A Circle of Trust: Remembering SNCC* (Rutgers: State University, 1998), 83.

18. Lewis, John with Michael D'Orso. *Walking with the Wind: A Memoir of the Movement* (New York: Simon & Schuster, 1998), 356.

19. Ibid.

20. Segrest was not indicted until November even though there were several witnesses to the killing. After Tuskegee Institute students organized a

protest march, Segrest was arrested and charged with murder. At the end of his trial in December, an all-white jury found Segrest not guilty.

21. News release issued from the SNCC Atlanta office, 4 January 1966 (SNCC papers, reel 14, 469).

22. Lewis, 358.

23. Ibid., 359.

24. "Statement by the Student Nonviolent Coordinating Committee on the War in Vietnam, 6 January 1966 (SNCC papers, reel 14, 472).

25. Lewis, 359. For details about the infiltration, see Carson, In Struggle. Over 2,800 pages of FBI reports are available online at the Freedom of Information Act homepage.

26. John Lewis, speech at memorial dinner of Council for American-Soviet Friendship, 26 January, 1966.

27. Lewis, 359.

28. Interview by Bob Hall and Sue Thrasher, "Julian Bond: The Movement, Then and Now," Southern Exposure, (3) 4, 1975, 11.

29. Ibid.

30. "Press Conference," 8 January 1965 (SNCC papers, reel 20, 959).

31. "Statement by Dr. Martin Luther King, Jr.," 12 January 1965 (SNCC papers, reel 20, 971).

32. Press Conference, 8 January 1965 (SNCC papers, reel 20, 959–963).

33. "Julian Bond," n.d. (SNCC papers, reel 24, 350).

34. Neary, 140. Bond was later elected to the Georgia Senate in 1975 and nominated for vice president at the 1968 Democratic National Convention. He eventually served four terms in the House and six terms in the Senate.

35. Henry Hampton, *Eyes on the Prize II: America at a Racial Crossroads, "Two Societies"* (Alexandria, Va.,: Blackside Inc. and the Corporation for Public Broadcasting, 1992).

36. Quoted in Greenberg, Cheryl Lynn, ed. *A Circle of Trust: Remembering SNCC* (Rutgers: State University, 1998), 165.

37. Forman, 481.

38. Forman, 481

39. Disputes between white police officers and blacks set off rioting in Newark, New Jersey for five days in July of 1967. Twenty-six people died and 1,500 were injured. The rioting spread to Detroit, where forty-three died and more than 2,000 were injured. Violence occurred in 128 cities that summer, resulting in approximately 80 casualties.

40. Forman, 486.

41. Ibid., 483.

42. SNCC press release containing the text of Forman's statement, 28 August 1967 (SNCC papers, reel 11, 352).

43. Ibid., 490.

44. Forman, 521.

45. "Joint Statement of the Student Nonviolent Coordinating Committee and the Movement for Puerto Rican Independence," 27 January 1967 (SNCC papers, reel 22, 348).

46. Forman, 492.

47. Ibid., 522.
48. William Mahoney, coordinator; Wilson Brown, printer; and Dena E. Malo-ney, secretary, "The Student Voice, Staff Meeting Report," n.d., but mentions 1967 (SNCC papers, reel 3, 1113–1114).
49. List of black publications (SNCC papers, reel 17, 318).
50. Forman, 497.
51. Ethel Minor, Report to Staff, 5 May 1967 (SNCC papers, reel 3, 1118).
52. Ethel Minor, SNCC Newsletter, 6 April 1967, 1, State Historical Society of Wisconsin, Madison (Howard Zinn papers, box 3, folder 3).
53. Ethel Minor, Report to Staff.
54. Notes from the Central Committee of SNCC, (SNCC papers, reel 3, 1277). By 1969, the group decided to give the records to the Martin Luther King Center in Atlanta whose officials promised security and granted the group rights to determine who might review the records
55. Criminal Disorder, 25 June 1969, 4013–14.
56. Forman, 473–474.
57. SNCC Newsletter, 6 April 1967, 4.
58. SNCC Newsletter, 6 April 1967, 2, State Historical Society of Wisconsin, Madison (Howard Zinn papers, box 3, folder 3).
59. Stokely Carmichael, speech at Spring Mobilization to end the war in Vietnam, 15 April 1967 (SNCC papers, reel 3, 57).
60. Ibid.
61. List of liberation publications (SNCC papers, reel 17, 318).
62. SNCC news release, 22 June 1967 (SNCC papers, reel 11, 349)
63. SNCC New York office news release, 18 August 1967 (SNCC papers, reel 11, 351).
64. Ibid
65. "Report from the Chairman," 5 May 1967 (SNCC papers, reel 2, 1129–1130).
66. Cited in Carson, 253. Brown in "We are Going to Build," *Movement*, June 1967, 1.
67. H. Rap Brown to "Dear Friends," n.d., but references August 1967 (SNCC papers, reel 3, 126).
68. Forman, 481.
69. Forman, 486.
70. "Statement on H. Rap Brown," n.d., (SNCC papers, reel 2, 1306).
71. Background, n.d., but mentions 18 September 1967, (SNCC papers, reel 3, 198).
72. Unsigned letter to Jean Wiley and Bob Smith, 13 October 1967, (SNCC papers, reel 2, 1044).
73. "Let Rap Rap," 21 February 1968, (SNCC papers, reel 11, 32).
74. "The History of Rap," (SNCC papers, reel 2, 1309).
75. Notes of the Central Committee of SNCC, Baltimore, Maryland, October (no year indicated officially, but 1968 is handwritten on front page), (SNCC papers, reel 3, 1276).
76. Ibid.

Bibliography

ARCHIVAL SOURCES

Alabama SNCC. 1965. Flier concerning LCFO election. (SNCC papers, reel 18, 760).

Alabama SNCC staff. Memorandum for "addressee." 2 August 1966. (SNCC papers, reel 20, 831).

An Address by the President of the United States, 'We Shall Overcome . . .'Remarks of the President to a Joint Session of Congress. 15 March 1965. Published by the Industrial Union Department of the AFL-CIO, Washington, D.C. (SNCC papers, reel 1, 1027).

At last, the paper you have been waiting for! What is the SNCC Research Department? 11, February 1965. (Mary E. King papers, State Historical Society of Wisconsin, Madison).

Ask yourself this important questions: What have I personally done to Maintain Segregation? SNCC flier based on advertisement appearing in the *Selma Times Journal*, 9 June 1963, (Howard Zinn papers), State Historical Society of Wisconsin, Madison.

Baker, Ella Jo to Anne Braden. 21 March 1960. (Martin Luther King, Jr., Center, Atlanta, Box 32). Cited in JoAnn Grant, *Ella Baker: Freedom Bound* (New York: John Wiley & Sons, 1998), 127.

Barry, Marion S. Jr., to field secretaries. n.d., (SNCC papers, reel 4, 924)

——— to Irving Dent. 11 August 1960. (SNCC papers, reel 4, 804).

——— to Richard M. Nixon. 18 August 1960. (SNCC papers, reel 1, 306).

——— and Claudia Rawles. 15 June 1963. Executive Committee Meeting. (SNCC papers, reel 3, 814).

Behind the hostile press campaign unleashed by the election of Stokely Carmichael: SNCC does not wish to become a new version of the white man's burden. 6 June 1966. *I.F. Stone's Weekly*. (SNCC papers, reel 20, 924).

Bellamy, Fay and Grinage, Ben. Report, 6 March 1965. Student Nonviolent Coordinating Committee Papers, 1959–1970, (Ann Arbor, MI: UMI, 1994). Available at the University of Southern Mississippi Library Cook Library, Hattiesburg, reel 10. Hereinafter "SNCC Papers."Reel 3.

———. The Press and Stokely Carmichael: A Little Ole Report by Fay D. Bellamy. n.d. (SNCC papers, reel 11, 312).

——— to the Editor of the *Herald-Dispatch*, Los Angeles. 24 May 1966. (SNCC papers, reel 2, 453).

———. 6 March 1965. (SNCC papers, reel 3).

Bennett, Lerone Jr. Stokely Carmichael: Architect of Black Power. July 1966. *Ebony*, 55–66.

Black Power with a Red Base. 12 September 1966. (SNCC papers, reel 7, 203).

Black Power: Notes and comment. The Student Nonviolent Coordinating Committee, Chicago, Illinois. 28 July 1966. (SNCC papers, reel 20, 859–863).

Bond, Julian to Anne Braden. 21 May 1962. (SNCC papers, reel 5, 663).

——— to reporters. 19 April 1962. (SNCC papers, reel 11, 701).

———. SNCC: What We Did. October 2000, Vol. 53, Issue 5, 14–29. *Monthly Review: An Independent Socialist Magazine*.

Braden, Anne to Charles McDew. 24 June, 1962.

——— to Mary E. King. n.d. (Mary E. King papers, box 3, M82445), State Historical Society of Wisconsin, Madison.

——— to Student Nonviolent Coordinating Committee. 31 October 1960. (SNCC papers, reel 4, 1090).

Campus program meeting. 16 February 1967. (SNCC papers, reel 3, 1096

Carmichael, Stokely to "dear friend." Fund raising letter. n.d. (SNCC papers, reel 2, 115).

———. Power and Racism. 1966. Exerpts reprinted from *The New York Review of Books*, (SNCC papers, reel 2, 106).

———. Summary of a statement regarding the Civil Rights Bill of 1966. 1 July 1966. (SNCC papers, reel 3, 68–69).

———. 15 April 1967. Speech at Spring Mobilization to end the war in Vietnam. (SNCC papers, reel 3, 57).

———. Who is Qualified? 8 January 1966. *The New Republic*, 19–22.

———. "Power and Racism," *The New York Review of Books*, 1966. (SNCC papers, reel 2, page 106).

———. What We Want. 22 September 1966. *The New York Review of Books*.

Clarke, Ruth to Julian Bond. 7 June 1964. (SNCC papers, reel 10).

Cobb, Charles. Towards a Theory for Communications. n.d. (SNCC papers, reel 11, 320).

Colley, John. Reporting for Workout Group #10, Raleigh, N.C.," 16 April 1960. (SNCC papers, reel 1, 1).

Congressional Record. Proceedings and debates of the 88th Congress, second session, Vol. 110, 22, No. 140. July 1964.

Dressler, Len. 31 July 1964. (SNCC papers, reel 10).

DeMuth, Jerry. Interview with Mrs. Aaron Henry. 2 August 1964, (Jerry DeMuth papers, State Historical Society of Wisconsin, Madison).

———. Violence in Alabama: The murders of Mrs. Viola Liuzzo and the Rev. James Reeb were part of a pattern that still persists in the most volatile state in the old Confederacy. June 1965, 7–10. *The New Republic*,

Explanation of Current Needs. 15 July 1963. (SNCC papers, reel 24, 642).

Face the Nation as broadcast on the CBS Television Network and the CBS Radio Network. 19 June 1966. (SNCC papers, reel 2, 1152–1165).

Financial Report: October 16 through November 22, 1960. 25 November 1960. (SNCC papers, reel 1, 195).

Forman, James to Mike Nichols. 14 February 1963. (SNCC papers, reel 5, 883).

——— to Madeline Cass. 21 November 1961. (SNCC papers, reel 10, 92).

Forman, Mim to Harry Belafonte. 27 May 1964. (SNCC papers, reel 38, 87).

Freedom Summer application. (SNCC papers, reel 12).

Freedom Summer and violence. n.d. (SNCC papers, reel 56, 198).

Friends of SNCC Groups. March 1965. (SNCC papers, reel 56, 357).

Fund Raising. 31 March 1962. (SNCC papers, reel 10, 356).

Fundraising flier from the Riverside Democrats, Inc., New York, New York. n.d., (Poor People's Corporation Papers, State Historical Society of Wisconsin, Madison, MSS, 72, Box 1).

Bruce Galphin. July 1967. Learning from SNCC, Reprint from *Atlanta Constitution* editorial page. Aframerican News Service. (SNCC papers, reel 17, 236).

Gleason, Ralph J. *The San Francisco Sunday Chronicle*, 23 September 1962. (SNCC papers, reel 14, 826).

Gospel for Freedom Festival program. n.d. (Vertical file, State Historical Society of Wisconsin, Madison, Box 47).

Hayden, Casey to Howard Zinn. 11 September 1963. (Howard Zinn papers, box 2, folder 11), State Historical Society of Wisconsin, Madison.

International Affairs Statement, Working Paper—SNCC History, n.d, but mentions June 1968 reorganization. (SNCC papers, reel 11, 339).

Inter-Staff Newsletter. 1 December 1962. (SNCC papers, reel 18, 30–35).

Interview with Stokely Carmichael, "It's very simple: We intend to take over Lowndes County." *The Movement*. March 1966. published by the Student Nonviolent Coordinating Committee of California. (SNCC papers, reel 56, 220).

Introduction to COFO Political Programs. n.d. (SNCC papers, reel 64, 1198).

Is this the party you want? n.d., (SNCC papers, reel 18, 759).

Jackson, James E. One Nobel Youth and Two Old Men. 16 January 1966. *The Worker* 209. (SNCC papers, reel 1).

Job descriptions. n.d. (Howard Zinn papers, State Historical Society of Wisconsin, Madison, box 2, folder 11).

John Lewis biography. SNCC Communication Manual, n.d. (SNCC papers, reel 10).

Joint Statement of the Student Nonviolent Coordinating Committee and the Movement for Puerto Rican Independence. 27 January 1967. (SNCC papers, reel 22, 348).

King, Edward B. to Jane Stembridge, Dated 7 June 1960, but most likely written 7 July 1960 based on dates appearing within the text. (SNCC papers, reel 4, 954–955).

King, Mary. WATS Report from Rita Schwerner. 25 June 1964. (SNCC papers, reel 15, 346).

———— and Mitchell, Francis. Memo to communications workers. 23 July 1964, (SNCC papers, reel 14, 840).

———— to Benjamin T. Spencer. 19 July 1964. (Mary King papers, State Historical Society of Wisconsin, Box 1, M12445).

———— to "Poppa." 21 June 1967. (Mary King papers, State Historical Society of Wisconsin, Madison, Box 3, M82445).

———— to Congressman Robert N.C. Nix. 19 May 1964. (SNCC papers, reel 13).

————. 14 November 1963. Working Paper. (SNCC papers, Reel 3, 815).

Komisar, Luch. Southern Idea: Poor People's Corporation Lets the Poor Speak Out, 22 July 1965. *The Village Voice.*

Kuettner, Al. *Kansas City Call.* 14 September 1964, State of Mississippi Sovereignty Commission Files. 2–166–3–21–1–1–1 Document Schwerner, Michael. Pages 1–1-1. Available at state archives in Jackson, Mississippi.

Leaders Call for Mass Action to Support Bond. SNCC press release. 11 January 1966. (SNCC papers, reel 14, 477).

Legal Newsletter. July 1964. (Mary King papers, State Historical Society of Wisconsin, Box 1, M82–45).

Lehac, Jane and Ned to Stokely Carmichael. 1 October 1966. (SNCC papers, reel 2, 221).

Letter to editors from communication staff. 15 July 1964. (Robert Beyers personal collection).

Lewis John to George Love. 28 July 1965. (SNCC papers, reel 1, 826).

————. 16 April 1964. Text of speech presented to the American Society of Newspaper Editors, Washington, D.C. (SNCC papers, reel 2, number 34).

————. 12 June 1964. Statement of SNCC Chairman: SNCC Shift National Headquarters. (SNCC papers, reel 12, 36).

————. SNCC Programs: A Report for 1965. November 1965. (SNCC papers, reel 1, 1155).

————. Memo to SNCC staff. 7 December 1965. (SNCC papers, reel 2, 25)

————. Statement on 1966. 30 December 1965. (SNCC papers, reel 1, 1163).

————. 26 January, 1966. Speech a memorial dinner of Council for American-Soviet Friendship.

———— and Donald Harris.14 December 1964. The Trip. (SNCC papers, reel 1, 1045).

List of black publications. n.d. (SNCC papers, reel 17, 318)

List of liberation publications. n.d. (SNCC papers, reel 17, 318).

List of press contacts to receive mailing of Mississippi Project communication. 31 August 1964. (SNCC papers, reel 13).

Literature and material request form. n.d. (SNCC papers, reel 38).

Lowndes County Alabama–Voter Education Program: A Proposal for Audio Visual Materials. n.d. (SNCC papers, reel 18, 694).

Mahoney, William. n.d., but mentions 1967. *The Student Voice*, Staff Meeting Report. (SNCC papers, reel 3, 1113–1114).

Meet the Press. August 1966. Transcript 21. (SNCC papers, reel 2, 71).

A Message from Chairman H. Rap Brown. 28 August 1967. (SNCC papers, reel 11, 31).

MFDP and Vietnam. Mississippi Freedom Democratic Party press release. 31 July 1965. (Howard Zinn papers, State Historical Society of Wisconsin, box 3, folder 5).

Minor, Ethel. Report to Staff. 5 May 1967. (SNCC papers, reel 3, 1118–1119).

———. Special Notice to Aframerican News Service Contacts. n.d. (SNCC papers, reel 17, 308).

Mississippi Project Parents Committee Newsletter. 1 August 1964. (Carolyn Goodman papers, State Historical Society of Wisconsin, box 1).

Mississippi Summer Project Fact Sheet. 1 August 1964. (Robert Beyers personal collection).

Mississippi Summer Project One Year Later, Southern Reporting Service News Release. 31 May 1965. (SNCC papers, reel 72, 414).

Morning Side Gardens Committee to Support the Mississippi Summer Project. n.d. (SNCC papers, reel 38).

Moses, Robert. Mississippi: 1961–1962. January 1970, *Liberation*, (14) 7. This newsletter appears to be strongly associated with SNCC and is available in the special collections of the Mississippi State University Library.

New York SNCC news release. 18 August 1967. (SNCC papers, reel 11, 351).

The New York Times, Sunday, 2 December 1962. (SNCC papers, reel 14, 827).

News of the Field, #1. 23 February 1966. (SNCC papers, reel 56, 242)

News from the Student Nonviolent Coordinating Committee. n.d. (SNCC papers, reel 4, 964).

Parks, Gordon. "Whip of Black Power," *Life Magazine*, n.d, but mentions Carmichael's fall 1966 resignation of the chairmanship, 76A. (SNCC papers, reel 20, 873–878).

Pauley, Francis. Report from Albany: Program Highlights of the Georgia Council on Human Relations. December 1961. (Howard Zinn papers, box 1, folder 3, State Historical Society of Wisconsin, Madison).

Poor People's Corporation Newsletter, Jackson, Mississippi. n.d. (Poor People's Corporation Papers, State Historic Society of Wisconsin, Madison, MSS, 72, Box 1).

Press Conference. 8 January 1965. (SNCC papers, reel 20, 959).

Press information, SNCC conference. November 29-December 1, 1963. (SNCC papers, reel 56, 497).

Princeton Freedom Center Newsletter. January 1965. (SNCC papers, reel 34).

A program for the Student Voice, Inc. n.d. (SNCC papers, reel 10, 169).

Progress in Mississippi Depends on You: A contribution in any amount will help this project. n.d. (SNCC papers, reel 38).

Prospectus for month of November–White Student Project. Zellner papers, State Historical Society of Wisconsin, Madison, box 11, folder 59.

Proposal by the Student Nonviolent Coordinating Committee. n.d. (Personal collection of Joan C. Browning).

Prospectus for Research Workshop. 12 April 1965, (SNCC papers, reel 16, 25).

Public Relations Report: June 13-July 31, 1960: Submitted August 5. (SNCC papers, reel 1, 327).

Publication list. n.d. (SNCC papers, reel 72, 396).

Recommendations of the Findings and Recommendations Committee. (SNCC papers, reel 1, 11).

Recommendations of the Temporary Student Nonviolent Coordinating Committee. 14–16 October 1960. (SNCC papers, reel 1, 65).

Recommendations Passed by the SNCC Conference Atlanta, Georgia. 14–16 October 1960. (SNCC papers, reel 1, 67).

Reese, Andrew J. Jr. Jackson Pupils Register Today. 20 August 1964, *Jackson Clarion-Ledger*, United Press International.

Report from the Chairman. 5 May 1967. (SNCC papers, reel 2, 1129–1130).

Report from the Committee on the Appeal for Human Rights. n.d. (SNCC papers, reel 4, 966)

Report of the Communications Section of the Atlanta Office. 1 August 1966. (SNCC papers, reel 3, 481–483).

Report on the publication of the first newsletter. June 1960, (SNCC papers, reel 1, 237).

Report on SNCC history, n.d., but mentions May 1967 and Brown's acceptance speech. (SNCC papers reel 11, 333).

Report on the Summer—Washington Office. 7 September 1964. (SNCC papers, reel 38).

Resume of the May and June Meeting reel of the Student Nonviolent Coordinating Committee. 1960. (SNCC papers, reel 1, 197).

Richards, Dona. Memo to SNCC staff regarding "A SNCC African Project," n.d., but author mentions that report was written in September, most likely 1965, just before the establishment of the International Affairs Division. (SNCC papers, reel 16, 385).

——— to "SNCC People." 10 October 1965. (SNCC papers, reel 17).

Roberts, Gordon. New Protest Set in Tense Albany. 14 December 1961, 1 *The Atlanta Journal*.

Schwerner, Rita. Statement to the press in Meridian. WATS Report, 24 June 1964. (SNCC papers, reel 15, 342).

Series of letters to SNCC leaders in Southern States. 16 June 1960. (SNCC papers, reel 1, 22).

Shayon, Robert Lewis. The Real Stokely Carmichael. 9 July 1966, *The Saturday Review*. (SNCC papers, reel 20, 897).

The Sleep and the Fearful, authored by "a housewife here in Albany." n.d. (Personal collection of Joan C. Browning).

Smith, Ruby Doris to Barbara Mohn. 20 December 1962. (SNCC papers, reel 25, 580).

——— to Sam Ellenport. 20 December 1962. (SNCC papers, reel 25, 600).

SNCC Announces an Opening. n.d. (Social action vertical file, Box 47, Wisconsin State Archives, Madison).

SNCC brochure. 1963. Special collections of the Mississippi State University Library, Starkville.

SNCC Chamber Concert Series. n.d. (SNCC papers, reel 24, 343).

SNCC Communication manual. (SNCC papers, reel 10).

SNCC field work at large: The Freedom Singers. n.d. (SNCC papers, reel 10).

SNCC to the editors of the *Atlanta Journal*. Regarding a 10 August 1960 article entitled "Brilliant Tactics," n.d. (SNCC papers, reel 1, 304).

SNCC to Roy V. Harris, editor of the *Augusta Courier*. 16 August 1960. (SNCC papers, reel 1, 306).

SNCC does not Wish to Become a New Version of the White Man's Burden. n.d. (SNCC papers, reel 17, 222).

SNCC Newsletter. 6 April 1967. State Historical Society of Wisconsin, Madison, (Howard Zinn papers, box 3, folder 3).

SNCC News Release. 2 December 1961. (Howard Zinn papers, box 1, folder 3, State Historical Society of Wisconsin).

SNCC News Release. 7 February 1962. (SNCC papers, reel 14, 654).

SNCC Press Release. 28 August 1967. (SNCC papers, reel 11, 352).

SNCC Programs for 1964. 23 February 1965. (SNCC papers, reel 3, 403).

SNCC Research Department. 11 February 1965. (Mary King papers, State Historical Society of Wisconsin, Madison, Box 1, M82–445).

SNCC Press Release. 22 June 1967. (SNCC papers, reel 11, 349).

SNCC Stand Presented by John Lewis. 3 June 1966. *The New York Post.*

Special Report: Selma, Alabama. 26 September 1963. (SNCC papers, reel 10, 3).

Staff Newsletter. 17 July 1965. (SNCC papers, reel 15, 31).

Staff Newsletter. 7 July 1964. (SNCC paper reel 15, 2).

Statement by Julian Bond to radio station WAOK. 8 January 1965. (SNCC papers, reel 20, 1066).

Statement by Dr. Martin Luther King, Jr., 12 January 1965. (SNCC papers, reel 20, 971).

Statement Submitted by the Student Nonviolent Coordinating Committee to the Platform Committee of the National Democratic Convention. July 7, 1960. (SNCC papers, reel 13).

Statement by the Student Nonviolent Coordinating Committee on the War in Vietnam. 6 January 1966. (SNCC papers, reel 14, 472).

Statement from SNCC in Support of Bond. 11 January 1965. (SNCC papers, reel 20, 971).

Strelitz, Ilene. Communications. n.d. (Mary King papers, State Historical Society of Wisconsin, box 1, M82–445).

Stembridge, Jane to David Forbes. 14 April 1960. (SNCC papers, Reel 4, 810).

———— to Bob Moses. 25 August 1960. (SNCC papers, reel 4, 835).

———— to "Jim." 1 February 1961. (SNCC papers, reel 4, 869).

———— to Dick Ramsey. 20 July, 1960. (SNCC papers, reel 4, 104).

———— to Amzie Moore. 15 August 1960. (SNCC papers, reel 4, 811).

———— to David Forbes. 14 August 1960. (SNCC papers, reel 4, 810).

The Student Voice, Albany, Georgia. 1 December 1961. (Howard Zinn papers, Wisconsin State Historical Society, box 1, folder 3).

The Student Nonviolent Coordinating Committee to "Congressmen." 3 August 1960. (SNCC papers, reel 4, 291).

Suckle, Mark to James Forman. 12 March 1964. (SNCC papers, reel 10, 165).

Thelwell, Mike to Elizabeth Sutherland. n.d. (SNCC papers, reel 3, 976)
————. Memo to Julian Bond, Mary King, and other press personnel. Spring 1964.
    (Howard Zinn papers, State Historical Society of Wisconsin, box 2, folder 6).
Unsigned letter to Bruce Hanson of the National Council of Churches. 18 May
    1964. (SNCC papers, reel 13).
Unsigned letter to Roy V. Harris. 16 August 1960. (SNCC papers, reel 1, 306).
Unsigned letter to Jane Stembridge from "Field Representative Bob." n.d. (SNCC
    papers, reel 4, 833).
Unsigned letter to Howard Zinn. 11 September 1963. (SNCC papers, reel 11, 2).
A Vote for the Lowndes County Freedom Organization . . . Is a Vote for Us. 1966.
    The Student Voice press, Atlanta. (SNCC papers, reel 18, 739).
Voting booklet. 1966. (SNCC papers, reel 18, 765–778).
WATS report. 24 June 1964. (SNCC papers, reel 15, 342).
Why Come Together. n.d. (SNCC papers, reel 18, 690).
Gayraud Wilmore, et.al. August 1966. Presbyterian delegation's report on Black
    Power, 1 August 1966. (SNCC papers, reel 20, 828–830).
Zellner, Dorothy Miller to the Atlanta police chief. 18 October 1962. (SNCC
    papers, reel 10, 163).
Zinn. Howard to Arnold Tovell. 17 September 1963. (Howard Zinn papers, box 1,
    folder 15), State Historical Society of Wisconsin, Madison.
———— to "Louie." 17 September 1963. (Howard Zinn papers, box 1, folder 15),
    State Historical Society of Wisconsin, Madison.

BOOKS

Belfrage, Sally. *Freedom Summer.* Carter G. Woodson Institute for Black Studies,
    University of Virginia, Charlottesville, 1990.
Bernays, Edward. *Propaganda.* New York: Liveright, 1928.
————. *Biography of an idea: Memoirs of Public Relations Counsel Edward L.
    Bernays.* New York: Simon and Schuster, 1964.
Burner, Eric R. *And Gently He Shall Lead Them: Robert Parris Moses and Civil
    Rights in Mississippi.* New York: New York University, 1994.
Carson, Clayborne. *In Struggle: SNCC and the Black Awakening of the 1960s.*
    Cambridge: Harvard University, 1981.
————, ed., *The Student Voice, 1960–1965: Periodical of the Student Nonviolent
    Coordinating Committee.* Compiled by the staff of the Martin Luther King,
    Jr., Papers Project.(Westpoint, Conn.: Meckler, 1990.
————. with David J. Garrow, Gerald Gill, Vincent Harding, and Darlene Clark
    Hine, *eds., The Eyes on the Prize Civil Rights Reader: Documents, Speeches,
    and Firsthand Accounts for the Black Freedom Stuggle.* New York: Pen-
    guine, 1991.
Chesler, Ellen. *Woman of Valor: Margaret Sanger and the Birth Control Movement
    in America.* New York: Simon and Schuster, 1992.
Cutlip, Scott M. and Allen H. Center. *Effective Public Relations.* Upper Saddle
    River, NJ: Prentice Hall, 1994.
Daniel, W. H. Daniels. *The Temperance Reform and its Great Reformers: An Illus-
    trated History.* New York: Nelson & Phillips, 1878.

Endres, Kathleen L. and Therese L. Lueck, eds. *Women's Periodicals in the United States: Social and Political Issues*. Westport, Conn.: Greenwood Press, 1996.

Fleming, Cynthia Griggs. *Soon we will not Cry: The Liberation of Ruby Doris Smith Robinson*. Lanham, Maryland: Rowman & Littlefield, 1998.

Forman, James. *The Making of Black Revolutionaries*. Seattle, University of Washington, 1985.

Furnas, J.C. *The Life and Time of the Late Demon Rum*. New York: G.P. Putman and Sons, 1965.

Grant, Joanne. *Ella Baker: Freedom Bound*. New York: John Wiley & Sons, 1998.

Greenberg, Cheryl Lynn, ed. *A Circle of Trust: Remembering SNCC*. Rutgers: State University, 1998.

Grunig, James E. *Excellence in Public Relations and Communication Management*. Hillsdale, NJ: Lawrence Erlbaum, 1992.

Halberstam, David. *The Children*. New York: Fawcett, 1999.

Hampton, Henry with Steve Fayer with Sarah Flynn. *Voice of Freedom: An Oral History of the Civil Rights Movement from the 1950s through the 1980s*. New York: Bantam, 1990.

Kerr, Austin K. *Organized for Prohibition: A New History of the Anti-Saloon League*. New Haven: Yale University, 1985.

King, Mary E. *Freedom Song: A Personal Story of the 1960s Civil Rights Movement*. New York: William Morrow, 1987.

Lewis, John with Michael D'Orso. *Walking with the Wind: A Memoir of the Movement*. New York: Simon & Schuster, 1998.

Lyon, Danny. *Memories of the Southern Civil Rights Movement*. The University of North Carolina, Chapel Hill, 1992.

McAdam, Doug. *Freedom Summer*. New York: Oxford University, 1988.

Moody, Anne. *Coming of Age in Mississippi*. New York: Dell, 1968.

Neary, John. *Julian Bond: Black Rebel*. New York: William Morrow, 1971.

Oppenheimer, Martin. *The Sit In Movement of 1960*, (Brooklyn, Carlson: 1989), 90–93.

Powledge, Fred. *Free at Last? The Civil Rights Movement and the People who Made It*. Boston: Little, Brown and Company, 1991.

Rose, Thomas John Greenya. *Black Leaders: Then and Now. A Personal History of Students who Led the Civil Rights Movement in the 1960's—And What Happened to Them*. Garrett Park, Maryland, Garrett Park, 1984.

Schultz, Debra L. *Going South: Jewish Women in the Civil Rights Movement*. New York: New York University, 2001.

Sellers, Cleveland. *The River of no Return: The Autobiography of a Black Militant and the Life and Death of SNCC*. Jackson.: University of Mississippi, 1990.

Sharp, Gene. *The Politics of Nonviolent Action*, Vol. 2. Boston: Porter Sargent, 1973.

Stoper, Emily. *The Student Nonviolent Coordinating Committee: The Growth of Radicalism in a Civil Rights Organization*. Brooklyn: Carlson Publishing, 1989.

The Student Nonviolent Coordinating Committee Papers, 1959–1972: A Guide to the Microfilm Edition, (Ann Arbor, Michigan, UMI, 1994).

Thompson, Mark, *Long Road to Freedom: The Advocate History of the Gay and Lesbian Movement* (New York: St. Martin, 1994)

Weiss, Andrea and Edwin Emery. *Before Stonewall: The Making of a Gay and Lesbian Community*. Tallahassee, Fla.: Naiad Press, 1992.

Zinn, Howard. *SNCC: The New Abolitionist*. Boston: Beacon , 1965.

SCHOLARLY ARTICLES

Burt, Elizabeth V. "Journalism of the Suffrage Movement: 25 Years of Recent Scholarship." *American Journalism (*Winter 2000): 73–86.

Hall, Bob and Sue Thrasher. "Julian Bond: The Movement, Then and Now." *Southern Exposure,* (3)4, 1975, 10.

Hon, Linda Childers "'To Redeem the Soul of America:' " Public Relations and the Civil Rights Movement." *Journal of Public Relations Research* 9 (3), 1997: 163–212.

Kern-Foxworth, Marilyn. "Martin Luther King Jr.: Minister, Civil Rights Activist, and Public Opinion Leader." *Public Relations Review* 18 (Fall 1992): 287–296.

McMillan, David W. "Sense of Community." *Journal of Community Psychology*, 24(4), 1996, p. 315.

McMillen, Neil R. "Black Enfranchisement in Mississippi: Federal Enforcement and Black Protest in the 1960s." *The Journal of Southern History*, 43(3), August 1977.

Stoper, Emily. "The Student Nonviolent Coordinating Committee: Rise and Fall of a Redemptive Organization," *Journal of Black Studies*, 8 (September 1977), 13–34.

INTERNET SOURCES

Julian Bond, "Civil Rights: Now and Then," Speech presented to the National Press Club, 29 May 1998.

James Forman, 25 April 2001, (SNCC listserve).

Biewen John and Kate Cavett. Interview with Robert Moses, Minnesota Public Radio, "Oh Freedom Over Me," 1994.

———. Interview with Betty Garman Robinson, Minnesota Public Radio, Oh Freedom Over Me, 1994.

Dorothy Zellner, SNCC listserve posting, 29 June 2001.

FBI-Freedom of Information Act–Student Nonviolent Coordinating Committee.

AUTHOR INTERVIEWS

Beyers, Robert. Telephone interview by author, 30 January 2000, Hattiesburg, Miss., and Oakland, Calif.

Bond, Julian. Email interview by the author, 13 May 2001.

Browning, Joan. Telephone interview by author, tape recording, 20 April 2001, Ronceverte, West Virginia and Hattiesburg, Mississippi.

———. Email interview with the author, 14 May 2001.

Currie, Constance. Telephone interview by author, 23 June 2001, Hattiesburg, Miss., and Atlanta.

Lyon, Danny. Email interview with the author, 12 May 2001.

Minnis, Jack. Personal interview with author, New Orleans, Louisiana, 12 December 2001.

Stembridge, Jane. Telephone interview by author, Hattiesburg, Miss., and Arden, N.C., 18 May 2001.

Zellner, Dorothy Miller. Telephone interview by author, Hattiesburg, Miss. and New York, 5 May 2001.

ORAL HISTORIES

Cobb, Charles. Interview with John Rachal. 21 October 1996. The University of Southern Mississippi Oral History Civil Rights Documentation Project.

Hamer, Fannie Lou. Interview with Neill R. McMillan on 14 July 1972. The University of Southern Mississippi Oral History Civil Rights Documentation Project.

NONPUBLISHED DISSERTATION

McBride, Genevieve Gardner. *No "Season of Silence": Uses of Public Relations in Nineteenth and Early Twentieth Century Reform Movements in Wisconsin.* (Unpublished doctoral dissertation, The University of Wisconsin, 1989), 18.

DOCUMENTARIES

Field, Connie and Marilyn Mumford. *Freedom on my Mind,* 1994 (Berkeley: Clarity Films).

Hampton, Henry. *Eyes on the Prize: America's Civil Rights Years, 1954–1965,* 1987 (Alexandria, Va: Blackside Inc., and the Corporation for Public Broadcasting).

———. Eyes on the Prize II, America at a Racial Crossroad, "Two Societies," 1990 (Alexandria, Va: Blackside, Inc; from Annenberg/CPB).

Index

www.ingramcontent.com/pod-product-compliance
Ingram Content Group UK Ltd.
Pitfield, Milton Keynes, MK11 3LW, UK
UKHW020431010325
455677UK00029B/1097